TAIWAN: CHINA'S LAST FRONTIER

Taiwan: China's Last Frontier

Simon Long

MACMILLAN

First published 1991

Published by
MACMILLAN PRESS LTD
Houndmills, Basingstoke, Hampshire RG21 2XS
and London
Companies and representatives
throughout the world

Printed in Hong Kong

London: Ma

British Library Cataloguing in Publication Data
Long, Simon, *1955 –*
Taiwan: China's last frontier.
1. Taiwan. Foreign relations with China, history 2.
China. Foreign relations with Taiwan, history
I. Title
327.51′249′051
ISBN 0–333–51292–8
ISBN 0–333–51293–6 pbk

To my Mother and Father

To my Mother and Father

Contents

Acknowledgements

My debts to those who helped me form the knowledge and opinions expressed in this book are too numerous to catalogue. However, I would like to express thanks to Georgina Wilde, my friend and editor at the Economist Intelligence Unit, who, unawares, set this book in motion. Basil Clarke and Michael Williams at the BBC Far East Service gave me the time to write it.

My editor at Macmillan, Belinda Dutton, and copy-editor Anne Rafique were models of professionalism and forbearance in dealing with a remote and unreliable author. But above all, I am indebted to Imogen Sharp, who made many invaluable comments on the manuscript, and helped me write it in many other ways besides. The errors are, of course, all my own.

Note on Romanisation

The question of how to transliterate Chinese names into English is a vexed one. The 'pinyin' system now standard on the mainland has made no inroads on Taiwan, which still refers to mainland leaders under the older 'Wade-Giles' system (Deng Xiaoping, for example, is known as Teng Hsiao-p'ing). To complicate matters further, many in Taiwan use yet other methods of spelling their own names in English. The author has opted in this book to follow no consistent system, but rather to Romanise in what seems to him now the most familiar form to the reader of English, e.g. Mao Zedong, not Mao Tse-tung, but Chiang Ching-kuo, not Jiang Jingguo, and Kuomintang not Guomindang.

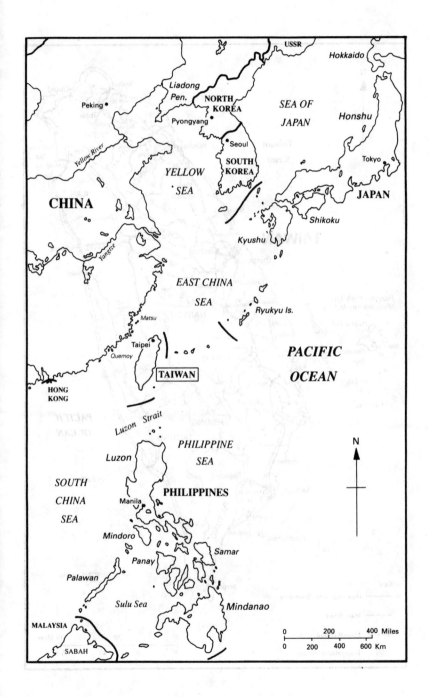

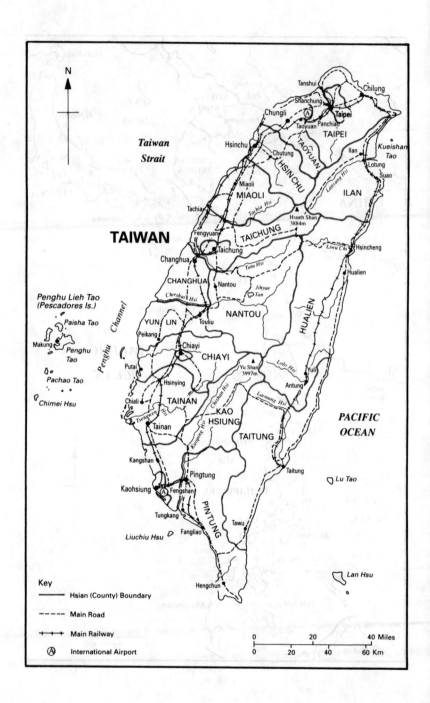

In the present and in the future we seek the peaceful unification of the motherland. We will not easily abandon this wish. But if this wish cannot be realised for a protracted period, and if it is clear that some elements in Taiwan are opposing unification with foreign encouragement, then we should re-examine the situation. If we're sure of our capabilities, then why not consider other means of unification? But we should be sure of the result. Unification is the last frontier for China. We must recover our full sovereignty.

Hu Yaobang, 1986 (at the time General Secretary of the Chinese Communist Party) [1]

Introduction

On the very night of the massacre, there was a mass rally
in Chiang Kai-shek's memorial in the centre of Taipei. The
crowd there sang songs, which, through a connection of
telephone lines were listened to by students in Tian An
Men Square, so they were overjoyed about the connection
of telephone lines. But suddenly, the other side, namely in
Peking, said, 'They opened fire', and the line was cut off.
The crowd in Chiang Kai-shek memorial suddenly became
silent, and they all wept.[2]

Thus Ma Ying-cheou, Chairman of Taiwan's ruling Nationalist Party's Mainland Affairs Committee described the events
of the early hours of 4 June 1989, in Taipei. That was how the
first news reached Taiwan of the Chinese People's Liberation
Army's brutal suppression of nearly two months of peaceful
pro-democracy agitation on the streets of Peking.

The scene he described would have been unthinkable just
months before. Who would have believed that the people of
Peking would so long have defied their government to pursue
their protests? Who would have believed that the old men of
the Chinese leadership would have sent tens of thousands of
armed soldiers in tanks and armoured personnel carriers
bearing automatic rifles to fire on unarmed civilians in the
heart of China's traditional capital? And who would have
believed that, in the middle of Taipei, in the memorial to the
fiercely anti-communist founder of Nationalist China on Taiwan, Chiang Kai-shek, the general public would be singing
songs in unison with communist students in Peking?

The Peking massacre marked the end of a chapter not just
in China's ten-year pursuit of 'reform and the open door'. It
also marked a turning point in relations with Taiwan, and
the end of another chapter in China's international image,
during which it had been possible to argue that the reintegration of China's 'separated territories' – Taiwan, Hong
Kong and Macao – could be achieved smoothly.

That telephone lines could be established with Peking was a
feature of a remarkable opening up of Taiwan to the mainland

in the late 1980s. Since 1979, China had been trying to woo Taiwan into acknowledging Chinese sovereignty with offers of autonomy and friendship. But the rival Nationalist government on Taiwan had refused any contact with the mainland; it saw the communists as rebels, bandits and usurpers of its proper position as the legitimate government of all of China. However, by the late 1980s, the Nationalists decided they had little to fear from allowing some tourist and commercial dealings with China, so by the time of the Peking massacre, the sense of kinship with mainland China went beyond the sense of ethnic and national identity that the Nationalists had tried to instil. Many had been to the mainland, had met long-lost family there, had made friends there, and felt involved in the struggle for democracy.

In Taiwan itself, some would argue that this is 'false consciousness'. Almost nine-tenths of the population have no parental or grandparental links on the mainland. They are ethnically Chinese, but in the way that many Australians are ethnically British. Taiwan's people had the dubious distinction from 1895 to 1945 of living in Japan's first colony of modern times. They have been ruled since 1945 by an élite of mainland-born administrators and soldiers who took refuge there when Chiang Kai-shek's armies were routed in the civil war of 1945–9 by Mao Zedong's communists. They had moved their government, still purporting to be the 'Republic of China', to Taiwan, and had built it up as a 'bastion for national recovery'.

Since then Taiwan's history has been one of remarkable economic achievement, accompanied by political repression, and growing diplomatic isolation. It has prospered financially but has seen its political status in the world dwindle, so that now all the world's major powers and diplomatic organisations, and all but a couple of dozen mostly tiny countries, recognise the claim of the Peking government to rule China, and that 'Taiwan is part of China'.

This volume will consider the relationship between Taiwan and China. It will examine Taiwan's history, and show that the ideal of national unity to which governments in both Peking and Taipei pledge loyalty is a dream with only tenuous roots in past reality. It will then consider the background of the Nationalist Party, or Kuomintang, which has ruled Taiwan since 1945, and claims to have had the right to rule all of China since 1928. As a background to the present relationship with China, economic and political developments in Taiwan since 1945 will be considered, as well as the way tensions across the 100-mile straits which divide them have ebbed and flowed since the founding of the People's Republic of China in 1949.

The last decade has been a period when tensions have been at a low ebb, when there has seemed no immediate reason why the peculiar status quo should not last. Peculiar, because two governments, each claiming legitimacy over a fifth of the world's population, have survived for so long without annihilating each other. I will argue, however, that this state of affairs cannot endure indefinitely, and that the present impasse holds the seeds of a transformation that will result either in confrontation, in the reintegration of Taiwan into China in some way, or in Taiwan's achievement of some form of separate nationhood. This last eventuality, independence in name as well as in fact, seems to me the least likely outcome. And I think that is a shame. There are 20 million people on Taiwan, who have made a good job of turning their island into a prosperous, booming, lively home. They have done this under the watchful eye of an overbearing communist neighbour, and increasingly abandoned by their ally, the United States, for whom they at one time promised to be an 'unsinkable aircraft carrier'. The author's bias is to feel they have a right to determine their own political future. That they are unlikely to be given that chance, seems to me one of the tragedies of the post-war era.

1 Geography and Early History

TOPOGRAPHY: THE BEAUTIFUL ISLAND

For Chinese historians, Taiwan has its own creation myth. Once upon a time, the story goes, fierce dragons lived at Wuhumen, Five Tiger Gate, guarding the seaboard entrance to the present-day port of Fuzhou, in China's south-eastern province of Fujian. One day, frolicking in the sea, they glided out through its depths and arrived at Taiwan. There, they began to cavort with especial abandon, ploughing through the earth itself. Where their heads surfaced at the north of the island, they threw up the bluff at Keelung. They then went writhing down the spine of the island, heaving up a jagged range of mountains. In a parting gesture, they gave a massive flap of their formidable tails, creating the sheer cliffs which mark the imposing south of the island, at the end of what is now called the Hengchun Peninsula.[1]

The dragons' adventure left an island of remarkable natural beauty, captured in its Portuguese name of *Ilha Formosa*, 'the Beautiful Island'. It is a small strip, the shape of a tobacco leaf, just 250 miles long, and 80 miles wide at its broadest point, tapering to a narrow promontory in the south. Its area is about 14 000 square miles, just more than Belgium, but slightly less than the Netherlands. Taiwan's modern population of about 20 million, however, is double that of Belgium and half as big again as that of the Netherlands. With the exception of Bangladesh, and the city-islands of Hong Kong and Singapore, Taiwan is the most densely populated self-governing area on Earth.

The straits which divide Taiwan from mainland China to the west are just over 100 miles wide. In between are many of the other 85 islands currently controlled by the Taiwan government. These include Penghu, the Pescadores, or 'Fishermen Islands', and the offshore islands of Quemoy and Matsu. Two hundred miles to the south of Taiwan lies the

1

northern tip of the Philippines archipelago. Seventy miles to
the north-west is the last of the Japanese-controlled Ryu-kyu
Islands. The southern island of Japan proper, Kyushu, is 700
miles away. To the west is the vast expanse of the Pacific,
with only the Hawaiian islands lying between Taiwan and the
coast of Mexico.

The mountainous spine of the island extends almost to the
eastern coast. In places, that coastline is in fact made up of
perpendicular cliffs 6000 feet high. Sixty per cent of the island
is mountainous, and only a quarter arable, with most of the
farmland lying in the lowlands on the western coast. But
Taiwan has always been a fertile home for agriculture, blessed
with a subtropical climate in all but the tropical southern tip
of the island, and a rich alluvial plain in the western lowlands.
The Tropic of Cancer bisects the island. Average temperatures
are in the 70s Fahrenheit, though in the central highlands,
where mountains are more than 10 000 feet high, snow falls in
winter. Its melting adds to the abundant rainfall which
averages 100 inches a year.

Apart from lavish supplies of water – providing plenty of
hydroelectric potential in the modern era – Taiwan is poorly
endowed with natural resources. Coal is the most important,
but many of the deposits are too small or inaccessible to be
worth exploiting. Some progress has been made at discovering
small hydrocarbon reserves both on-shore and off-shore, but
today Taiwan has to import more than nine-tenths of its
energy needs. Gold, copper, marble and dolomite are all
present under Taiwan, but again, have been of little economic
importance.

When the first Europeans began to disembark on Taiwan in
the sixteenth century, they found one large forest. More than
200 species of trees still flourish, and cover more than half the
island's surface. That is after four centuries of deforestation,
first from the slash and burn agriculture of the primitive tribes
who were the earliest inhabitants, then from the more sophisticated agricultural methods of the European and Chinese
immigrants.

PRE-HISTORY: BEFORE THE CHINESE

Even Taiwan's early history is a political issue. Both governments claiming to represent China today see the island as an

inalienable part of Chinese sovereign territory. History is an awkward encumbrance to this belief. Most of Taiwan's present inhabitants were born there, of parents likewise natives of the island, with no immediate family links on the mainland. Although the vast majority are ethnic Chinese, even these native Taiwanese are relative newcomers to the island, descendants of immigrants from south-eastern China from the seventeenth to nineteenth centuries.

The origins of the island's earliest inhabitants are less clear. The 'aboriginal' tribes, who now make up less than one per cent of the population, have far deeper roots on Taiwan. Two different groups settled in the island. Long before Christ, people known as Taiyals and Vonums lived in the north. Historians have tended to ascribe to them an origin that suited contemporary political reality. For the Japanese colonialists of the late nineteenth century they were 'Lonkius', the descendants of a people who had fled the cold north and settled in the Kurile archipelago to the north of Japan, through Japan and the Ryu-kyu chain, and south as far as Formosa. Ethnically, this theory goes, they are linked to the 'hairy' Ainu people of the northern Japanese island of Hokkaido. Distinguished Western ethnologists have reinforced this view. For the Chinese, however, the Lonkius are a mainland Chinese people. They are said to have reached Taiwan as early as 1700 BC, as a shortage of agricultural land under the Shang dynasty led primitive tribesmen eastwards from present-day Guizhou province, in south-western central China, and finally sent them across the straits in the search for new land to farm. As evidence for this theory, historians have pointed to the Taiyal myth that the tribe is the result of a union between a princess and a dog. Early in this century, aboriginal tribes in Guizhou were said also to worship the image of a dog as the founder of their tribe.

The second group of early inhabitants are of less controversial ancestry. Their languages and customs have much in common with those of early Malay and Filipino peoples, and they are of Malayo-Polynesian ethnic stock. In the centuries before Christ, these people drifted north, through South-east Asia, and reached Taiwan by way of the Philippines. It seems that for some centuries, the Malays and the Lonkius co-existed at different extremities of the island in mutual ignorance of the other's presence. Then in the seventh century after Christ, the Malays moved northwards, gradually extending their settlements over much of the island, and forcing the Taiyals into the foothills of the northern end of the central highlands.

A Dutch visitor in the seventeenth century described the aboriginal inhabitants of Taiwan in the following terms:

> The inhabitants are very barbarous and savage, the men being generally very tall and exceedingly robust, in fact almost giants. Their colour is between black and brown, like most Indians, but not so black as the Caffirs. In summer they go about perfectly nude, without any feeling of shame. On the contrary, the women are very small and short, but very fat and strong, their colour being between brown and yellow. They wear some clothes, and possess a certain degree of shame, except when they wash themselves, which they do twice a day with warm water.[2]

He described them as engaged in subsistence agriculture, with the women as 'total drudges', doing most of the work. They grew rice, a type of millet, a mysterious fruit, and caught shrimps, crabs and oysters. They built their villages both in the lowlands and in the hills, and moved often, as they slashed and burned to make new planting land. The men seem to have been an idle lot, doing little other than making occasional hunting forays for wild boar and deer. Tribes were often at war with one another, collecting heads as trophies, or with the immigrant Chinese who by then were trading clothing, wood and other items for meat and animal hides.

EARLY CONTACTS WITH THE MAINLAND

Until the collapse of the Ming dynasty in 1662, rulers of mainland China had by and large ignored Taiwan. It was seen as part of the Ryu-kyu chain, and, in the dynastic records of the sixth century Sui dynasty, was referred to as 'Tai Liu-chiu', or Great Ryu-kyu (although later it was also known as 'Lesser Ryu-kyu'). It was under the expansionist rule of the Sui Emperor Yang-ti that mainland China first tried to bring Taiwan into its fold. In 605 one Shu Kuan was dispatched by the Emperor to investigate reports that in clear weather a smoky haze could be seen across the Taiwan strait. Shu Kuan met a peaceful group of Taiwanese, but, unable to find any way of making himself understood, kidnapped a few islanders and reported back to the Emperor. His interest awakened, in 611 Yang-ti sent another expedition, this time under Ch'en Ling, accompanied by one of the captive islanders now trained for rudimentary interpreting. Ch'en had a less pacific welcome. The tribe Shu Kuan had met had been driven back inland by another tribe and had taken refuge in the hills. Their aggressors were bellicose, and when Ch'en demanded tribute on behalf of the Emperor, he was sent packing.

That was the last 'official' Chinese contact with Taiwan for several centuries, and since the Malay tribes there had long since ceased to be great seafarers, there were few other opportunities for exchange. Towards the end of the twelfth century, however, several hundred Taiwanese began appearing in some of the small seacoast villages of Fujian province, looting and pillaging. This was the start of several centuries of Taiwan- and Ryu-kyu-based piracy. Meanwhile, on the southern Chinese seaboard, traders and would-be migrants were growing bolder, venturing first to the Pescadore islands and Penghu, staging posts to Taiwan, and then establishing trading posts and settlements in Taiwan itself. They met resistance, and the purpose of the late twelfth-century piracy seems to have been to secure iron for weapons to beat off the invaders. But the mainlanders persisted, and started growing sugar-cane and tea as well as rice on Taiwan, shipping it back to Fujian. The migratory trickle gathered momentum in the dying years of the Sung dynasty in the second half of the thirteenth century as Hakka Chinese from Fujian and Guangdong provinces fled the advance of the Mongol, Yuan dynasty, under which the Hakka were subject to the persecution which afflicted them periodically for centuries.

This first wave of mainland emigration pre-dates what Chinese historians have regarded as the true starting-point of Taiwan's history. That is the year 1430, during the Ming dynasty, which year marked the accidental landing in Taiwan of Wan San-ho, better known as Cheng He, the greatest of the Ming explorers. He was driven to Taiwan by a storm on a voyage back from Thailand. He was treated kindly by the tribespeople he met, who furnished him with supplies to reach the mainland. Cheng He gave the Emperor, Ming Hsuan-tsung, a glowing account of the island, despite its 'strange and barbarous' people. He also took back herbal remedies that impressed Chinese physicians with their apparently miraculous efficacy in curing Cheng He himself from a disease thought to be mortal. But the brief flurry of imperial interest did not seem enough to prompt another expedition, and Taiwan once again dropped out of the official imperial histories, this time for about a century. Taiwan became mainly known as a hotbed of piracy, as, especially in the sixteenth century, Japanese pirates mounted ever more ambitious raids on China's coast, sometimes using Taiwan as a base. As early as 1380, Ming founder Hung-wu had written to the Ashikaga shogun reproving him for his tolerance of piracy. 'You stupid Eastern barbarians! Living so far across the sea . . . you are haughty and disloyal; you permit your subjects to do evil.'³ In 1563, pirates expelled from their base on Namoa Island on the Guangdong border, took refuge on Taiwan, which was to remain an important pirate lair until the arrival of the Dutch, followed by Chinese and then Manchu forces in the seventeenth century.

EARLY FOREIGN CONTACTS

By then, the Japanese pirates were not the only non-Chinese foreigners to have encountered Taiwan, although they were at the time the ones to have the biggest impact. During the Ashikaga dynasty in Japan, in the fourteenth to sixteenth centuries, Japan was often torn apart by civil war. Many people moved around Japan to flee the incessant combat and significant numbers took to sea. Of these, a large proportion were attracted by the trade and piracy opportunities afforded by China's seas. First in the Pescadores and Penghu, and then from Taiwan itself, with Keelung established as a headquarters, they raided the China coast, where scarcely a village on the Fujian coast escaped their attentions. Sometimes they ventured further afield, as far as Thailand. Their booty – silk, porcelains, spices, herbal medicines – was then traded legitimately with their homelands to the north.

Gradually, the lucrative pickings of piracy began to attract more orthodox traders, although the distinction between trade and piracy was blurred. A ban on maritime trade in the sixteenth century had been imposed by the Ming to try to stop piratical depredations. The effect was to make all sea-borne commerce for a while tantamount to smuggling, and to encourage traders to arm themselves. In 1567, the maritime ban was replaced by a system of licensed trading ships.

Taiwan, regarded by the pirate-trader settlements as an unclaimed land inhabited by feeble savages, became an attractive duty-free port. Its location, on the sea-routes from southern China and South-east Asia to Japan, gave Keelung and other Taiwan harbours an early role as entrepot ports. Chinese traders from the vibrant ports of Quanzhou and Zhangzhou in Fujian used Taiwan as a resting place in the arduous voyage to Japan. In 1592, merchants from Nagasaki, Kyoto and Sakai received special permission from the Shogun to engage in foreign commerce. They made their headquarters on Taiwan, at a town which at that time bore the same name. With the Tokugawa reunification of Japan in 1600, the value of Taiwan to the encroaching European explorers encouraged the first Tokugawa shogun, Iesayu, to try to formalise Japanese control of Taiwan. The Ryu-kyus were subjugated by the Shimazu realm of southern Kyushu in 1609, and the Ryu-kyu kings, whose capital was at Okinawa, became Japanese vassals. But by then, the Ryu-kyus had a tributary relationship with the Chinese Empire, which the Japanese left intact, in order not to disrupt the profitable trade. An effort to conquer Taiwan from the Ryu-kyus at the culmination of the subjugation campaign failed. Six years later, Iesayu sent the Governor of Nagasaki to try again, with a force of 3000 men. But resistance from the native tribes and the by then considerable Chinese population again deterred the Japanese. From 1653 on, Japan withdrew into national isolation, and its contacts with Taiwan dissolved.

In the sixteenth century, the China seas had also begun to see European ships. From the Chinese point of view, the first arrivals, the Portuguese, whose first expedition left for China in 1514, were just so many more barbarians and pirates. But by 1557, they had been granted the island of Macao, off Guangdong, as a base. Although they gave Taiwan its name,

Formosa, the Portuguese did not settle there for long, although some accounts speak of a Portuguese settlement at Keelung in 1590. The Portuguese were followed into these newly charted waters by the Spanish, who established themselves in Manila in 1571. In the seventeenth century, their dominance was to be supplanted by that of the British.

But it was the Dutch, among the Europeans, who took Taiwan seriously, if only by chance. In 1595, Cornelius Houtman had managed to open up trade with Java, leading to the formation of the Dutch East India Company, and the annexation of the Dutch East Indies. The China trade enticed the company, but the Chinese persistently refused Dutch requests to establish a trading post in China, although by this time they had worked out a *modus vivendi* with the Portuguese. Frustrated by this failure of diplomatic efforts to break into the China market, the Dutch began to make preparations to fight their way in. In 1622, after several fruitless expeditions to China, the Dutch captain Reyerszoon was sent there again, either to conquer Macao and so replace the Portuguese, or to open up trade in some other way. After initially failing in the first mission, he began to build a naval base in the Pescadores, while an advance party established a settlement on the tiny island of Taoyuan, off the south coast of Taiwan. The threat of serious war galvanised the Chinese into finding some sort of accommodation with the Dutch. In 1623, after a number of small clashes with Chinese vessels on the mainland coast, Commander Sonck arrived from Batavia (Jakarta) to conclude terms in Amoy (now Xiamen, in Fujian province). He was negotiating with the crafty governor-general of Fujian and Zhejiang, Xiong Wen-can. Xiong hit on the ruse of offering the Dutch a trading post in Taiwan. The Dutch, apparently, thought they were being handed a bigger and better Macao. the Chinese, on the other hand, imagined they were disposing of the Dutch problem by directing them to a remote and disease-ridden haunt of pirates. It was perhaps the first instance of what was to become a feature of Taiwan's history – its handing over by one foreign power that did not control it to another with no obvious claim to sovereignty.

TAIWAN UNDER THE DUTCH: 1624–62

In 1624, the Dutch founded their Taiwan settlement at Fort Orange, later called Zeelandia, or, in Chinese, Anping, the port to the present-day city of Tainan, in the south-west of Taiwan. Encouraged to find they were in unclaimed territory, and by their achievements in the East Indies, the Dutch decided to turn Formosa into a full-blooded colony. They were delighted with their new acquisition. The port at Fort Orange offered comfortable access to their naval and trading vessels. From there, they would be able to harass both the Spanish trading out of Manila, and the Portuguese from Macao. The island appeared bountiful, and its people, who by now included an estimated 25 000 Chinese, seemed easily pacified by the offer of 30 000 deerskins annually. The Japanese merchants, by now relatively few in number, were placated with promises that their business would not be disrupted. The aborigines were, with some foresight, courted as eventual allies in any conflict with the Chinese or Japanese.

The Dutch built up a flourishing trade, both on the island, with the Japanese and Chinese merchants, and in Japan and China themselves. Raw silk and sugar were shipped to Japan; silken ware, porcelain and gold to Batavia; rice, sugar, deer-skins, deer-horns and drugs native to Taiwan were sold to China, along with imported products like paper, spices, amber, tin, lead and cotton. They fortified the island with 25 military centres, including a series of forts on the central and northern coasts. Bricks for the defences were imported from Batavia. The preponderance of military men among the 1000 or so Dutch colonisers created a need for labour and mainland Chinese were aggressively dragooned into crossing the straits. Sometimes they were enticed with promises of seeds, tools and oxen. Some would only come for the growing season, and then return to the mainland. The Chinese population, concentrated around Fort Orange, reached an estimated 50 000 by 1662.

The Dutch also brought Christianity, of an austere, Calvinist variety, to the island. The early missionaries, Candidius and Junius, had remarkable success and by 1635, 700 Formosans had been baptised. The following year, a Dutch school was set up, teaching Formosan children to write in roman letters. But the missionaries' zeal was sometimes unwelcome to the military authorities. The Dutch East India Company in 1660 sent an order from India to stop the practice of public whipping and banishment for idolators, adulterers and fornicators. Not only might this antagonise the aboriginal population at a time of pressure from the Chinese, it would also provoke the Japanese, at the time engaged in a persecution of Christianity, partly as a result of Dutch policies in Formosa. Japan, however, was still an important client of the East India Company.

The Dutch reign in Formosa was never untroubled. Made uneasy by the presence of their commercial rivals straddling important sea-lanes, the Spanish established settlements in the north of the island in 1626, when they built Santissima Trinidad at the entrance to what is now Keelung harbour. Although they never aimed at a rival colonisation, seeming content with the safeguarding of Spanish commercial interests, the Dutch Governor of Formosa saw the Spaniards as a threat. In 1642, they were driven out, and by 1650, Dutch control of Taiwan was almost complete, a short-lived prosperous heyday before they themselves were expelled 12 years later. In one year, the Dutch earned 300 000 guilders from taxes, 4 million guilders from the China trade out of Taiwan, and 980 000 guilders from the raw silk trade with Japan alone.

There had also been tensions with the Japanese. In 1628, Yamada Yahei, a Nagasaki merchant pirate, attacked the Dutch with a force of 500 men, in reprisal for the treatment of the Japanese on the island. The Dutch had reneged on their pledges not to interfere with trade: one of their administration's first acts was to impose a duty on two staple exports, sugar and rice. The incensed Japanese argued that, as earlier arrivals in Taiwan, they should be exempt. The bitter row at one point threatened the entire Japan–Netherlands trade. Yahei was inspired in particular by an incident where a Japanese district officer, *en route* to Fuzhou to trade, was forced by Dutch intervention at the Pescadores to abandon his voyage. Yahei even captured Nuyts at one point and obliged him to negotiate. But the discussions yielded little, and the Japanese gradually withdrew from Taiwan.

Resentment among the Chinese population also boiled over in two rebellions, in 1640 and 1652. Both were suppressed

with considerable brutality. Apart from the merchants' disaffection, the Chinese farmers and workers were angered as
well, by licence fees for deer-hunting and fishing rights, by a
capitation tax for every household, and by the forced labour
and assimilation to which they were subject. The Chinese
uprisings were put down with the help of the aboriginal
population, in dealing with whom the Dutch showed greater
sensitivity.

THE KONGA INTERREGNUM: 1661–83

Thus, by the middle of the seventeenth century, the Chinese
claim to Taiwan was unformulated. Taiwan was an outpost, a
haunt of savages and pirates and in no way incorporated into
the Chinese polity. Unlike Tibet and Mongolia, it was not
visited by Mongol armies. Indeed, Chinese foreign policy, in
so far as the Sino-centric world view of the Chinese emperors
can be characterised as such, had always been far more
interested in China's internal, central Asian borders, than in
maritime advances. Nor was Taiwan part of the network of
'tributary' relationships which the Ming Empire established
with its neighbours, such as Korea, the Ryu-Kyu Islands,
Annam (Vietnam), Thailand, Burma and a host of minor
peripheral states. Taiwan was hardly worthy of notice.

It was the collapse of the last truly 'Chinese' dynasty, the
Ming, that was to bring Taiwan to a position of importance in
Chinese affairs. It was also to sow the seeds of a potent
historical parallel for the Nationalist government on Taiwan
after 1949, struggling against the historical odds to recover the
mainland from the 'bandits'. In the seventeenth century, a
man known as Koxinga did this three centuries before Chiang
Kai-shek, as Taiwan became the last bastion of Ming resistance against the consolidation of the Manchu Ch'ing dynasty.

'Koxinga' is, in fact, a Dutch corruption of 'Guoxingye', or
'Lord of the Imperial Surname', a title bestowed on Cheng
Ch'eng-kung. He was the son of Cheng Chih-lung, a famous
Fujianese pirate, who had surrendered in 1628 and helped the
Empire against Japanese pirates. Koxinga's mother was a
Japanese noble. He became a great favourite of the Ming
court in the 1640s, as it retreated south in the face of Manchu

incursions. In 1646, Koxinga's father defected to the Ch'ing. He himself, however, resisted their blandishments, and gathered an army, which he based in Amoy (Xiamen) and on the offshore island of Quemoy. Having established 72 military bases in Fujian, and having developed an extensive civil arm of government as well, in 1658–9, he led a major counter-offensive against the Ch'ing. However, he failed in a bid to recapture Nanking and retreated in disarray back to Amoy and Quemoy. Here he found his freedom of manœuvre too constrained, and so turned his attention to Taiwan. In 1661, hearing that the Batavian fleet had left Taiwan under the guard of only a small garrison, Koxinga invaded with a force of 900 ships and 25 000 men. On 1 February 1662, a treaty was signed with the Dutch Governor, Frederick Coyett, ending Dutch rule on Taiwan.

Koxinga's plans for leading a drawn-out campaign to oust the Ch'ing and restore the Ming in some form were thwarted by his death at the age of only 38 in June 1662, some say by suicide. His son, Cheng Ching, carried on the struggle. In 1663–4, his remaining mainland forces were driven out by the Ch'ing with Dutch help, but he still held Taiwan. The Ch'ing resorted to a cruel scorched-earth policy. To isolate Taiwan from mainland sources of supply, and to make coastal raids unattractive, coastal areas in Fujian, Guangdong and Zhejiang were forcibly evacuated to a distance inland of 10 miles or more.

Thrown back on Taiwan itself, Cheng imposed for the first time a Chinese-style regime on the island. He based himself at Zeelandia, now renamed Anping, and divided Taiwan into one prefecture and two districts. Officials were appointed, and educational systems set up to train an imperial type of mandarinate. Their regime was, like that of the Dutch, harsh and repressive, and exacted a heavy toll in taxes on the native and Chinese population. But clandestine emigration from the mainland continued, and the Chinese population of the island doubled to an estimated 100 000 by 1683. Chinese farmers and soldiers colonised more of the south-west of the island, reclaiming land and vastly increasing agricultural output. Trading with Japan – selling mainly rice and sugar – carried on, as did extensive smuggling with the mainland. The Manchu isolation policy forced Taiwan to develop a new level of economic advance and self-sufficiency.

But the dream of recovering the mainland did not fade. In the 1680s, the Cheng regime became involved in the so-called 'Revolt of the Three Feudatories'. This was an anti-Ch'ing rebellion by some of their former Chinese collaborators in the south, who resisted full incorporation into the newly vigorous empire. In 1683, the Ch'ing finally mustered its naval forces for a concerted attack on Taiwan. The rebels were defeated. Taiwan became part of China, or, strictly speaking, of Fujian province, of which it was made a prefecture in 1684. This was also the final chapter in the Ch'ing conquest of all of China, a historical memory less often evoked on Taiwan today than that of Koxinga's doomed resistance struggle.

THE 'WILD EAST': TAIWAN 1683–1850

Even with the Ch'ing victory over Koxinga's son, Taiwan did not become 'part of China' in the full sense. It was a remote island, seen as barbarous, lawless and rebellious. Between 1714 and 1833, the island experienced three 'Great Rebellions' against the Ch'ing, and dozens of smaller outbreaks of resistance to continental rule. It was a place where 'there was a minor revolt every three years, and a major one every five years'.[4] When not at war with the mainland, Taiwan was constantly prey to strife between the various ethnic groups and Chinese clans now occupying the island. Its rice and sugar made it an ever more important 'granary' for the swelling mainland population. But for the unfortunate members of the imperial service posted there, it was a career graveyard. Apart from dealing with truculent residents and the ever-present marauding pirates, the officials had to dwell on an island with a reputation for being disease-ridden. Even the scourge of opium, that was later to have such a debilitating effect on all of China, is said to have been present in Taiwan in some areas as early as 1620. Already suffering a career set-back simply by being there, many officials in Taiwan took consolation in trying to make their fortunes. Official corruption became endemic. This, and the brutality accompanying the quashing of the constant rebellions, fuelled resentment against Ch'ing officialdom.

Besides the hapless visiting mandarins, Taiwan was home to at least five significant groups of people. Under Dutch tutelage, some of the aboriginal tribes had become, in the Chinese terms of the time, 'civilised', living on the plains and taking part in trade and other intercourse with the Chinese immigrants. Other tribes had retreated into the hills, and maintained a separate and antagonistic culture. As late as 1871, when some Japanese castaways were killed by tribes-men, the Peking government felt justified in disclaiming authority for all but Taiwan's western seaboard. The Chinese immigrants were also split into three sometimes mutually hostile groups. The first were the Hakka – literally 'guest people'. The Hakka's origins are not entirely clear. They seem to have migrated from northern and central to southern China during the twelfth century, but to have retained a separate language and cultural identity. They were subject to discrimi-nation, even persecution, on the mainland. Only with the reign of the first Ch'ing Emperor K'ang Hsi were they allowed to hold jobs in the civil service. They could not own land. The tough, physically quite large Hakka had begun to drift to Taiwan at the time of their twelfth-century migration. They were joined by a steady stream of migration from coastal Fujian, of a people known as the 'Hoklo'. They spoke Fujian dialects, and lived in traditional Fujian style. Finally, a third group of Chinese immigrants, from Guangdong province, settled in the port towns, thus in general keeping a distance from the land jealousies that fuelled Hakka–Hoklo conflict. The Cantonese likewise kept a separate identity, but numer-ically were far less important than the other two Chinese groups.

This five-part division was further complicated by the strong clannishness of many of the Chinese. Clans from the ports of Zhanghou and Quanzhou were especially dominant. But, given the inadequacies of Ch'ing rule, and the lawless-ness of Taiwan, Chinese communities often banded together on Taiwan on the basis of a common surname, for mutual protection against rival clans, aboriginal tribes or government extortion. The very same pressures led to a burgeoning of the secret societies that were so long a feature of anti-imperial rebellion in China. Perhaps the most famous of all of these, the Triads, are believed to have originated among the Fujianese immigrants in Taiwan in the early years of the Ch'ing.

As a result of a ban on free emigration to Taiwan, a lucrative immigration racket was created for the officials, selling passports to those fleeing the increasing deprivations of south-eastern China. Fujian is a relatively barren province, and as farmland became ever more inadequate to feed China's exploding population in the late eighteenth and early nineteenth centuries, reports of the fertile paddy of Taiwan made the trip across the straits look an attractive option. According to a Chinese census of 1818, the population on Taiwan had risen to more than 2.5 million. This seems to be an overstatement, since an 1887 census produced an almost identical result. Nevertheless, through immigration and natural growth, Taiwan's population was growing, and becoming overwhelmingly Chinese in ethnic origin. Many Chinese emigrants left their wives and children behind, hoping to return once they had amassed a little fortune. Often, they took aboriginal wives, or sometimes were joined years later by family from the mainland.

Taiwan, as we have seen, was not at this stage a Chinese province, but a prefecture and military district of Fujian. The imperial regime had two main interests in the island: keeping down insurrection, and importing rice, sugar and other products. Nor were the insurrections minor matters of a few discontented locals taking up arms. In 1722 a humble duck-farmer who led one revolt declared the Chinese Empire at an end and installed his own dynasty, driving the Ch'ing officials back to Fujian. Later, a contemporary French observer wrote in 1789 of the Great Rebellion that had broken out two years earlier:

> The troubles in Formosa are ended at last, but at the cost of a shameful and expensive war to China. She has lost at least a hundred thousand men, destroyed by disease or the swords of the rebels; and she has expended two millions of taels.[5]

That rebellion, like so many others, had its roots in a secret society uprising, intensified by clan rivalries. At one time, the rebels controlled almost the entire island and it took nine months of constant battling for the imperial army to quell the unrest.

The huge cost of maintaining its garrisons in Taiwan against this perpetual local resentment was mitigated for the imperial dynasty by the economic benefits of colonisation. Farming in Taiwan began to develop along lines similar to the mainland. Settled tenant farmers gradually acquired their own land, opening up new arable fields, as irrigation and flood control systems began to protect the south-western plains from the uneven distribution of rain. The principal exports were sugar and rice, sold to both Japan and China, as were Taiwan's long-prized deer products. Early in the eighteenth century the abundant forests were declared a government monopoly. This gave officialdom a new opportunity to rake off profits from the lucrative camphor business. In the 1720s, the decapitation of upwards of two hundred people for felling camphor trees was an important spark in an earlier rebellion.

The Chinese-style administration set up under Koxinga and his son was replaced by an equally sinicised administrative structure under the Ch'ing, although the examination system instituted by the Ming loyalists for training a mandarinate on Taiwan was scrapped. However, the direct role of the government in the administration of Taiwan and the exploitation of its agricultural surplus was minimal. The officials, who until the end of the eighteenth century were almost all sent from mainland China, were a by-word for incompetence and venality. Apart from camphor taxes and 'passport fees', there was money to be made in customs bribes, court fees and salt taxes. The governor of Fujian rarely visited his Taiwan prefecture, less still the imperial censors charged with disciplining the civil service. So the mandarinate on Taiwan had little hindrance in pursuing extortion as compensation for a hardship posting. Correspondingly, the inhabitants had little redress against arbitrary abuse of imperial power. This only strengthened the tendency towards clan, secret society and other forms of subversive social organisation, which in many cases took on the character of local governments.

TAIWAN JOINS INTERNATIONAL POLITICS: THE NINETEENTH CENTURY

In the eighteenth century, following the expulsion of the Dutch from the island in 1662, Taiwan seemed to slip off the edge of European maps of the world. A handful of bold adventurers landed on the island, and wrote colourful reports of its beauty and wildness, but it no longer figured largely in the European trade with Asia. Then, in the early nineteenth century, China's traditionally inward-looking foreign policy was challenged by the advent of the gunboats and commercial fleets of the European, and later American, sea-powers. Taiwan became one more chip in the great bargaining game these powers played among themselves, and with the crumbling Manchu Empire. Britain, France, Prussia, Russia, the United States and Japan all at some point contemplated annexation, colonisation or purchase of the island.

In the early decades of the century, a trickle of foreign ships again began to think of landing in Taiwan. As early as 1662, the British had secured trading rights in Taiwan, and indeed sold munitions to the Ming resistance under Koxinga's son. But no regular trade was to develop until the 1850s. Taiwan's former anchorage at Anping had undergone a natural transformation, hiding it from the crow's nests of passing ships, and so there was no obvious port of call. Taiwan's isolation, however, was brought to an abrupt end by the Opium War of 1840–42, when British gunboats forced the Chinese Empire into yielding trading concessions, and the right to supply the snowballing opium market with the produce of Indian poppy fields. Taiwan was shelled as a sideshow in that war, but it came to prominence because of one of the first in a series of incidents confirming the island's reputation as a savage backwater. This was the islanders' inhospitable custom of cutting the heads off foreign visitors. In 1842, when two British ships were wrecked off Keelung, 197 survivors were executed, apparently on orders from Peking. The British protested to the governor in Fujian, but, satisfied with Hong Kong and the other prizes won in the Opium War, were placated by the demotion of some of the officials involved. Any thought of annexing Tawain was put in abeyance, largely so as to avoid antagonising Prussia, which was also showing some interest in the island. British interests in Taiwan thereafter were solidified by the 1858 Treaty of Tianjin and subsequent agreements through the early 1860s, opening powers on Taiwan to foreign foreign trade (Tamsui, Ta-kao – the present-day Kaohsiung – Anping and Keelung). They became 'treaty ports', like those on the continental seaboard; foreigners not only had access, but also enjoyed 'extra-territorial' privileges of effective exemption from Chinese justice. Britain at one time toyed with the idea of turning Taiwan into a penal colony, like Australia, but its interests there were largely defensive, designed to stop the Russians or the Japanese from establishing a menacing presence too close to their port of Hong Kong.

For the Russians had, in fact, won a concession on Taiwan before the British. In 1858, there was a welter of humiliating treaties signed by the Peking Government with foreign powers, after the second major war with the Western powers accelerated the process of dismembering the empire. In their treaty, the Russians gained the same rights as other foreigners at the five existing 'treaty ports' – Canton, Amoy (now Xiamen), Shanghai, Ningbo and Fuzhou – but they added two to the list, one on Taiwan, and one on the southern Chinese island of Hainan. In 1880, it was believed in Peking that Russia might declare war on China, partly in order to annexe Taiwan. Russian warships in the channels north of Taiwan provoked the rapid fortification of Keelung and Kaohsiung, but suddenly one day the Russians withdrew never to return.

The United States, too, was beginning to forage for concessions in eastern Asia – or at least its traders were. In the 1850s, American merchants based in the treaty port of Canton explored Taiwan, built a port there and persuaded Peter Parker, the American Commissioner in Canton, to urge the State Department to take over Taiwan. Some even went so far as to raise the Stars and Stripes. They were backed by no less a figure than Commodore Matthew Perry, whose 'black ships' had in 1853 'opened Japan'. He saw the advantages of the island as a coaling station between Japan, southern China and the East Indies. It would give the United States a trading base to rival Britain's at Hong Kong, or Portugal's at Macao. Townsend Harris, Washington's first envoy to Japan, recommended outright purchase of the island. But the State Department dustily reminded these would-be expansionists that government policy of the time foreswore 'territorial aggrandizement or the acquisition of political power in that distant region'.[6]

France also became involved in the future of Taiwan. The new strengthening of the imperial defences and discipline on

Taiwan that had manifested themselves in the anti-Russian deterrence of 1880, were also in evidence in the Sino-French war of 1884–5. In another humiliation, China lost its traditional suzerainty over Annam (Vietnam), and had to allow French commercial penetration into the southern interior provinces. In August 1884, a naval battle off Fuzhou resulted in the rout of the Chinese fleet. Taiwan was blockaded by the French, the Pescadores were seized, and Keelung occupied. The imperial forces on Taiwan fared much better than their counterparts on the mainland in the land war, following astute preparations by the forward-looking official then in charge of the prefecture, Liu Ming-ch'uan. Once they had won the war on the mainland, the French withdrew.

Naturally, these foreign encroachments aroused hostility in Taiwan. Not only did aborigines continue to behead shipwrecked sailors and others, but anti-foreign sentiment took hold among the Chinese population on Taiwan as well. In the 'Formosan Incident' of 1868, a mob assaulted foreign merchants, who were engaged in trying to break the monopoly on the camphor trade. Typically, the incident led to a British punitive expedition, which blew up Chinese defences at Anping, and exacted 40 000 taels of silver in indemnities. All the imperial powers complained at one time or another to Peking about the lawlessness and savagery of Taiwan. Similarly, it was to be anti-foreign violence on Taiwan that provided Japan with its first pretext for trying to acquire the territory.

In 1871, some aboriginal tribesmen, as was their wont, beheaded some Japanese castaways. The Chinese reaction to Japanese complaints about this was indicative of China's ambiguous and unresolved attitude to Taiwan even at this late date. First, China protested that since the sailors were from the Ryu-kyu Islands, a long-standing Chinese tributary, and since Taiwan was part of China, the incident was, in the present-day parlance of Peking, an 'internal matter'. But then, when the Japanese persisted in demands that order be enforced on Taiwan, China resorted to claiming that its sovereignty only extended to the approximately one-third of the island that was 'civilised' – the cultivated western seaboard. So in 1874, Japan sent an expeditionary force, threatening to occupy the 'uncivilised' two-thirds of the island, and then offer to purchase the remainder. Japan's motives were in part pre-emptive, fearing that a Western power might establish itself on Taiwan as a beach-head for military action against Japan itself. Correspondingly, Britain was nervous at the prospect of Japan sitting astride sea-routes so close to Hong Kong, and brought pressure to bear on China to insist on its sovereignty over the whole island. China acquiesced, and was obliged yet again to pay an indemnity for the beheadings and the cost of the Japanese expedition.

EARLY MODERNISATION: SELF-STRENGTHENING ON TAIWAN

The reorientation of Chinese foreign policy as it faced mounting coastal challenges inevitably led to a reappraisal of Taiwan. It became more important in Peking's eyes primarily for military reasons, but, increasingly, economic self-interest also dictated a firmer hand over the lawless outlying island. This reassessment of Peking's interests in the island coincided with the 'self-strengthening' movement of the last decades of the nineteenth century. Imperial officials, notably Li Hung-chang, began to try to shore up the crumbling imperial edifice by a programme of reform and selective Westernisation. In this new climate, a series of progressive imperial administrators began to tame Taiwan, and to introduce the first modernisation of the island.

Shen Pao-chen, an Imperial Commissioner, spent a year on Taiwan after the Japanese partial occupation of 1874. He installed coastal batteries and made plans for a mechanised coal-mine at Keelung. This new interest was pursued by Ting Jih-ch'ang, Governor of Fujian from 1875 to 1877. Ting had a scheme to turn Taiwan into a major naval base and to construct a north–south railway to facilitate troop movements, but these ambitious plans were thwarted by a shortage of financial backing.

More progress was made, however, during the time of Liu Ming-ch'uan, a protégé of Li Hung-chang and former military commander, who had distinguished himself in the anti-French war. Liu inaugurated a radical programme of reform and modernisation of Taiwan. Having served in the wars against the Nien and Taiping rebellions, Liu gave improving the island's defences a high priority. But it did not stop there: he supervised the construction of the first railways – 42 miles of track between Taipei and Hsinchu – which were completed in 1894. This was more than a tenth of the total length of railway track in China at the time. Under Liu, an east–west road was also built, starting from Chang-hua in the west and crossing the mountains. Both road and railway were aimed at improving economic extraction – especially at opening up more of the forests for the camphor and timber industries – and at improving military readiness to combat foreign aggression and the still restive aboriginal population. Liu developed the coal-mines and shipping industry, established telegraph communications between Taipei and Tainan, and had a cable sunk under the sea to the Pescadores and Fuzhou. In 1887, he switched on electric light in Taipei, which thus became the first Chinese city to be electrified. Land was reclaimed; the sulphur and silk industries were promoted. From an under-developed backwater, Taiwan had suddenly become perhaps the most progressive region of China.

Liu waged more than forty campaigns against the 'savages', and introduced new, modern training for the army, after the manner of his patron Li Hung-chang. He also had to contend with Chinese uprisings, most notably in 1888 in Chang-hua, provoked by his efforts at tax reform. Liu also tried to improve the performance and quality of his officials by recommending special emoluments for those who served well on Taiwan, in the same way as those sent to the other frontier in north-western Xinjiang were rewarded. In a parallel effort, he tried to restrain official corruption by impeaching a prominent official, and by trying to increase the efficiency of tax collection, commissioning a thorough survey of land holdings to overcome the widespread evasion of land taxes. He taxed camphor at the distilleries in the hills and imposed a variety of other 'likin' duties.

Besides the financial support given Liu, the most concrete signs of the new official consciousness of the importance of Taiwan were twofold. In 1875, the ban on emigration from the mainland was lifted. Then, twelve years later, Taiwan's status was up-graded. It became the twentieth province of Ch'ing China, with Liu Ming-ch'uan as its first Governor. His seat, for the first time, was at the present-day capital, Taipei.

But the reformists like Li Hung-chang were of fluctuating influence in Peking. As the star of his patron, Li Hung-chang, waned, the antagonism Liu had built up for himself among the literati officials, the land-owners and the merchants of Taiwan undermined his position. Some of the Taiwan gentry had, in fact, backed Liu with money and political support, and part of the reason for his comparative success in the early years of his governorship was that the Taiwan élite was not so hidebound by traditional conservatism, vested privilege and resistance to change as the landlord–gentry class in China proper. But, like reformers on the mainland, Liu also found he was nibbling away at too many entrenched interests. In 1890, he put a characteristic proposal to the imperial court. The idea was to raise capital for the Keelung coal-mine by receiving an investment from a British merchant in return for a twenty-year coal and kerosene monopoly on Taiwan. The rejection of the plan gave Liu's enemies the chance to move against him. He was criticised and, in October 1890, dismissed from his rank, though he kept his duties. Disillusioned, Liu resigned the governorship in June 1891.

He left a province that had seen considerable economic growth, largely driven by foreign trade. Taiwan was still an agricultural community, with rice and sugar much the most important exports, followed by tea and camphor. Opium and textiles were the largest imports. A primitive manufacturing industry developed in the processing of agricultural products, and a more integrated economy began to take shape as large landowners diversified into trade. A new élite class of land-owning gentry, comprador tradesmen and literati officials emerged and a lucky few of the peasant farmers who made up most of the population were able in a few generations to aspire to the privileges of the gentry. More and more, the élite aped the manners, life-style and ambitions of their counterparts on the mainland. Some would have their sons educated in classical learning, so that they could compete in the imperial examinations for entry into the mandarinate.

So, except perhaps for the fact that foreign trade represented a more important part of its overall economic activity, Taiwan was by 1895 much more like mainland China than it had ever been. Clan rivalries were less intense now, and the aboriginal wars more one-sided. It was a Chinese-dominated community with a landlord gentry élite comparable to that on the mainland, and an official class now somewhat less adrift from the mainstream of bureaucratic career advancement. It was a peasant economy with, apart from some food-processing, no manufacturing industry and no working class.

But these similarities still did not make it an integral part of China. It had been formally part of China for over two hundred years, but a full province for less than a decade. For most of those two hundred years, Taiwan had been neglected and despised by Peking and its rulers. They, in turn, were resented and perpetually resisted by the population on Taiwan, including the aboriginal tribes, which were either assimilated and lost their identities, or gradually lost ground and retreated into more and more inaccessible mountain lairs in the interior. But resistance had also come from the immigrant Chinese community, much of which had rarely recognised the rule of Peking's representatives, let alone paid heed to the edicts of the distant northern capital. By the 1890s, much of Taiwan's traditional xenophobia was directed more at the mainland than at European visitors. After all, the foreigners tended to have the same interest in developing Taiwan's economy without submitting to the imperial 'squeeze' on profits. The seeds of resistance to the forthcoming Japanese occupation were deeply embedded, not so much in Chinese nationalism, but in an ethnic consciousness limited to the island itself.

THE JAPANESE ANNEXATION AND THE REPUBLIC OF TAIWAN: 1895

It will be recalled that in 1874 the Japanese had already tried to wrest Taiwan from China, and that it was partly the intervention of other foreign powers that at that time forced China to make explicit its still vaguely formulated claim to sovereignty over the whole island. In 1895, another great power intervention to stop China giving too much away to Japan resulted in Japan taking Taiwan almost as a booby prize in a war fought at the other end of China.

The Sino-Japanese war broke out in 1894 over Korea. China was engaged in putting down a rebellion in what it still regarded as its tributary. For Japan, this was another chance to push for the concessions it wanted in China. It joined the war, notionally to protect Korean independence, but in reality to protect and further its own interests in Korea and in China. The war was fought at sea and in Manchuria, and Japan occupied the Liaodong Peninsula, giving it control of the ports of Dairen and Port Arthur. Yet again, despite the reforms and modernisations introduced by Li Hung-chang, China's army and navy were overwhelmed, the Japanese poised to march on Peking, and the empire had once again to sue for peace. In the peace agreement formalised as the April 1895 'Treaty of Shimonoseki', Japan secured recognition of Korean independence, the opening of four more treaty ports, the right of Japanese nationals to build factories in China, a sizeable indemnity, and the cession of Taiwan, the Pescadores, and the Liaodong Peninsula.

The Sino-Japanese war was a turning point. It was almost the final nail in the coffin of Ch'ing credibility as holders of the 'mandate of heaven'. The economic concessions won by the Japanese were then extended to all the foreign powers, stifling Chinese entrepreneurship and industrial investment by opening industry to all-comers. Japan was left the dominant power in north-east Asia, with control from Korea to Taiwan. The disintegration of imperial China seemed near to completion, and the war was followed by a scramble for concessions in China among the imperialist powers.

The treaty was followed in a week by the 'Triple Intervention'. Russia, France and Germany warned Japan that the Liaodong Peninsula must be handed back to China. Russia was the instigator of this move, alarmed at Japan's growing naval capability, and envious of its possession of the warm-water ports of Dairen and Port Arthur. France, a partner in the Dual Alliance, was treaty-bound to support Russia, and Germany, anxious to placate Russia in the east so as to forestall expansionism to the west, colluded. Russia gave a disclaimer about its own territorial intentions in Manchuria (only to dishonour it two years later in the rush for Chinese concessions), and Japan faced the threat of war with three major powers. Liaodong was handed back to China in exchange for an increased indemnity, further crippling the imperial finances, already dangerously in hock to British

financiers, and Taiwan and the Pescadores thus achieved the
dubious distinction of becoming Japan's first fully-fledged
colony. By this time Chinese claims to tribute from the Ryu-
kyu Islands had lapsed, and Japan had formally annexed the
archipelago in 1879. But that was less a colonisation than a
southern extension of Japan proper, and a formalisation of a
long-standing relationship.

Before the Shimonoseki Treaty was signed, Japan had
already taken practical steps to press home the demand for
Taiwan. In March 1895, Penghu and the Pescadores were
occupied, in the same way as the Dutch, Koxinga and the
Ch'ing had all used the Pescadores as a staging post to
Taiwan itself, and Taiwan was put under a naval blockade.
But on Taiwan, the Japanese encountered fierce resistance.
Local reaction to the Treaty of Shimonoseki was one of a
sense of betrayal, presaging the anger felt at twentieth century
betrayals by the great powers. Emboldened by their relative
success in fighting the French, and proud of the improvements
made on the island under Liu Ming-ch'uan, Taiwan's residents were not prepared to hand over to a foreign power in a
treaty negotiated without reference even to the emperor's
representatives on Taiwan, let alone to its residents. The
Chinese governor of Taiwan province, T'ang Ching-sung, was
persuaded to declare the island a Republic, and to lead the
resistance. He did the first, on 25 May, and made himself the
first president. However, he did not seem to have the stomach
for the fight, and was simultaneously offering the island to
first Britain, and then France, in return for protection against
the Japanese. T'ang's curious behaviour hints at the degree of
anti-Japanese racism that was to become such a potent force
in China's nationalist struggle over the next five decades. He
had no reason to think that rule from London or Paris would
be preferable to rule from Tokyo, and experience suggested
that the latter could hardly be worse than neglect and misrule
from Peking. But to be under the sway of an allegedly
culturally inferior 'dwarf' people from the north was a telling
blow to Chinese ethnic self-esteem. Failing to rally any
international support, however, T'ang fled to the mainland,
leaving his new-born Republic as a disorganised, anarchic
resistance movement, and the imperial garrison making hasty
preparations for flight.

The invasion of Taiwan began when Japanese troops landed at Keelung on 30 May. They reached Taipei in less than three weeks and hoisted the Japanese flag there. But it was October before Japanese troops had extended their control over the island. A second 'Republic' was declared by a Chinese general who pledged to hold the line against the Japanese at Tainan, but the Japanese shipped in reinforcements from the Pescadores to meet the southward advance of the army. Of this army, 14 000 men had reached Changhua, but only half of them had survived the next fifty-mile stretch. Taiwan's reputation for diseases was proving itself again, and the Japanese imperial army succumbed to a variety of tropical ailments. But, by the time they reached Tainan, the Republic's second 'President' had also escaped as a fugitive to the mainland, embezzling as he went the contributions he had extorted from landlords and gentry. On 21 October, the Japanese took Tainan. Sporadic armed resistance to the Japanese was to continue as a guerrilla war for another decade, but with the capture of Tainan, they were in virtual control of the island, and were to remain so until 1945.

TAIWAN UNDER THE JAPANESE: 1895–1945

Perhaps because it was Japan's first real colony, Taiwan was ruled with a rod of iron. Still smarting from the humiliation of the 'Triple Intervention', which had seemed to suggest that the Western powers did not think it fit to join the club of imperialist colonisers, Japan was anxious to avoid serious trouble on Taiwan. It wanted to prove it could manage an overseas possession more efficiently than Britain, Germany, France and the others who had been in that business for much longer. The result was a rule of harsh brutality when it came to crushing resistance, of ruthless organisation in exploiting the economic benefits of colonisation, and of stifled economic and political development among the islanders themselves.

The Japanese era on Taiwan can for convenience be divided into three periods. There was the initial consolidation of rule, a time of, in effect, martial law, when Taiwan was ruled by military men, whose first priority remained security in the face of the rumbling guerrilla war. From 1919 to 1936, the

Japanese administrators were civilians, and there was some liberalisation of political controls as more and more Taiwanese became assimilated into the structures of the Japanese Empire. Then, from 1937, when Japan launched full-scale war on continental China, a new form of martial law re-emerged, and Taiwan's development became subordinated to the needs of the Japanese war effort.

The key elements of Japanese rule were put in place under the rule of the Governor from 1898 to 1906, General Kodama Gentaro, and his civilian administrator, Goto Shimpei. By the time Kodama took over, 16 000 Japanese civilians had arrived in Taiwan, to add to the large military garrison, and to impose Japanese rule on the population of some 2 500 000. At Shimonoseki, the Japanese had granted the Taiwanese two years leeway to choose their sovereign allegiance. In this breathing space, an estimated 200 000–300 000 Taiwan residents, mainly the recent arrivals under the brief period of free emigration since 1875, returned to the mainland. Those who stayed behind were deemed to have opted for citizenship of the Japanese Empire.

A pervasive system of social control was installed, based on the traditional Chinese 'bao-jia' system, which can be traced on the mainland even today in the activities of the 'neighbour-hood' committees as the state's eyes and ears at the grass-roots. Under the Japanese system, households were grouped in tens, known as 'ko', and further amalgamated as 'ho', groups of ten 'ko'. The 'hoko' system demanded mutual responsibility from the members to prevent crime, organise community service and prevent subversion. Although hoko members were Taiwanese, the Japanese police were able to keep a close watch on the elected leaders. More than three-quarters of the police force, and all its senior officers, were Japanese. This was the first time in Taiwan's history that state control had so thoroughly penetrated to the local level. It was one way of undermining the social bases of the surrogate forms of civil organisation, like clans and secret societies, that for so long had been the seedbeds of Taiwan's endless rebellions.

Another was the sheer ferocity of the repression. In one campaign alone, against unrest in Tainan district in the summer of 1896, thirty villages were razed to the ground when Japanese troops panned out from the town of Taulok, under orders to kill every living thing within a five mile radius. Such savagery was a feature of the first few years of Japanese occupation, and tended to drive more people to join the rebel bands still hiding out in the hills. Under General Kodama such mass terror tactics were supplanted by a less random but equally ruthless suppression of resistance. Kodama had grand plans for the strategic role of Taiwan, seeing it as a possible base for a Japanese push into South-east Asia, where the Spanish grip on the Philippines already appeared tenuous. He was restrained by more cautious heads in Tokyo, but in the 1940s, a version of his vision was to be realised.

Besides asserting imperial control, the main task of the Kodama–Goto administration was to integrate Taiwan's economy into the Japanese Empire. By the time they arrived, the improvements made under Liu Ming-ch'uan had fallen into decay – even his prized railway from Taipei to Hsinchu was in disuse – so a programme of rapid infrastructural building was started. Roads and railways were built; harbours were dredged; telegraph lines were extended; irrigation works were resumed and advanced. The aim was to harness Taiwan's potential as an agricultural supplier for Japan. Sugar and rice were still the main crops. New high-yielding rice seeds were introduced, along with fertiliser. Through farmers' associations and the hoko network, advances in agricultural techniques were widely disseminated. The land-tax and ownership system was reformed. Traditionally in Taiwan, most farmers were tenants and taxes were payable by the landlord, who, as Liu Ming-ch'uan found, would rarely meet the true tax bill. Now, the landlords were bought out, given government bonds in exchange for their entitlement to rent, and the tenants became owners of their own land, and responsible for land tax. Hence the farmers themselves had to increase their productivity to ensure they could meet their tax liability.

The reforms were a success. By 1905, the colony had become financially self-supporting, and was exporting 90 per cent of its sugar crop and a fifth of its rice, almost all to Japan. These early reforms set a pattern that was to distinguish Taiwan's experience of colonisation from that of many other primary product producers in the developing world. It remained first and foremost a nation of smallholders, rather than a plantation economy managed by expatriate bosses representing colonial or multinational interests. But Japan did take direct financial control of much of the output. Sugar was refined in Japan, or, later, in Japanese-owned refineries in Taiwan. Sugar production was organised around fifty Japanese-owned sugar mills. Government monopolies were set up in camphor, salt, liquor, tobacco and opium.

Japan also set about dismantling the cultural and educational inheritance of Chinese imperial rule. A gradual process of assimilation saw restrictions imposed on the traditional Chinese schools run by classically trained literati, and the promotion of Japanese-style schools for the children of the gentry and literati, to woo their offspring away from residual loyalty to China, and inculcate them with a sense of 'Japaneseness', and of loyalty to the Emperor. This policy helped win influential collaborators from among the pre-Japanese élite, and some Chinese families secured important monopolies and became thriving and influential business people. Japan was in effect following a two-tier policy of rigid social organisation and repression among the bulk of the population, while working hard at assimilating the most powerful elements of the society it had taken over.

This process of assimilation was to be accelerated once Taiwan received its first Japanese civilian government, under Baron Den Kenjiro, who ruled for four years from 1919. The emphasis was on education, with the role of the Japanese schools enhanced, and the departure of several thousand Taiwanese for further education in Japan itself. A nugatory degree of local autonomy was introduced. In 1921, nine Taiwanese were included in a 'consultative council', and a process of slow liberalisation began, culminating with an unrealised 1935 plan for an elected assembly on Taiwan to give the island greater autonomy. In 1924, Taiwanese were for the first time made eligible for military service. In the early 1930s, a policy known as 'kominka' was pursued. It envisaged total assimilation, or 'changing into the emperor's subjects'. This reflected a growing sense of urgency in Tokyo to stamp out Taiwanese nationalism at a time when, from 1931, in full control of Manchuria, plans were being laid for the expansion of the Japanese Empire – the 'Greater East Asian Co-Prosperity Sphere'. But Japan faced a dilemma. On the one hand, the growing ultranationalist ethos in Japan precluded the proposition that aliens could in some way become 'true Japanese'. On the other hand, the alternative to assimilation was to preserve a separate Taiwanese identity, leading either to continued disaffection on the island, or to granting greater local autonomy, which Tokyo was always reluctant to do other than in token measures.

Throughout the Japanese rule, a 'home-rule' movement in Taiwan continued to gather support. The guerrilla wars of the early years resurfaced in anti-Japanese uprisings, notably the 'Musha' revolt of 1930, a bloody uprising by aboriginal tribesmen in the mountain hinterlands of Tai-chung. More than two hundred Japanese died, and twenty days of vicious reprisals left hundreds of tribesmen dead, officially by suicide, supposedly hanging themselves in their huts which were then burnt. The aborigines felt, with justification, that they were the worst treated of all the Taiwanese, and that even the harsh lives of the ethnic Chinese coolies were preferable to the discrimination they faced. But at the other end of the Tai-wanese social spectrum there was also persistent agitation against Japanese rule. As Taiwanese began to travel abroad and mix with other expatriate students, ideals of freedom, democracy and even socialism took hold. A small and short-lived 'Taiwan Communist Party' was founded in Shanghai in 1928.

The most eminent of these bourgeois nationalists was Lin Hsien-t'ang, a scion of a prominent Taiwanese clan which had in fact been prominent among those who had benefited from collaboration with the Japanese. Lin travelled widely in the first three decades of the twentieth century, and mingled with two of the intellectual founders of modern Chinese national-ism, Liang Ch'i-ch'ao and Tai Chi-t'ao. Both tried to per-suade him to adopt a reformist path rather than seek self-determination, in which China, now wracked by warlordism, disunity and intermittent civil war, would not be able to offer support. Lin became a force for moderation in the Taiwan home-rule movement, which was frequently split, treading a narrow path between collaboration and revolution. He was jailed for a time by the Japanese, but also at times scorned by more radical Taiwan nationalists. The resistance to the Jap-anese showed all the problems of disunity, lack of leadership and clan or local loyalties which had for centuries made

Taiwan so difficult to govern. But the experience of Japanese colonisation did at least provide a single focus for the resentment of the disaffected.

The creeping Japanese-sponsored liberalisation of the years between the World Wars came to an end in 1936, and once again the Japanese governors became military men. As Japan became bogged down in a long drawn out and costly war of attrition on continental China, Taiwan's role became that of, firstly, supporting the war effort on the mainland, and then of serving as a stepping stone to South-east Asia. In 1941, now a member of the tripartite pact with fascist Italy and Nazi Germany, Japan launched its offensive against the European and American South-east Asian colonies. For the first time some industrialisation other than food-processing was allowed on Taiwan. Taiwanese-owned firms were taken over by the Japanese, and new chemicals, aluminium, machine-tool and textile factories were built. The war turned against Japan, and the sea-lanes became more hazardous for the imperial fleet. So there was no choice but for Taiwan to develop greater self-sufficiency in industrial and consumer goods, which hitherto, in the classic imperialist mode, had been imported from Japan, which had in return creamed off the agricultural surplus. Taiwan could process the raw materials extracted from the conquered territories in South-east Asia, and serve as a stockpile, refuelling station and garrison for the imperial forces. The 'kominka' programme was stepped up, and dissent suppressed with a new severity and thoroughness. Taiwanese youths were called up to serve as soldiers or navvies, or to defend Taiwan against anticipated invasion. This did not materialise, though the island was bombed heavily during 1944. At this stage, with defeat looming, Japan made a last-ditch effort to woo Taiwanese allegiance in what was seen as the forthcoming battle for Taiwan. In 1945, elections would give Taiwanese full representation in Japan's national parliament, and Taiwan would become a full prefecture of Japan proper.

But, as always in Taiwan's history, its fate after the war was decided not by its people, but by distant statesmen, parcelling it out as part of an accommodation where other considerations weighed heavy. On 1 December 1943, in Cairo, Allied leaders Roosevelt and Churchill issued a joint declaration with China's National leader Chiang Kai-shek. At the end of the war, Japan would be divested of all 'stolen' territories, and the Pescadores and Taiwan would be 'restored' to China. That pledge was reaffirmed at Potsdam in 1945 by Britain, the United States and the Soviet Union. On 14 August, the Japanese Emperor, making his famous observation that, following the atom-bombing of Hiroshima and Nagasaki, 'the war situation has developed not necessarily to Japan's advantage', gave his surrender broadcast. Taiwan was thus spared an Okinawa-style American invasion.

Towards the end of the war, Japan had toyed with various ideas on Taiwan. In 1944, with the prospect of defeat already staring them in the face, some Japanese strategists argued in favour of using Taiwan – and Korea – as bargaining chips – territories which could be handed to the Allies to forestall invasion of Japan itself. In 1945, some of the Japanese Emperor's advisors had urged a second 'Taiwan option', of luring the Americans into a costly and bloody invasion of Taiwan, thereby strengthening Japan's negotiating position when it finally had to sue for peace.

But these schemes came to nought. On 9 September, the Japanese in China formally surrendered at the Nationalists' capital of Nanking. Six Taiwanese were invited over for the ceremony, and took the opportunity to petition the Chinese for 'special status' for Taiwan, 'in order to ensure the continued prosperity of the island'. Forty years later, the communist government in Peking was to be pushing just such an option. But in the 1940s as in the 1980s, the Nationalists insisted on the full integrity of Taiwan as a Chinese province. Any illusion that the ending of the Japanese occupation meant greater autonomy for Taiwan, was shattered when in October, Chiang Kai-shek's armies arrived in Taiwan on American ships. On 25 October, the Japanese commander signed the document formally retroceding Taiwan to the Nanking government. Taiwan had lost one foreign occupation and gained another which did not even acknowledge itself as such.

2 The Kuomintang

THE KUOMINTANG IN 1945

The Chinese 'government' which took the Japanese surrender in southern China at Nanking, and which dispatched troops to reclaim Taiwan, was that of the 'Nationalist Party', the Kuomintang, or KMT, under its leader, and national president, Generalissimo Chiang Kai-shek. Even in 1945, the KMT's control of mainland China was far from total. The Japanese surrender had removed them from occupation of most of the eastern seaboard, and enabled the KMT to move back to their pre-war capital at Nanking, from their retreat in the western province of Sichuan, at Chongqing. But during the war the strength of the KMT's notional allies in an anti-Japanese 'United Front', the Chinese Communist Party, had grown from an estimated 40 000 political and military activists to 1.5 million. They controlled bases and extensive 'border regions' in north-west China around Yenan, in the Shandong Peninsula, in southern Manchuria, in the north Chinese plains of Hebei and Henan, in Hunan, in Jiangxi, and in the coastal province of Jiangsu among other places. KMT influence in Manchuria was so limited that the Soviet Union, having declared war on Japan just days before the end of the war, was authorised by the KMT to move into Manchuria to accept the Japanese surrender there. The Americans had to airlift 500 000 KMT troops to the north-east to sustain the myth of the KMT as a 'national' government. Besides areas controlled by the communists and the Soviet Union, large parts of China were still effectively under the sway of fractious warlords, who may have detested communism and paid lip-service to obeying the KMT government, but were no government's pliant subjects.

Nevertheless, at the time, few but the most prescient observers and optimistic communists expected that the KMT would, within four years, have caved in to abject defeat in the ensuing civil war. The KMT enjoyed overwhelming firepower – perhaps three-to-one in terms of front-line soldiers, and five-to-one in weaponry. Just as important, the KMT enjoyed the support of the country which had emerged undisputedly as the world's most powerful nation, the United States. Even the Soviet Union was co-operating with the KMT in accepting the Japanese surrender. The communists' success in mobilising patriotic resistance to the Japanese was unlikely, it was thought, to replicate itself in turning China's people against its legitimate government, the KMT. By this time the KMT had been in power over a 'united' China for two decades. Its leader, Chiang Kai-shek, had appeared at Cairo with the leaders of the free world, and he and his family had been fêted in the United States as fighters for freedom and democracy. China had won its Japanese war, even if as much due to the efforts of the communists and the atom bomb as to the KMT's own fighting capabilities. With even Stalin adopting a cautious, arms-length relationship with the communists, the KMT were apparently assured of power, and their government became a founder member of the United Nations, and permanent member of its Security Council.

That all this should wither so quickly into a series of disastrous military defeats reflects failures of leadership, organisation, ideology and economic management. The roots of these failings can be traded right back to the KMT's origin as the confused offspring of the turbulent nationalism and republicanism of the dying days of imperial China.

SUN YAT-SEN AND THE ORIGINS OF THE KMT

By the end of the nineteenth century, the Chinese empire was doomed. The voracity with which foreign imperialists were carving up China robbed the Ch'ing dynasty of any credibility as a permanent government. The reforms instigated by progressive officials to keep China's 'essence' intact, while making use of Western techniques to modernise and strengthen China, were as hopeless as that of Deng Xiaoping and his colleagues almost a century later. Like Deng's regime, too, imperial China had no way of filtering out the ideological influences of westernisation from the technological benefits they hoped it would bring. So, in the years around the turn of the century, a variety of small, Western-influenced revolutionary organisations sprang up.

One of these was the 'Hsing Chung Hui', the 'Revive China Society'. It was formed in 1894 by Sun Yat-sen and a hundred or so overseas Chinese in Hawaii, at that time a republic. Sun was a native of Guangdong province, between Macao and Guangzhou. He was of peasant stock in a region of long revolutionary traditions and of persistent anti-Ch'ing resentment. The area had, in all China, the longest experience of foreign contacts, and Sun, born in 1866, had been educated in Honolulu, and had become a Christian. With these Western ideas in his head, he became a rebel on returning home in the early 1880s. He was expelled to the British colony of Hong Kong in 1884, for desecrating village idols. In Hong Kong, he acquired a medical training and the sobriquet 'Doctor'.

In 1894, Dr Sun, like many other ambitious and patriotic young men, had taken a proposal for economic and political reform to Peking, to present it to the modernising imperial statesman Li Hung-chang. Unsurprisingly, Li spurned the opportunity of meeting the upstart and Dr Sun turned away from the reformist route, and became one of China's first professional revolutionaries. In 1895, he organised a small branch of the 'Hsing Chung Hui' in Hong Kong, with the idea of capitalising on the national unrest sparked off by China's humiliation in the Japanese war, to drive out the Ch'ing. At this time, although suffused with a vague republicanism, Dr Sun, like most of his contemporaries and like his anti-Ch'ing revolutionary antecedents, was inspired more by the nationalist antipathy to what was still seen as a foreign, un-Chinese, Manchu rule. The 1895 plotted revolution ended in farce, when arms ferried in cement barrels to Canton were seized by a forewarned police force, and the revolutionary fighters arrived a day late, also to be greeted by the police.

This fiasco was to be the first of several. The successful 1911 Wuchang uprising was the eleventh attempt at armed insurrection. But Dr Sun's reputation as the natural leader of the revolution was already well in the making. Forced to go into exile, he travelled widely, and in 1896 gained more fame when the imperial government tried to kidnap him in London. But it was in Japan in particular that he made his base, vying for support among the overseas Chinese and sympathetic Japanese with the reformist intellectuals K'ang Yu-wei and

Liang Ch'i-ch'ao. Both Dr Sun and Liang Chï-ch'ao visited Taiwan a number of times during these years. The economic progress made under Japanese rule was another source of inspiration for what might one day be possible on the mainland. K'ang and Liang were much more able thinkers than Dr Sun, but lacked the charisma and energy that was to carry Sun through repeated abortive uprisings and a political and ideological programme that was at best sketchy and at worst downright naïve. Nor was the K'ang–Liang line, of constitutional reform within the imperial framework, one with the popular appeal of Sun's call for revolution. In fact, the empire was disintegrating anyway. What none of these theorists addressed with sufficient clarity was the question of what to put in its place.

Nevertheless, Dr Sun collaborated for a while with the others, borrowing their ideas when they suited him, and in 1903 he began to write articles himself. The slogan he came up with, and was to elaborate in the 1920s as his political testament to the KMT was 'The Three Principles of the People'. These are usually summed up as 'Democracy', 'Nationalism' and 'People's Livelihood'. This is somewhat misleading, 'Nationalism', or 'minzu-zhuyi', incorporates both nation and race, so that even today, Taiwanese can feel inspired by pan-Chinese 'nationalism' even if they oppose reunification with the mainland. 'Democracy', 'minquan', translates as people's rights or power, and thus did not necessarily at the time have its Western connotation of electoral choice. Thirdly, 'People's Livelihood', a term borrowed from classical Chinese, in origin meant no more than that the people should have enough to eat, wear and meet their tax obligations. This principle was fleshed out by another slogan which was adopted by the communists long before the KMT made it law on Taiwan in the late 1940s – 'land to the tiller'. China was overwhelmingly a peasant society, and it was to be in the countryside that the KMT would lose the civil war. Ruefully surveying their history on the mainland, the KMT on Taiwan would come to the conclusion that their failure to institute a proper land reform had been a prime cause of their loss of power.

In other words, the 'Three Principles' were not, even in summary form, a plan for action. Rather they formed slogans around which large sectors of the Chinese intelligentsia and others could rally, for the very reason that they were so vague. Later, in the 1920s, their flexibility also enabled Dr Sun to declare them sufficiently compatible with the aims of the Communist Party for the first 'United Front' to be formed.

Dr Sun did, however, produce two other sorts of idea. One was for the organisation of government, and it is still followed on Taiwan today. Borrowing the imperial term for the branches of government, he said there should be five 'yuan', or constitutional arms of government: executive, legislative, judicial, examination and control (or inspectorate). This is a kind of crude amalgam of Montesquieu and Confucius – of a conventional Western concept of the separation of powers, with traditional Chinese adjuncts, like examination boards for the civil service, and the censorate, for keeping officialdom up to the mark. Second, Sun expounded the concept of a three-stage transition to republican government. In the first stage, the Ch'ing would be overthrown. All the excrescences associated with the decadent empire would be wiped out – foot-binding, opium-smoking, geomancy, bureaucratic extortion and excessive taxation. This would be followed by a period of military rule, a transitional phase of what Dr Sun called 'political tutelage'. Because, in Dr Sun's words, the Chinese people had been 'soaked in the poison of absolute monarchy for several thousand years', the Chinese were short of democratic experience. In this period, they would be embued with democratic values by a firm but far-sighted government under idealistic revolutionaries. The period of political tutelage was to last six years. Thereafter, the military government would surrender to a government elected by the people.

Dr Sun's ideas are important not so much as concrete contributions to Chinese political thought, but because of their abiding influence in Taiwan and mainland China. He is still regarded in both Peking and Taipei as the father of modern China. The Republic of China on Taiwan sees itself as a continuation of the Republic of China which was to be inaugurated with Dr Sun as its provisional President on 1 January 1912. Its official data still describe the years in the old imperial fashion, with 1912 as year one of the new dynasty. Meanwhile, the communists in Peking look on Dr Sun as the leader of a bourgeois revolution. That, in accordance with classic Marxist historiography, had to precede their own socialist revolution. Into the 1980s, Dr Sun's statue and relics were revered in both Chinas. On the mainland, his widow, Soong Ch'ing-ling, held senior if not very powerful posts under the communists, culminating, for a fortnight before her death in 1981, with the honorary Presidency of China. In Taiwan, her sister, Soong May-ling, the widow of Chiang Kai-shek, was a rallying point for conservative opinion into the late 1980s, when she was well into her nineties. The KMT still spoke of 'reunifying China under the Three Principles of the People'. Vestiges of Sun's ideas of political tutelage surfaced on the mainland as the theory of 'neo-authoritarianism', that what China needed was, on the model of South Korea, Singapore, and Taiwan itself, a period of strong government before democratic freedoms could be bestowed on an unprepared people. The Chinese uniform of the Cultural Revolution, known outside China as the 'Mao suit', is known in Chinese as a 'Sun Yat-sen suit'.

Back in the early 1900s, however, Dr Sun was just one of a number of active apprentice revolutionaries striving for the support and finance of overseas Chinese communities to back their plans for an uprising that would topple the Ch'ing from its increasingly precarious perch, and inaugurate a brave new world of reform, modernisation and self-respect in China. Then in 1905, under Japanese pressure, Dr Sun started to assert some degree of organisation and centralisation on these mushrooming revolutionary cells, under his leadership. In Japan, he set up the 'Revolutionary Alliance', the 'T'ung Meng Hui'. It was the largest such grouping yet, attracting membership from a number of student groups which had extensive connections in almost every province of the mainland. Dr Sun could attract backing from his well-established network of international contacts among overseas Chinese, and sympathetic foreigners, especially Japanese, and from the secret societies, the Triads, who were to be a crucial element of KMT history.

As the Revolutionary Alliance gathered a few thousand members overseas, events gathered a new impetus. The defeat of Russia by Japan in the 1905 war made the Chinese revolutionaries yet more painfully aware of their country's backwardness, and of the failure of 'self-strengthening'. For the first time, the 'white' races had been defeated. Anything seemed possible. In 1900, foreign intervention to suppress the Boxer uprising, an originally anti-Manchu secret society revolt which had been turned by the dynasty against the imperialists, seemed to push the regime of the Empress Dowager Ci Xi to the very brink of annihilation. The reforms of the last days of the Ch'ing, which in 1905 scrapped the old examination system in a bid to present its policies as modern, were too little, too late to salvage a corrupt and demoralised officialdom, and an out-gunned and disorganised army. In 1908, the Empress Dowager died, leaving a child emperor under the control of a venal regent. A military man, Yuan Shih-k'ai, emerged as the one strong man in the enfeebled dynasty. For a century, the dynasty had been embattled. At home there had been a series of bruising internal rebellions, notably the massive Taiping uprising of 1850–64, which raged over half of China and led to tens of millions of deaths. Abroad, China's territorial integrity had been abused time and again by the encroachments of foreign commercial interests that the dynasty had proved powerless to resist. Now, it was facing repeated abortive putsch attempts mounted by the T'ung Meng Hui. Finally, the emperor was found to have no clothes, and a revolution that was more like a minor riot ended five millennia of imperial history.

On the 'Double Tenth', 10 October 1911, it was an attempted rebellion by some military officers at Wuchang on the middle Yangtze in central China that sparked the final downfall of the Ch'ing. Like so many attempted uprisings of that period, the plot was discovered, forcing the officers to revolt to save themselves. However, they found they were knocking at an open door; the local commanders fled, and one of the officers pronounced himself the head of an independent regime. Within two months, all the provinces of central and south China had followed suit, along with the north-west. The imperial government called on Yuan Shih-k'ai for assistance. In the 1890s, when eclipsed in semi-disgrace, Yuan had founded a modern fighting force, the Northern (Beiyang) Army. He had then put this army at the disposal of Ci Xi against the reformists arrayed against her in 1898. Now, however, negotiating for the empire, he arranged its abdication.

Sun Yet-sen was in the United States at the time, and read of this turn of events in the newspapers. He hurried back to China in time to be inaugurated as the first president of a new Republic on 1 January 1912, in Nanking. But, back in China for the first time in years, Dr Sun then offered to step down in favour of the strong man and potential 'political tutor' Yuan Shih-k'ai. Yuan agreed to support Dr Sun's demands for political reforms, and, in particular, for a parliament. He appeared to have the strength and prestige to force through such measures. National unity seemed the priority, both, on the one hand, to withstand the centrifugal tendencies so manifest in Chinese history when dynasties fall, and, on the other hand, to attract foreign support and deter any foreign power from seeking to capitalise on the change of dynasty by invading. Sun Yat-sen himself took charge of a railway project. If his ideas do not mark him out as a great revolutionary thinker, his behaviour at the crucial juncture of the 'revolution' he is now credited with leading, does not suggest a great strategist either. As a tactician, fund-raiser and cajoler of disparate forces, however, Dr Sun was a past-master.

But the idea that Yuan Shih-k'ai, a mandarin general brought up in the old traditions, could prove to be the man to usher China into a new age of democracy was far-fetched and soon proved illusory. One of the revolutionary leaders now back from abroad, Sung Chiao-jen, drafted a new constitution, providing for a two-tier national legislature, and for provincial assemblies, popularly elected, if only on a very small franchise. In August 1912, he also engineered the merger of the Revolutionary Alliance with four smaller groups to form the 'Nationalist Party'. In 1914 and 1919, Dr Sun himself was to preside over two further major reorganisations, disbanding the T'ung Meng Hui in 1914, to form the Chinese Revolutionary Party, and then in 1919, to found the 'Chinese Nationalist Party', the Kuomintang or KMT that was to be his vehicle until his death. In 1912–13, national elections were held in China. Under the Constitution, the Prime Minister would come from the majority party. The KMT's campaign, masterminded by Sung, was targeted at the voting gentry élite. When KMT duly won its majority, Sung saw himself as a prospective leader of parliament and began to think of whittling away the powers Yuan Shih-k'ai had arrogated to himself. However, Yuan Shih-k'ai had him assassinated in March 1913. This precipitated a 'second revolution', easily suppressed by Yuan, who then banned the KMT, dissolved parliament, abolished the provincial assemblies and announced he would be President for life. In 1915, he said he would become emperor. For the young idealists of the stillborn KMT, it was back to the drawing board.

THE KUOMINTANG REORGANISES: 1916–28

Yuan Shih-k'ai's dynastic aspirations provoked a new insurrection and eight provinces in the south and west declared their opposition. Then in June 1916, Yuan died. However, instead of giving the abortive Republic a second lease of life, Yuan's death also buried hopes of a unified Republican China. The Republic continued to exist in name, with a president in Peking, the product of a usually rigged election in parliament. But the President's position in fact relied on the support of whatever warlord happened to be in control of the capital at the time. The effective sway of his government extended no further than the outskirts of Peking and China disintegrated into a score or more of warlord-run satrapies, ruled by whichever strongman had the resources to field the most ruthless and efficient army, and often at war with each other.

With chronic internal disunity now exacerbating China's external weakness, the revolutionary movement in China gathered new force. On 4 May 1919, protests at the ceding of German concessions in China to Japan at the Versailles Conference at the end of the First World War spread to a national 'May 4th Movement'. Inspired by aggrieved patriotism, the movement became a nationwide campaign for 'science and democracy', and for the popularisation of Chinese culture and the eradication of the feudal traditions by which China's modernisation and very survival as a sovereign state were threatened. Out of that intellectual movement, one strand began taking inspiration from the Bolshevik revolution to the north. In July 1921, in Shanghai, a dozen delegates representing a paltry 57 members formed the Chinese Communist Party (CCP). One of the most obscure of the delegates was the Hunanese, Mao Zedong.

Of all the various groups which sprang up in the intellectual ferment of the period, the CCP was not, numerically, that important. It had at the time, however, one very strong card. It was the Chinese representative of a movement which had waged a successful revolution in the vast land to China's north. For revolutionaries seeking international backing for the ousting of the plethora of corrupt, violent and repressive regimes which now ruled China, the Soviet Union seemed the obvious choice. For the Soviet Union, isolated and beleaguered and seeking to promote the creation of friendly regimes in other countries, the CCP did not seem to offer great hope.

Out of this conjunction of interests emerged the first United Front between the CCP and the KMT, and the reorganisation of the KMT which was to enable it to unify China. After the failure of his Republic, Dr Sun Yat-sen and his supporters regrouped in Canton, with the unreliable backing of a local warlord, and the continued support of some of his foreign and secret society connections. Dr Sun then made overtures to the Soviet Union and in January 1923, he signed an accord with the Soviet envoy Adolf Joffe. Later that year, the man who was to usurp Dr Sun's mantle, Chiang Kai-shek, was sent on a mission to Moscow. The Communist International began sending advisors to China, and the Comintern's English-speaking international agitator, Mikhail Borodin, whose career spreading the Comintern's line spanned a dozen countries, arrived in Canton in September 1923 to act as Dr Sun's personal advisor. The result was the Kuomintang's Reorganisation Conference of January 1924.

This put into effect the Sun–Joffe accord. In essence, the Soviet Union was acknowledging that it was too early to expect a mature communist party to develop in China. Instead it would put its weight and technical support behind Dr Sun and the 'bourgeois nationalist' revolutionary party, the KMT. The Soviet Union also renounced some of its tsarist concessions in China, and disavowed any future imperialistic intentions in Outer Mongolia. Under instructions from Moscow, the CCP would co-operate. Its members, however, would join the KMT as individuals, so that the CCP would be no more than a bloc within the KMT, rather than a partner in a true 'United Front'. The Soviet Union would provide arms and military advice. A military academy was set up in Canton in late 1923, the Whampoa Academy, under Chiang Kai-shek, where he could build an army that was modern, well-organised and loyal to him. The Soviet Union provided 3 000 000 roubles as well as some 40 Soviet officers as instructors and advisors, and the curriculum included political indoctrination as well as military training.

The strategy worked, if not in the way the Soviet Union hoped. The support for the KMT regime at Canton became a weapon in the battle for Lenin's legacy between Stalin and Trotsky. Stalin believed that once they had completed their task in the process of revolutionary history, the KMT could be discarded 'like a squeezed lemon'. More pertinently, Trotsky wrote that the CCP–KMT pact was an alliance with the devil, and that 'it is absurd to suppose that the devil will be converted . . . and that he will use his horns not against the workers and peasants, but exclusively for good works'.[1] Leninist theory had backed the 'Stalin' line. In his 'Theses on the National and Colonial Question', Lenin had written, 'The Communist International must be ready to establish temporary relationships and even alliances with the bourgeois democracy of the colonies and backward countries.' However, he had gone on to warn about too close a relationship. 'It must not, however, amalgamate with it. It must retain the independent character of the proletarian movement, even though this movement be in the embryonic stage.'

The KMT reorganisation of 1924 had a more lasting impact on the party than simply in preparing it for victory in its battle for national reunification in the 1920s. The party became a Leninist one, whose outlines can still be seen in Taiwan today. The organisational principle was of 'democratic centralism'. That is, it was a mass party, formed in a tight pyramid structure, whose local cells owed obedience to directives from the centre. The central organs of power were, and are, a Central Committee of about 200 members, who in turn delegated day-to-day decision-making power to an Executive, or Standing Committee, analagous to the 'politburos' of Marxist–Leninist parties. In government, it tried to manage a one-party state, and established party supervisory committees at every level of government. It developed mass propaganda organs, preparing itself for power as the party embodying the firm authoritarianism needed for what its Marxist advisors regarded in the context of communist parties as the dictatorship of the proletariat. But the KMT was a bourgeois, or even feudal, party in terms of the sectors of society from which it drew its power base. In Dr Sun's theory, it was preparing itself for the authoritarian transitional phase of 'political tutelage'. One of the many great historical ironies of Taiwan's current situation is that it has been ruled by a party whose two most striking characteristics are on the one hand its ideological commitment to anti-communism and, on the other hand, its communist party-style organisational structure.

In January 1924, Lenin died, leaving behind a disputed succession. Just over a year later, in March 1925, Sun Yat-sen also died. The Kuomintang was facing two great questions. Should Dr Sun's line of co-operation with the Soviet Union and the CCP be continued? And who should take Dr Sun's place as leader of the KMT? On his deathbed, Dr Sun had signed a 'political testament', calling on the party to follow his ideas, and a letter to the Soviet Union, pledging the party to 'keeping in close touch' with Moscow. But the KMT's leadership, almost all from merchant, gentry or landlord families, were not natural allies of proletarian revolutionaries. An influential group of right-wingers, known as the 'Western Hills' group, demanded the expulsion of CCP members from the party, and the dismissal of Borodin and all other Soviet advisors. The KMT split, but the Whampoa clique around Chiang Kai-shek was looking ever the stronger faction. Yet another faction within the KMT took a more leftist line than Chiang, in which, naturally, they could play on the support within the KMT of the CCP. This faction looked to a veteran stalwart of the anti-Manchu agitation, Wang Ching-wei, who was with Dr Sun at his deathbed and had written down the 'testament'. He saw Chiang as an upstart and himself as the natural successor.

In the end, both of the two central questions facing the KMT were resolved by Chiang Kai-shek's victory in the inner party power struggle. Chiang was a military man turned politician. The son of a salt merchant from near the treaty port of Ningpo in Zhejiang province, he had received military training in Japan in the early 1900s, and began his rise in the nationalist military struggle against Yuan Shih-k'ai. He had joined the T'ung Meng Hui in Japan and met Sun Yat-sen there. In 1922, he had helped Sun escape by boat from Canton when an alliance with a local warlord turned sour. This encounter cemented him in Sun's esteem, and secured him the mission to the Soviet Union, and then the top job at the Whampoa Academy. Now, he tried to capitalise on the legitimacy his association with Dr Sun gave him. A story was put about that Dr Sun died with Chiang's name on his lips. As with the Lenin letter casting doubt on Stalin, or Mao Zedong's purported note to Hua Guofeng – 'with you in charge, I am at ease' – it seemed essential to justify or negate the revolutionary succession by reference to the founding father's final wishes. Then Chiang proposed marriage to Sun's widow, Soong Ch'ing-ling. She refused, and was presumably outraged – not only was Chiang married already, but he had also earlier proposed to Ching-ling's younger sister May-ling. In 1927, when Chiang, the common military man, was close to becoming undisputed dictator of most of China, he proposed to Soong May-ling again, and was accepted. At a stroke, he married into Dr Sun's 'dynasty', and into one of the wealthiest and most powerful families in Shanghai, the Soongs.

With its new organisational and military muscle, the KMT went from strength to strength from its base at Canton, while the warlord armies continued to rampage around the country. But the CCP was also becoming a force in its own right. Both organisations were helped in attracting support by the 'May 30th' movement. On that date in 1925, thirteen demonstrators in Shanghai were killed by the British-officered police force. Less than a month later, fifty-two more died in Canton, also to foreign bullets. A wave of patriotism washed across China, leading to boycotts of foreign goods, strikes by newly formed trades unions, and to a recruitment bonanza for both the KMT and the CCP. By the time of the KMT's second National Congress in January 1926, more than a third of the delegates were also CCP members. Chiang Kai-shek abruptly alleged a plot, and purged some CCP leaders and Soviet advisors. Meanwhile, he still protested his allegiance to the alliance with Moscow.

Stalin, despite the evidence of Chiang's willingness to dispense with his communist partners, apparently still thought he was in control of the relationship. But later in 1926, Chiang's 'Revolutionary Army' launched the 'Northern Expedition', a military push to reunify China. Warlords resisted, but in many cases only half-heartedly, and communist agitators in the countryside turned the expedition into a social revolution as well as a military conquest. The armies reached the Yangtze in late 1926, and moved the KMT capital to Wuhan. Then Chiang moved east to Nanking and Shanghai. Workers in Shanghai wrested control from the local warlord, and greeted the Revolutionary Army as one of liberation. Chiang mobilised his contacts among the thuggish underworld of the secret societies against the worker-pickets. On 12 April 1927, they were disarmed, and a 'White Terror' ensued, as Chiang turned viciously on his notional communist allies. Thousands died. Chiang set up his government at Nanking. For a while, the 'left' KMT in Wuhan, including Wang Ching-wei and Sun Yat-sen's widow Soong Ching-ling, carried on some semblance of the United Front, but that too soon crumbled. By the end of 1928, China was virtually united under Chiang Kai-shek's leadership, and the communists, who had seemed almost on the point of leading successful urban insurrection in China's main ports, became a bedraggled band of fugitives hiding in remote hill-lands.

THE KUOMINTANG IN POWER: 1928–37

The Kuomintang government of Chiang Kai-shek which, for a brief nine-year period, controlled most of China is referred to nowadays in the official Taiwan media as 'the best government China ever had'. This is so much of an untruth as to undermine the KMT's quite justifiable claims to real achievements on Taiwan itself. Chiang's rule on the mainland was a corrupt, brutal dictatorship, which flirted with fascism, and presided over economic devastation, social misery and national humiliation. In his own account of himself, *China's Destiny*, Chiang was to lay all the blame for this at the door of international communism and foreign imperialism. That his own personal failings and the regime's early loss of direction also played a part is, however, undeniable. Throughout the period, the KMT was preoccupied with three threats: that of internal division; that of communist revolution; and that of Japanese invasion. In preferring to concentrate on these three dangers in that order of priority, Chiang and his advisers were not just making a strategic miscalculation; they were also recognising that their interests were ever more closely enmeshed with those of foreign imperialism than with those of China's workers, or, in particular, peasantry.

On 3 October 1928, the KMT Central Executive Committee adopted a provisional constitution, called 'An Outline of Political Tutelage', and the five-yuan structure of government was put in place, under Chiang Kai-shek as President of the Republic. But the 'unification' achieved by the northern expedition was far from complete. Many of the old northern warlords had shrewdly kept their power bases more or less intact by co-operating with the KMT. They now continued to operate as semi-independent fiefdoms. Notable among these were the 'young marshal' Chang Hsueh-liang in the northeast, the 'Guangxi clique' in central China, the 'Christian general' Feng Yu-hsiang in the north-west, and Yen Hsi-shan in Shanxi. They steadfastly resisted attempts to merge their considerable armed forces into a national army dominated by Whampoa-trained Chiang loyalists.

Quite apart from its military limitations, Chiang's regime was also plagued by internal factionalism. The Western Hills faction was continually at odds with the 'left' KMT of Wang Ching-wei, which twice set up short-lived rival governments. The admixture of fractious warlords with squabbling politicians was a potent disincentive to strong government action. Chiang represented a third KMT faction, sometimes siding with the right, sometimes with the left. The uncertainty surrounding his own position made him, and hence the KMT government, dependent on four important sources of support: there was the Whampoa-trained army; the Shanghai underworld 'Green Gang', with its lucrative squeeze on so much of China's business, and in particular on the opium trade; the related power of comprador capital, especially in Shanghai, where Chiang's family links with the Soong dynasty assured him of access to the world of international high finance; and finally, there was international capital, in particular from Britain and the United States, needed to bail out an ailing and mismanaged economy. The KMT government became the tool of soldiers, gangsters, big business and of foreign capital. Even if it had been motivated to do so, it would have found it hard to move decisively and effectively against Japanese incursions.

The KMT's ideology under Chiang took a sharp turn to the right. He became disillusioned with the older Western models of democracy, and increasingly attracted by the rising power of the fascist leaders in Germany and Italy. In 1932, he began building up a fascist-style personality cult. The so-called Blueshirts were formed of a few thousand loyal and enthusiastic army officers. They were to devote themselves to Chiang's interests in the manner of Mussolini's or Hitler's acolytes. In 1934, a 'New Life' movement tried to link the revival of traditional Chinese Confucian ideals with Chiang's own dictatorship. It was a defensive move. Natural disasters, financial incompetence and the failure to introduce a land reform had all contributed to economic hardship in much of the country. The government was manifestly failing to preserve China's territorial integrity. Some source of legitimacy for the regime had to be found.

The KMT did, however, make a concerted effort to quash once and for all China's communist movement. The bankruptcy of Soviet policy in China following the Shanghai massacre was made complete with the failure of subsequent attempts to lead urban-based insurrections. Within the party, a struggle for power grew up between an 'internationalist' line represented by 28 'returned Bolsheviks' – students who had spent time in the Soviet Union – and various other factions. The drift to the countryside by communist remnants gathered pace, and with it, the power and influence of Mao Zedong, who had led peasant insurrections in his native Hunan province as early as 1927. In remote, usually mountainous, 'border' regions, out of the reach of the main KMT centres of control, the communists began to regroup as a rural, peasant-based revolutionary movement. In 1930, Chiang started his 'bandit extermination' campaigns, directed at the eight major communist bases, which stretched from the 'Central Soviet', in southern Jiangxi and western Fujian, to the Oyuwan Soviet, straddling Hupei, Henan and Anhui. Mao Zedong emerged as an outstanding strategist of guerrilla resistance warfare, and of peasant-led revolution. Although Party support had been all

but wiped out in the 1927 terror – there were only about
10 000 Party members by the end of that year – in the
countryside, with an enlightened policy of winning over all
sections of the peasantry, the Party now began to find new
adherents. It claimed 300 000 members by 1934 and the
KMT eradication drive was stepped up. In 1932, two of the
southern bases were evacuated. Then in 1934, in the largest
'encirclement' campaign so far, involving some 750 000
nationalist troops, with aircraft and German military advisers,
the KMT's armies forced the communists to abandon their
Jiangxi bases. The resultant 'Long March' to comparative
safety in Shanxi in the north-west wrote the Party's finest
hour in its own history books, although it came close to
destroying it as a political and military force. Of 100 000 Red
Army members who began the epic trek, perhaps no more
than a tenth survived. But in the course of the march, Mao
Zedong gained control of the Party, and it developed the
strategy that was to prove fatal to the KMT.

While, like the Ch'ing emperors before him, Chiang Kai-
shek was committing his military strength to stamping out
internal 'chaos', the creeping dismemberment of China by
foreign powers was gathering pace. In September 1931, after a
presumably stage-managed explosion on a railway train and
ensuing shooting incident, Japan began the siege of Mukden,
now known as Shenyang, in Manchuria. That touched off the
invasion of Manchuria and other parts of northern China, and
the establishment of the Japanese puppet kingdom of 'Man-
chukuo', under P'u Yi, the last Ch'ing emperor, who had lost
his throne while still an infant. The five-month campaign to
gain full control of Manchuria in full swing, in January 1933
the Japanese opened a second front, fighting a successful two-
month battle around Shanghai to break a boycott of Japanese
goods. In 1933, Japan expanded its dominion out of Manchuria into Inner Mongolia. There was no gainsaying its
ultimate ambition to establish a protectorate over much, if not
all, of China. The communists declared war on Japan in 1932.
But even the Central Committee of the Communist Party had
had to flee a clandestine existence in Shanghai for the Jiangxi
Soviet in 1933, and it was not until 1935 that the declaration
of war became a formulated strategy rather than a propaganda bonus in its civil war with the KMT.

The KMT, meanwhile, avoided full-scale confrontation with Japan. After the 'Mukden Incident', the KMT appealed to the League of Nations, which proved ineffectual. In 1933, Japan withdrew from the League, cocking a snook at the body, the very purpose of which was undermined by its helplessness in the face of Japanese aggression in Manchuria. Nor would Chiang commit his armies to a war of resistance. His policy was summed up in the slogan 'Unification and *then* resistance'. But public opinion was increasingly impatient of this. Students especially, in the May 4th traditions, campaigned against Japan. In 1936, a National Salvation Association was founded to campaign for active resistance, and Soong Ch'ing-ling, Mme Sun Yat-sen, lent her name to it. Capturing the popular mood, the CCP launched an appeal for a 'Second United Front', this time against the Japanese. In the extraordinary 'Xian Incident' of December 1936, Chiang Kai-shek was kidnapped by the young marshal Chang Hsueh-liang. Chang's armies were supposed to be rooting out communists around Xian, but would rather have been fighting the Japanese in their home provinces of Manchuria. After nearly two weeks in captivity, Chiang Kai-shek was freed, apparently on the intervention of the future communist prime minister Zhou Enlai. The price of the ransom seems to have been Chiang's support for bringing the KMT into a United Front. In July 1937, another fabricated incident, this time at Marco Polo Bridge outside Peking, saw the onset of full-scale Japanese invasion, and the start of an eight-year period of CCP–KMT alliance, that had more the character of a civil war in waiting than of a genuinely concerted patriotic united front.

THE SECOND UNITED FRONT: 1937–45

China became divided in three. The north-east and much of the coastal region was under Japanese occupation. In the north-west, from their capital at Yenan, the communists controlled the smallest portion. The KMT, meanwhile, having moved its capital west from Nanking first to Hankow, and then to Chongqing in Sichuan, controlled the rest, large tracts of mainly inhospitable terrain in the west. So swift was the Japanese invasion that Nanking fell in December 1937, with the massacre of tens of thousands of civilians, while the KMT was contemplating suing for peace. The erstwhile leftist 'Wang Ching-wei', despairing of China's chances of winning the war, advocated an anti-communist united front with Japan, and became the head of a Japanese puppet regime.

Whereas, from Yenan, the CCP instituted land reforms and developed a mass base, the KMT in Chongqing were more like an occupation force. Cut off from their roots in the Shanghai secret society underworld and big business, they resorted to printing money to finance themselves. Rather than reform land ownership and win the support of the peasantry, they relied on a shifting and unreliable pattern of alliances with local land-owners and warlords. Intellectuals defected to the CCP in a steady stream north. Still, even with Japanese troops occupying vast tracts of the Chinese heartland, the leadership seemed as much concerned with forestalling the communist threat. In the most notorious example of this, in January 1941, several thousand communist soldiers who had encroached beyond the southern banks of the Yangtze, were slaughtered by the KMT in what was known as the 'New Fourth Army Incident'. That effectively spelled the end of the United Front, whose international basis had been sorely tested by the Nazi–Soviet pact of August 1939.

However, with the bombing of Pearl Harbour in Hawaii in December 1941, the Japanese gave Chiang Kai-shek his strongest card – full-blooded US commitment. Until then, China had fought virtually alone. The most significant outside support had come from the Soviet Union, which had offered the KMT a non-aggression pact in August 1937, and by the end of the following year had supplied 1000 planes, 2000 pilots and 500 military advisors. The US in the same period, still isolationist in outlook, had provided just US$120 million in non-military aid, and a further US$50 million to prop up China's inflated currency. As US–Japanese relations worsened, the lend-lease programme became available to China in March 1941. With Pearl Harbour, the Anglo-American declaration of war on Japan, and the Chinese war declaration against the Axis powers, the Chongqing government became part of a worldwide alliance. The allies created a China–India–Burma theatre of war, with Chiang Kai-shek as supreme commander of the China theatre. An airforce made up of American mercenaries had flown for the KMT even before Pearl Harbour. Now it was incorporated into the US Fourteenth Air Force. The KMT became ever more dependent on large infusions of US aid, weapons, material and advice, although Chiang constantly grumbled that the support was not enough. Indeed, the 'hump' airlift from Burma to KMT-controlled Kunming in Yunnan was at the very extremity of the United States' strategic reach. General 'Vinegar Joe' Stilwell was sent from the US to be Chiang's Chief of Staff. Stilwell was to be one of the loudest of those voices urging US caution in backing Chiang. He was constantly frustrated in his efforts to urge Chiang to mobilise some 400 000 of his best troops, who spent much of the war blockading the communists in the north-west, rather than confronting the Japanese advance from the east. Stilwell and some US foreign service staff began to sense that the US was backing a loser in what was inevitably going to be a civil war.

For all Stilwell's scepticism, however, the KMT regime became the public face of China. Chiang and his wife Mayling became emblematic of 'Free China', striving to save the ancient empire not just from the yellow peril but from the red menace as well. The popular image of the Chiangs, fostered especially by the almost personal sponsorship of *Time* magazine publisher Henry Luce, and the appeal of an apparently non-communist national liberation government, held sway over both public opinion, and government policy. American support could not win the war against Japanese aggression for the KMT on Chinese soil. It could, however, help lay the foundations for the situation in 1945, where, as we have seen, the KMT seemed poised to take its place at the tables of the great nations, as the party ruling a reunited China, including the province of Taiwan.

3 Taiwan's Political Development: 1945–86

THE KMT TAKEOVER OF TAIWAN

It was in keeping with imperial tradition that the man appointed by the KMT to be the new Administrator General of Taiwan, Chen Yi, should earlier have been in charge of Fujian province. And it was in keeping with the decadence of KMT rule that Chen Yi was a corrupt general, with a history of brutality and quiet collaboration with the Japanese. As such, he was relatively well known on Taiwan. Links between Taiwan and its mainland neighbour survived the Japanese war and in 1935, about 60 000 Fujian workers lived on Taiwan, mainly for casual seasonal labour. Some had signed up with the labour brokers in Taiwan precisely in order to escape the regime of Chen Yi. Similarly, large numbers of expatriate Taiwanese in Fujian returned to what seemed the lesser evil of Japanese colonialism across the Straits.

Chen was an old crony of Chiang Kai-shek, who had sent him to Fujian in 1933 to 'reconstruct' the province after the collapse of a local independence movement. Chen Yi instituted a harsh regime, aided by KMT officials like Yen Chia-kan, later to become Prime Minister and, briefly, President of the Republic of China on Taiwan. Under Chen, the Soong dynasty exerted a tight economic grip on Fujian through a system of monopolies justified as 'necessary state socialism'. They controlled banking and shipping, and left Chen Yi to squeeze as much as he could out of trade. Chen Yi, who was married to a former Japanese geisha, carried on a clandestine trade with Japan even after all-out war began in 1937. In 1935, he attended a conference in Taipei to mark the fortieth anniversary of Japanese rule, after which the KMT government enlarged its consulate in Taiwan, and official relations between the KMT and the Japanese administration on Taiwan grew positively cordial. Chen's Japanese links provoked widespread resentment of his rule, and protests which were mercilessly repressed.

53

Chen Yi's Japanese affiliations even began to worry the KMT in 1942, and he was recalled to Chongqing, amid rumours that he might defect to the Wang Ching-wei puppet government in Nanking. But he served out the war in the senior post of Secretary-General to the Executive Yuan, before being given his Taiwan assignment in 1945.

The final war years had been hard on Taiwan. Many Taiwanese were dragooned into military service, or forced labour in the South-east Asian conquests. The expectation of greater local autonomy led to an air of optimism about the prospects for nationalist liberation. But there was soon friction between the native Taiwanese and the steadily accelerating influx of mainlanders. Many were carpet-baggers, trying to make their personal fortunes out of confiscated Japanese assets. The new arrivals moved into the offices of the Japanese colonial administrators, thus blocking the Taiwanese themselves from advancing in government, and from fulfilling their illusory hopes of greater self-rule. The mainlanders held all but a token few of the top positions in Party, government and army. Since they owned no land or business, they had no choice but to make their living initially in the administration – in effect, by exploiting the surpluses created by the native islanders.

In February 1947, simmering resentment against the mainland immigrants boiled over into a near-revolution. Like so many of Taiwan's domestic disturbances since, this had its origins in a commercial dispute. A woman selling cigarettes on the black market was beaten up by an agent of the monopoly bureau. A passer-by who tried to intervene was shot. This, the 'February 28th Incident' escalated into an island-wide revolt demanding political and economic reforms. The Taiwanese protestors were given an assurance by the KMT that troops would not be used to suppress the revolt, while Chen Yi played for time. On 8 May, that pledge was broken and some 10 000 troops shipped over from the mainland to deal with the crisis went on a fortnight-long rampage of execution, rape and pillage. Between 10 000 and 20 000 people died. The slaughter seems not to have been wholly indiscriminate – the Taiwanese social and intellectual élite was especially targeted and a generation of potential Taiwan nationalist leaders was wiped out. The incident poisons mainlander–Taiwanese relations to this day. Chen Yi was transferred to Zhejiang, and later, in 1950, executed by the KMT on a Taipei racecourse. But other KMT officials were rewarded for their part in the butchery. An official account of the February 28th Incident was published in 1967, attempting to portray it as a revolt not against the KMT, but against Chen Yi, acknowledged as a despot. Even now a call for a thorough and open reassessment of this cancer at the core of KMT rule on Taiwan is still one of the political opposition's most commonly voiced demands.

At the time, the remnants of a political opposition fled, first to Hong Kong, where they split into two camps. One, a procommunist faction, ended up on the mainland as a 'Taiwan Democratic Self-Government League', echoing the CCP's calls for the 'liberation' of Taiwan under communist sovereignty. The other faction moved to Tokyo, where it degenerated into various squabbling sub-factions, mostly agitating for total independence. On the island itself, pro-independence activities were strictly banned.

Political repression was, as on the mainland, combined with economic prodigality. The island was looted to line the pockets of the KMT élite, and to back the war effort on the mainland. Entire factories were dismantled and shipped to China. The Japanese-built infrastructure, already damaged by the American bombing of 1944, sustained another heavy blow. Chen Yi used the Bank of Taiwan to print money to cover the deficits his administration was running. As on the mainland, hyper-inflation loomed. In August 1948, emergency measures were taken in KMT-controlled China. A new currency was issued (at a value of one new dollar to three million old dollars!), wage and price rises were restricted, and the government began the compulsory purchase of gold, silver and hard currency. These reforms prompted a speeding up of capital flight from the mainland. Some found its way to Taiwan, adding to the inflationary pressures already there. In August 1948, prices on Taiwan rose 1145 per cent.

As the KMT tottered to defeat in the civil war on the mainland, the exodus of mainlanders to Taiwan became a flood. By the end of 1949, some two million had crossed the Straits, joining a Taiwanese population at the time of just six million. On Taiwan, the KMT faced the twin threat of Taiwanese uprising and communist invasion. In April 1948, the KMT enacted 'The Temporary Provisions Effective During the Period of Communist Rebellion', suspending some constitutional provisions, and giving the President extraordinary powers, including that of declaring martial law. In May 1949, as first Hankow, and then Shanghai fell to the communists, an 'Emergency Decree' on Taiwan was promulgated, effectively imposing martial law. It was to be almost forty years before it was lifted.

DEFEAT ON THE MAINLAND AND THE 1946 CONSTITUTION

As the KMT tightened its hold on Taiwan, it was losing its grip on the mainland. A CCP–KMT truce agreed at the end of 1945 proved short-lived, as fighting between rival Chinese troops soon broke out in Manchuria, where the Soviet Union began dismantling Japanese plant and removing it wholesale to the Soviet Union. The KMT continued its arms build-up, while the CCP consolidated its position on the ground. Proposals for a National Assembly to be held in April, attended by both CCP and KMT delegates, to draw up a constitution, were shelved. In June, another truce was announced, but it lasted just a fortnight. By the end of the year, civil war was raging in earnest, and the communists had appealed to the United Nations to halt 'American infringement of Chinese territorial integrity and security'. The Cold War had broken out, and the CCP charged that the US was using the KMT as a pawn to gain control of China as a base for attacking the Soviet Union. Over the next three years, the civil war went the way of the CCP far quicker than anyone had anticipated. Demoralised in the cities by inflation, and in the countryside by the KMT's siding with exploitative landlords, the civilian population soon became disenchanted with KMT appeals to self-sacrifice for democracy and freedom. Despite its generous allowance of American arms and advice, the army, too, was at a low ebb. Mass defections meant that the American weaponry often ended up with the Red Army.

Meanwhile, the growing reliance of the KMT on American support made it essential that it did something to brush up its image as a democratic government. In November 1946, the

National Assembly convened, boycotted by the CCP and most third party delegates. On 25 December 1946, the National Assembly adopted a national constitution, to go into effect exactly a year later. This is the constitution by dint of which the KMT still claims legitimacy over Taiwan, China, various disputed islands, and the Mongolian People's Republic.

The 1946 Constitution has its origins in Sun Yan-sen's inchoate theories. The people are given four powers: suffrage, recall, initiative and referendum. Administrative power is, as before, shared between five 'yuan' – Legislative, Executive, Judicial, Control and Examination. The Legislative Yuan is the law-making body, made up of elected members, with powers to oversee the work of the Executive branch. The Executive Yuan is headed by a prime minister, appointed by the president, and approved by the Legislative Yuan. The separation of functions between prime minister and president is left vague in the Constitution. However, since the president has generally also been chairman of the Kuomintang, in practice the division of labour works rather like that between heads of party and government in communist systems – the party leader is responsible for general policy issues and for ideological direction, while the prime minister is the hands-on administrator, concerned especially with economic policy. The heads of the various ministries under the Executive Yuan, together with certain other officials, form the cabinet. The Control Yuan, which monitors the bureaucracy for efficiency, and the absence of corruption, is also elected, but indirectly by provincial and municipal councils. A third elected body, the National Assembly, has limited constitutional powers. It chooses the head of state, the president, and his deputy, and it alone can amend the Constitution.

From 21 to 23 November 1947, a three-day popular election by secret ballot was held, to choose representatives for the National Assembly. The government claimed that 20 million people voted (out of a total Chinese population of about 540 million), and that KMT delegates won almost all the seats. Similarly, in May 1948, Legislative Yuan and Control Yuan elections were held on the mainland. 3045 members were elected to the National Assembly (of whom 2961 showed up for the first session in March 1948), 773 to the Legislative Yuan, and 180 to the Control Yuan. The April 1948 'Temporary Provisions', as subsequently amended by the National Assembly, gave these delegates the right to hold their seats in the Chinese legislature indefinitely, on Taiwan, until such time as 'free and fair', 'national' elections could be held on the mainland again. Forty-two years later, some of those elected were still occupying these seats, in Taipei, in theory, pending the KMT's triumphant return to Nanking. The presence of these ageing mainlanders was to be both a potent symbol of the KMT-imposed political system. The 1947–8 elections thus acquired a status as the first and last true expression of the political will of the Chinese people. This was at odds both with the tiny proportion of the population who actually had a chance to exercise their franchise, and with the evidence that was to come to light of widespread electoral anomalies and malpractice.

In the late 1940s, it was gradually becoming apparent that the KMT might have to make Taiwan its bolt-hole. In December 1948, Chiang Kai-shek sent his son, Chiang Ching-kuo to Taiwan to head the provincial party organisation. Ching-kuo's task included a revamping of the security system, and he set up the Political Action Committee, which became the overseer of the KMT's extensive public security apparatus. Along with Ching-kuo, Chiang Kai-shek sent a trusted sidekick, the general Ch'en Ch'eng, to be the new provincial governor, and he began very quickly to tackle land reform and the stabilisation of the local currency. In late 1948, the KMT suffered a disastrous defeat at the hands of communist armies in the Battle of Huai-Hai, for control of Xuzhou, the last important nationalist military enclave north of the Yangtze. 500 000 of Chiang's best troops were lost, two-thirds of them taken prisoner. If Chiang had any thought of negotiating for peace (and at this time, the CCP still controlled only a third of China), he was deterred by the uncompromising communist attitude to him and 45 other KMT 'war criminals', whom they promised to punish if and when captured. But on 21 January, Chiang resigned the Presidency to which the National Assembly had elected him in April the previous year. The Vice-president Li Ts'ung-jen took over. He had been elected by the National Assembly in the teeth of Chiang's opposition, but later complained he was hamstrung by Chiang's control of all the important levers of power, especially as Commander-in-Chief of the armed forces. This continued to be true in the period of Li's presidency, and by June Chiang was in active charge of the Party, although he was not to resume the presidency until March 1950.

In August 1948, the Party moved its headquarters to Taipei. The treasures of the Ch'ing dynasty from the Forbidden City in Peking and other palaces around China had already been packed in crates and moved south, as Peking fell without a shot being fired in January 1949. Now this, the finest collection of Chinese art in the world, was shipped to Taiwan, too. On 1 October 1949, Mao Zedong proclaimed the establishment of the People's Republic of China from the gate of the Forbidden City in the communists' new capital, Peking. By the end of 1949, communist control extended over almost all China. Tibet, Taiwan and the southern island of Hainan remained 'unliberated'. Chongqing fell on 30 November. The KMT moved its capital to Chengdu, and on 8 December to Taipei. Chiang Kai-shek followed on 10 December.

THE KMT CLEANS UP ITS ACT ON TAIWAN

In the early 1950s, the KMT in Taiwan seemed to have learnt the lessons of its catastrophic failures on the mainland. The chaos of the Chen Yi period was followed by a purge of the Party and government that brought, if not political liberalisation, then at least stability and economic recovery. In this, it was inestimably helped by US support after the start of the Korean War in June 1950. After equivocating over whether the KMT remnants were in any way worth supporting, the US now committed itself to defending Taiwan from communist invasion, and to fostering its development and international status as 'Free China', and a bulwark in the global war against communism. The US provided a military shield, an economic lifeline, and a plethora of advisors and technicians whose counsel could, in the circumstances, scarcely be ignored. The KMT was forced to reform by the sheer desperation of its plight, and by the expectations of its most important paymaster.

US backing relied on the government on Taiwan representing a real alternative to communism as practised in Peking. To match up to this reputation, and to sustain its own legitimacy on the island, the KMT had to superimpose a governmental structure designed for all of China. The branches of government set up under the 1946 Constitution, and the National Assembly-men and legislators elected in 1947 and 1948 were all transported to Taiwan. With the exception of a few local appointees, the non-elected branches of government were staffed out of the hundreds of thousands of unemployed refugees who had fled the communists. In March 1950, Chiang Kai-shek reclaimed the Presidency, prompting the ousted Li Ts'ung-jen, then in New York for medical treatment, to berate him as a dictator, and threaten to return to Taiwan to overthrow him. The next day Li had lunch with President Truman. But the Korean War threw the US willy-nilly behind Chiang, and his new Prime Minister, Ch'en Ch'eng. Ch'en had been replaced as governor of Taiwan province by K.C. Wu, the American-educated former mayor of Shanghai. Wu's main job seemed to be to draw up plans for local autonomy and reorganisation as a carrot for US aid administrators.

In addition to the National Assembly and the five 'yuan', government in Taiwan included various security agencies not directly in the ambit of any of the yuan, and a 'provincial' level administrative tier. Of the security organs, the most important were – and still are – the National Security Conference, and its bureaucracy, the National Security Bureau. This sits atop a pyramid of intelligence-gathering and security organs, and has always been run by military men. It is accountable directly to the President, not the legislature. In addition, the KMT has its own internal security apparatus. Of the 'provincial' organs, the most important was the 'Provisional Provincial Assembly', created in 1951, with a Governor appointed by the President, and 55 members indirectly elected by county and municipal assemblies. Since 1959, it has been elected by popular suffrage. Based in Wu-feng, 100 miles south of Taipei, it fulfilled in name the KMT's promise of greater local autonomy. But its powers were – and are – limited, sandwiched between the national-level branches of government and county and municipal governments. A reorganisation in 1950 divided Taiwan into five municipalities, and sixteen counties. Magistrates and mayors are directly elected, and have considerable say in local affairs. The provincial government, however, had one key function – it was notionally in charge of the Taiwan Garrison Command, the military agency charged with enforcing martial law. Although a civilian government was established relatively quickly on Taiwan, it remained on a war footing, with 600 000 men – more than 7 per cent of the population – under arms in the early 1950s. The implicit support of the military has remained crucial for Taiwan's leaders to the present day.

In setting up this complex administrative structure, the KMT remained true to its Leninist organisational principles, setting up parallel party organisations at every tier of government. The Party approved all major government decisions, and the Standing Committee of its Central Committee operated like a politburo, or supervisory cabinet. The KMT membership organised itself in party cells in schools, factories or government organisations, and played a supervisory role. The Party also took responsibility for the selection of candidates for the local-level elections, and for ensuring the victory of the 'right' one.

But the KMT began to change. No longer so beholden to the Soongs, two of whom had exiled themselves in the US, or to the secret society 'Green Gang' thugs, Chiang Kai-shek was, in the early 1950s, able to purge the Party of many of its more outrageously corrupt elements. His son's spadework in the spying business gave him a good insight into potential opposition both within and outside the Party. Chiang Kai-shek in August 1950 dissolved the Party's Central Executive Committee, and replaced it with a 'Reform Committee'. This did the groundwork for the Party's Seventh National Congress in October 1952, which elected a new and 'cleansed' Central Committee. It was the most thorough reform of the Party since the first National Congress in 1924, and was to set the line which basically ran Taiwan until the KMT's next major shake-up, at its Thirteenth Congress in July 1988.

POLITICAL DEVELOPMENT IN THE 1950s AND 1960s: MAINLANDER DICTATORSHIP

For all its self-cleansing in the early 1950s, the KMT on Taiwan remained a one-party dictatorship imposed on the people of Taiwan. The political structure just described remained essentially frozen for two decades. Two small pro-government parties – the Young China Party and the China Democratic Socialist Party – were permitted, but opposition parties were banned. Under martial law, constitutional guarantees of personal freedom were suspended, and the Taiwan Garrison Command had the right to try suspected political prisoners in camera. The pervasive security apparatus rooted out and persecuted the two types of subversive. The first were those with communist sympathies. The experience of mass KMT defection to the CCP on the mainland in the late 1940s had shown the extent of communist infiltration of the KMT's own ranks. In the tense years of the 1950s, when communist invasion at times seemed an imminent threat, it was assumed that the CCP also had agents working to undermine the KMT in Taiwan. These suspects were largely mainlanders. The second class of subversive was that of Taiwan nationalists, opposing the KMT from a 'Taiwanese' perspective, as an alien élite imposed on Taiwan. To call for independence remained seditious, since it was at odds with the 1946 Constitution. Pro-independence activists were ruthlessly suppressed.

For three decades the KMT continued to be dominated by a mainland political élite, and mainlander–Taiwanese tension was an abiding feature of political and social life. Although precise figures for the numerical breakdown between the two groups are hard to come by, since official statistics try to disguise the divide, most estimates in the late 1980s assumed that 'mainlanders' made up 10–15 per cent of the population of about 20 million. This includes not just those born on the mainland, but those born on Taiwan of mainland-born parents who, clearly, are now much the more important component of the mainlander population numerically. Neither sector of society was homogeneous. We have seen that the pre-1945 population of Taiwan was composed of the descendants of a small aboriginal population (numbering no more than a quarter of a million by 1989) and various waves of mainland emigration, speaking various Chinese dialects, and in some cases preserving a distinct cultural identity. Similarly, the 'mainlanders' who arrived in the late 1940s came from all over China. Hence there is no greater ethnic divide between mainlanders and Taiwanese than there is within the ranks of the mainlanders themselves. Nevertheless the two groups have remained remarkably distinct and although inter-marriage has, of course, diminished the differences, this has not happened on the scale that might be expected.

Linguistically, the Taiwanese speak a dialect close to the Hokkien spoken in Fujian province. The mainland émigrés of the late 1940s speak a variety of regional dialects. In the 1950s and 1960s, the government promoted 'mandarin Chinese' as the national dialect. This is the north Chinese dialect, spoken in its purest form in Manchuria, and known in communist China as 'standard language' (*putonghua*), in South-east Asia as 'Chinese' (*huayu*), and in Hong Kong and Taiwan as 'national language' (*guoyu*). Since most were learning it as a second language, at first many Taiwanese in fact spoke a purer form of mandarin than the mainlanders, who might speak a variety of the dialect heavily coloured by their regional origin. But by the second and third generations of post-1945 mainlander, they were speaking mandarin as a first language, whereas Taiwanese still speak their own dialect at home. Reluctance by mainlanders to learn Taiwanese dialect as a second language, rather than English or Japanese, perpetuated a linguistic and social division. This is one quite important factor in the persistence of the mainlander–Taiwanese gulf into generations where even the vast majority of mainlanders were born on Taiwan and do not share their parents' or grandparents' personal and emotional links with mainland provinces. In the elections in 1989, some opposition candidates made a point of making speeches only in 'Taiwanese'.

But the essential split between mainlander and Taiwanese was not and is not cultural or linguistic, but political and social. Mainlander domination of the political system excluded Taiwanese from positions of authority in government or army. A survey in 1967 showed that mainlanders held 82 per cent of the positions in the military, police and national security agencies, and 34 per cent in public administration and the professions. The elected organs of government, National Assembly, and Legislative and Control Yuans remained mainlander preserves until 1969. The foundation of this discrimination was the 1946 Constitution, and the notion of Taiwan as a 'bastion for national recovery' – the base from which the KMT would win back the mainland.

Even within the KMT, there were considerable disagreements over this. Although, even today, all prominent members in the Party will pay lip service to the idea of eventual reunification with the mainland, there was from the very early days a debate over strategy. On the one side were those who saw reunification as the overriding policy goal, to which Taiwan's internal development should be subordinated. On the other were those who argued that the best basis for national recovery was a strong and prosperous Taiwan, and that hence attention should be concentrated on questions of internal development. The achievement of Chiang Kai-shek on Taiwan was that he managed both to be the hope and symbol of the 'reunification first' school of thought, and the tacit supporter of the 'developers'. Thus the structure of government was devoted to reunification. Military plans were constantly refined. In 1954, in an abandoned Japanese-built opium hospital in Taipei, the 'Planning Commission for the Recovery of the Mainland' was founded. It provided a sinecure for mainland officials, and began a task still being elaborated 35 years later – of drawing up detailed administrative plans for the KMT's reorganisation of each and every mainland province, and of the Mongolian People's Republic. Meanwhile, Chiang left the administration of Taiwan itself in the hands of the Prime Minister Ch'en Ch'eng, supported by a clique of able economists.

The corollary of the preponderance of mainlanders in politics and administration, was the dominance of commerce and agriculture by Taiwanese. The same 1967 survey showed only a 6 per cent mainlander representation in commerce, and 1 per cent in agriculture. As the economy began its rapid advance, improvements in living standards helped mitigate the effects of political discrimination. Even industrialisation was not accompanied by widespread labour unrest despite exploitative working conditions. Partly this was a function of repressive labour legislation and harsh social control. But in part it also reflected the opportunities opening up in a fast-growing economy. Many workers saw themselves not as life-long wage slaves, but as potential entrepreneurs earning their start-up capital.

Taiwanese disaffection was also partially contained by a Taiwanisation of the KMT. After the 'home rule' reform of

1950, there were elections for a wide range of local councils, magistrates and mayoralties. Since only Taiwanese would win a popular vote, since the KMT was the only party, and since one of the prime responsibilities of the Party's local cells was the manipulation of the electoral process to ensure acceptable candidates were voted in, the KMT had no choice but to recruit among the Taiwanese population. The KMT was and is a mass party, with some 2.5 million members by 1989. Its membership gradually became overwhelmingly Taiwanese, and a generation of politically motivated young Taiwanese were co-opted into the Party. Although, as in communist societies, party membership is an important path to preferment, membership does not carry the cachet and élite status of that of some ruling communist parties. Partly this is a matter of numbers. The KMT truly is a mass party – with 12.5 per cent of the entire population of Taiwan as members by the late 1980s – in a way that, say, the Chinese Communist Party (less than 5 per cent of the mainland's population in 1989) is not. Partly, the opening of the KMT to Taiwanese membership in the 1950s, and 1960s, at a time when the levers of political power and social status were still firmly manipulated by mainlanders, in itself undercut party membership as a badge of élite status.

Nevertheless, despite the blanket suppression of Taiwanese nationalism, including the slaughter in the late 1940s of its natural leaders, and despite the co-opting of the Taiwanese population through the medium of local elections, a persistent strain of anti-KMT Taiwanese opposition never entirely vanished. Non-KMT independent candidates stood in local elections and would attract the protest vote. This was tolerated, so long as it did not pose a serious threat to KMT control. But in 1960, Lei Chen, a mainland-born intellectual and editor of the journal *Free China* was sentenced to ten years in jail when he tried to form an opposition party. He was jailed for allegedly harbouring a communist agent on his staff. The next year, Su T'ung-chi, a Taiwan-born provincial assembly deputy was sentenced to life imprisonment convicted of plotting an armed rebellion. Similarly, in 1965, a prominent professor, Peng Ming-min, was sentenced to eight years in prison along with two associates, for publishing a manifesto calling on Taiwanese to unite to overthrow the Chiang dictatorship. Peng's sentence was later commuted, having provoked considerable international interest, and he escaped to the United States.

None of these incidents in themselves amounted to a very serious threat to KMT power. But dealing with them severely was both in accordance with Chiang's dictatorial instincts, and evidence of the residual unease in the KMT about the depth of anti-KMT resentment bubbling away under the apparently serene surface of one-party rule. What it meant for the Taiwanese independence movement was its virtual extinction as a domestic political organisation, and its survival as a largely exile body, with its roots among Taiwanese expatriates in, especially, Japan and the United States. In the 1960s and 1970s, the profound factionalism of these groups was to worsen. As country after country recognised the Peking government, the exiled independence movement was more and more to base itself in the United States. There, one extremist faction turned to a Marxist-oriented liberation ideology, and resorted to terrorism. By one count, they engaged in 26 incidents of violence between 1970 and 1983, of which the most notorious was the attempted assassination of then Vice-premier Chiang Ching-kuo in New York in April 1970.

THE BIRTH OF THE OPPOSITION: 1969–86

There was thus a structural tension built into the political system of Taiwan, between its purported role as a national system, and its actual function, the maintenance of KMT control over just Taiwan. By the end of the 1960s, another equally severe strain emerged, and seemed to necessitate reforms: the dichotomy between Taiwan's rapid economic advance and its ossified political structure. As in so many developing countries, economic progress bringing higher living standards, greater access to education and an internationalisation of outlook, also brought a demand for more meaningful political participation. This phenomenon was especially acute in the case of Taiwan, first, because of the reliance on the United States with its democratic traditions and, second, because of the increasing dependence of the economy after the 1950s on international trade. In the early 1970s, Taiwan, having seen a terrifying ultranationalism take hold of the CCP, found its world of diplomatic make-believe disintegrating about it. Henry Kissinger, Japanese Prime Minister Tanaka and President Nixon all went to Peking. Taiwan lost its seat at the United Nations. The KMT's legitimacy and *raison d'être* seemed under attack from without as well as within.

No longer could the political aspirations of the Taiwanese be fobbed off with the often-rigged and always tightly controlled local elections. But nor did it seem, at the time, could fundamental reform of the elected organs of government take place without putting into question the very basis of the KMT's claim to power. An uneasy compromise was reached, of a limited 'Taiwanisation' of the executive branch of government, and an even more limited democratisation of the legislature. In 1969, the first Taiwanese-born provincial governor, Hsieh Tung-min, was appointed, following a succession of mainlander generals. Hsieh was later to become Deputy Premier and, in 1978, Vice-president, as then President Chiang Ching-kuo accelerated the process of Taiwanisation. His advance was mirrored at lower levels of government by a large number of Taiwan-born administrators.

In 1966, the National Assembly passed a constitutional amendment, allowing the President to hold so-called 'supplementary' elections to the National Assembly, the Legislative Yuan, and the Control Yuan. Before this, it had been an article of faith that fresh elections could not be held until the mainland was liberated and a free national poll was possible. In 1969, the first supplementary elections were held. Mortality had already taken a heavy toll of the membership of these bodies. Of the 2961 National Assemblymen who had attended its first session in 1948, only 1393 were still serving in 1971; in the Legislative Yuan, the survivors were 434 out of 759; in the Control Yuan 69 out of 180. The 1969 elections were only a token effort. Fifteen Taiwanese were voted into the National Assembly, 11 into the Legislative Yuan, and two onto the Control Yuan. But in 1972 and 1973, in further supplementary elections, the Taiwan seats were increased to 53 in the National Assembly, 51 in the Legislative Yuan, and 15 in the Control Yuan.

These elections saw some non-KMT candidates succeed. Opposition parties remained illegal under martial law, but independent candidates could stand, and the opposition thus became represented by these men, known as 'dangwai', or 'those outside the party', whose first spokesman was the Legislative Yuan member K'ang Ning-hsiang, first elected in 1969. The opposition also consistently won seats in local elections. In 1964, independents won the mayoralties of Tainan, Keelung and Taipei. The most prominent opposition figure in this regard was Henry Kao, who twice embarrassed the KMT by winning the election for Taipei's mayor. In 1967, before he had completed his second term, the government changed the rules, and made Taipei a 'special municipality', with a mayor appointed by the President. The same tactic was used in 1979 in Kaohsiung, which had become an opposition stronghold. The damage done to the KMT's image by deposing an elected mayor in Taipei was limited by making Henry Kao the first appointed mayor.

However, the cautious liberalisation of the political climate, combined with the seemingly disastrous international moves towards de-recognition of Taiwan, took the lid off the carefully contained intellectual discussion about Taiwan's future. In 1971–3, a political debate of unprecedented openness was waged among intellectuals, students and writers. What amounted to a kind of latter-day May 4th Movement was sparked by the United States' decision in 1971 to hand over to Japan the Diaoyutai or Senkaku Islands, which the US had administered along with Okinawa. As with the May 4th Movement, perceived government weakness in the face of Japanese territorial claims was the starting point for a movement not just for nationalist resistance, but for domestic political reform as well. It was bolstered by the return to Taiwan of a number of exiled political activists, although many now began to think of moving the other way, and making preparations for deserting what seemed to be a sinking ship by moving their capital overseas. The autocratic style of the KMT, and, in particular, the far-reaching restrictions on freedoms of expression and association under martial law, provided a natural cohesion to what was in fact a potentially highly fragmented opposition movement. A kind of manifesto for this movement was published by fifteen prominent intellectuals associated with the magazine *Daxue* in October 1971. It was argued that, in the face of the painfully felt betrayal by its international supporters, the United States and Japan, Taiwan should look on reunification as only an ultimate goal, and

> build Taiwan into a paradise, and make it appealing to Chinese people in all parts of the world ... We must concentrate our effort on building an economy, and making the people prosperous, protecting human rights, and establishing the rule of law as well as an open society with pluralist values.[1]

Twenty years later, such a manifesto would not have looked out of place in a KMT propaganda publication; it represents the new orthodoxy. In 1971, however, it was, if not seditious, because it retained the ultimate goal of national reunification, then at least subversive. In contrast to its earlier practices of immediate and vicious reprisals against its opponents, the KMT, increasingly under the influence of Chiang Ching-kuo, adopted a more subtle approach. The movement was at first tolerated, but then the KMT moved against the most outspoken of the young intellectuals. The media were warned to show caution, a number of academics lost their jobs, and the heat was taken out of the movement without a major confrontation.

In 1975–7, however, following the death of Chiang Kai-shek in 1975, and the assumption of power by his son, who had emerged as a force for moderation, the opposition regained momentum. Chiang Ching-kuo released about two hundred political prisoners, but, even on his own admission, 254 remained in jail, of whom more than a third had been arrested in the political agitation of the mid-1970s. In 1975, the *Taiwan Political Review* began to publish anti-government articles. Late the following year, the editor found himself sentenced to ten years imprisonment for sedition. Nevertheless, there was a sudden flowering of the media. Intellectual opposition to the KMT generally stayed within the constitution by refraining from pro-independence activities, but was harshly critical of some of the social injustices and hardships inflicted on Taiwan's people in the name of rapid economic growth. Meanwhile, as in the May 4th movement, literature itself was becoming a battle-ground for political reformers, as a group of young Taiwanese writers started a 'xiang-tu', or 'nativist' school, which emphasised Taiwanese cultural identity.

This intellectual movement came to a political head with the 'Chung Li' incident of November 1977. Perhaps predictably, given the orientation over three decades of Taiwanese political life towards local elections, it was a four-yearly magistrate's election in Taoyuan county that provided the spur. It was contested as an independent by Hsu Hsin-liang. He had been both a rising star in the KMT, and an activist in the 1971–3 reform movement. A critical memoir of his days in the Provincial Assembly had made him a celebrity. It also made sure the KMT did not nominate him for the Taoyuan elections. He ran anyway, as an independent, and won an overwhelming majority, which the KMT allowed to stand. But that was only after a mob of 10 000 people protesting at repeated KMT attempts to rig the election had attacked the police station, and gone on the rampage. The incident broke many of the taboos that had kept political life in Taiwan within strict bounds. For the first time since the late 1940s, there had been concerted and violent street protest against the government. And KMT attempts first to co-opt, then to coerce Hsu had failed, as had the Party's efforts to manipulate anti-government feeling by stage-managing a fraudulent election. The next 'supplementary' elections, due in December 1978, were postponed for two years. That same month, the US handed the KMT an excuse for even tighter repression, by less than a week later announcing the establishment of diplomatic relations with the People's Republic of China.

The KMT organised a witch-hunt against alleged perpetrators of the Chung Li incident, but it in fact hastened the development of an organised opposition. The 'dangwai' began to belie their name through behaving more and more like an opposition party. New magazines sprung up, a new one hitting the news-stands almost as the Taiwan Garrison Command used martial law to close down the last. Of these magazines, three can be singled out as representing different strands of dissident opinion, still evident today. *China Tide* (*Xia-chao*) adopted a more Marxist-influenced perspective on Taiwan's ills, criticising the role of foreign capital, and concentrating on demands for social welfare as well as political liberty. *The Eighties* represented the more moderate stream of 'dangwai' opinion, around K'ang Ning-hsiang. The '*Formosa*' group, led by Shih Ming-teh, Yao Chia-wen, Hsu Hsin-liang and others was later to emerge as the precursor of the avowedly pro-independence 'New Tide' faction of Taiwan's first opposition party, the Democratic Progressive Party (DPP).

Even in the late 1970s, the *Formosa* group opened offices around Taiwan, and acted like a political party. On 10 December 1979, international human rights day, the *Formosa* group overstepped the stretched limits of KMT tolerance with a mass rally in Kaohsiung. They were encouraged by the emergence on mainland China of a 'Democracy' movement, that had been suppressed by Deng Xiaoping earlier that year. In the US, President Carter's human rights rhetoric also led them to think that the KMT would not dare take too violent action against them. Meanwhile the revolution in Iran also seemed to presage the downfall of dictatorial US-backed autocrats around the world. What exactly happened at Kaohsiung is still open to dispute. Like the Kwangju massacre in South Korea, it has become a touchstone for the opposition, a litmus test of whether government is prepared to face up to its past by telling the truth. There was a riot, followed by a bloody street battle, and the *Formosa* group ended up with stiff jail sentences, largely for sedition. Hsu Hsin-liang escaped to the US; Shih Ming-teh, who has an American wife, Linda Gail Arrigo, became Taiwan's most celebrated prisoner of conscience; and Yao Chia-wen emerged from jail to lead, for a year in 1987–8, the Democratic Progressive Party.

In the next elections, in 1980, the opposition did surprisingly well, in view of the restrictive laws on campaigning, and the massive organisational superiority of the KMT. There were fewer allegations of ballot box stuffing and blatant vote-buying, but the opposition still complained that the KMT used neighbourhood chiefs distributing small gifts to sweeten up voters. Nevertheless, the 'dangwai' won 27 per cent of the votes. This still only gave them nine seats in the Legislative Yuan. But that number was to fall in the next elections, in 1983, to just six, although the KMT share of the vote fell slightly, to 71 per cent. By now, the KMT was better organised, and more effective in stopping KMT members from standing for election without party endorsement against the official candidates. The protest vote remained important, however. The wives of two jailed dissidents were elected. Yao

Chia-wen's wife, Chou Ch'ing-yu, won more votes than any-one else in the six-yearly 1980 National Assembly election, and in 1983, Fang Su-min, wife of imprisoned dissident Lin Yi-hsiung won sympathy votes for her husband's plight and a seat in the Legislative Yuan. But in 1983, the unofficial leader of the opposition, K'ang Ning-hsiang, lost his seat. Already he was a victim of the infighting within opposition ranks that was to plague the Democratic Progressive Party in later years.

CHIANG KAI-SHEK AND THE SUCCESSION PROBLEM: THE SON ALSO RISES

While the stifled opposition was learning to breathe again in the 1960s and 1970s, the KMT faced the problem of the succession to Chiang Kai-shek. As in many autocratic systems, the KMT's centralised pyramidical structure made it probable that his death would put the whole stability of the regime at risk. In Taiwan, the problem was to a certain extent mitigated by Chiang's personality. An increasingly austere, aloof and even eccentric figure, he was not the object of mass popular affection. To the extent that he represented the brutality of the KMT's acquisition of Taiwan, he was even a symbol of dictatorship and mainland oppression. Never an impressive orator, his thick Zhejiang accent made him unintelligible to many Taiwanese. On the other hand, his presence as the elected leader of all of China, made him, in the KMT's eyes, an important guarantor of its international status and domestic legitimacy. It is perhaps not surprising that as in other states where, after nationalist 'liberation', power is concentrated in the hands of one political party – Romania, North Korea and Singapore, for example – the succession struggle involved the dictator's own family.

For most of his later life, Chiang Kai-shek was grooming his son to take over from him. In many ways, Ching-kuo was both an unlikely successor to a right-wing dictator, and, subsequently, an even more unlikely advocate of the dramatic reforms he pioneered in his last years. Arrested as a dangerous anti-imperialist agitator in Peking in the 1920s, Chiang Ching-kuo then spent twelve years in the Soviet Union. He returned with a Russian wife, an antipathy to communism, yet a lifelong respect for, and expertise in, the techniques of Leninism. In the years of the anti-Japanese war he held several posts in the north-east. In the civil war from 1946, he found himself in Shanghai, posted by his father to try to bring order amid economic chaos, hyper-inflation and collapsing morale.

Then, as we have seen, Chiang Ching-kuo was sent as part of the advance guard to Taiwan, in late 1948, as security lieutenant to Chen Cheng. It was thus he more than anyone else who was responsible for the merciless suppression of the Taiwanese home-rule movement in the aftermath of the February 28th uprisings. Thereafter, he gradually worked his way around most of the key organs of power, in retrospect as part of a process of grooming by his father. In the 1950s, he served for a short while as Chairman of the KMT's provincial party organisation, and then as political commissar in the Ministry of Defence. He kept his security co-ordinating role, but later in the decade, was moved from Defence to become Chairman of the Vocational Assistance Commission for Retired Servicemen, an important job in keeping the backing of the KMT old guard. He was also Chairman of the China Youth Anti-Communist National Salvation Corps, which was to serve him in good stead when his image later shifted, in response to opposition advances, to that of the face of KMT moderation, and the sponsor of a rejuvenation programme. In the 1960s, he went back to the Ministry of Defence, as Deputy Minister in 1964, and Minister the following year. In 1967, he took on an economic portfolio, as Chairman of the influential Commission for International Economic Co-operation and Development. In 1969, his destiny as his father's designated successor was spelled out, by making him vice-chairman of the Executive Yuan, effectively vice-premier. The one other figure of comparable stature as a contender for the succession, Ch'en Ch'eng, had died in 1965. In 1972, Chiang Ching-ko became Prime Minister, and under him the office became the real ultimate authority rather than the presidency, as his ailing father relinquished most of his authority to him.

But it was in the Party above all that Ching-kuo had his power base, working his way up its hierarchy concurrently with his government responsibilities. He was on his father's 'Central Reform Committee' from 1950 to 1952, then on the 'politburo', the Central Standing Committee. When Chiang

Kai-shek died in 1975, Ching-kuo became party chairman, confirming him as the real successor, even though the presidency, in accordance with the Constitution, passed to the vice-president Yen Chia-kan (one of the KMT bureaucrats who had come with the butcher Chen Yi to Taiwan in 1945). At the next National Assembly presidential election, Chiang Ching-kuo duly became president and the balance of power between the presidency and the premiership shifted again.

By the time he died in January 1988, Chiang Ching-kuo seemed to have become a genuinely popular leader. His death was mourned with real grief in almost all sectors of society. His background as a security tsar and Party hitman seemed forgotten. There were perhaps three reasons for this. First, Ching-kuo enjoyed something of the common touch that his father never laid claim to. Second, he was responsible in his final years for sweeping reforms both of the domestic political scene, and of the Government's policy to the mainland, which were widely popular. Finally, for the old guard whose life histories had been dictated by loyalty to his father, Ching-kuo was still a powerful symbol of the irredentist dream of reunification with the mainland.

4 Taiwan's Economic Development

INTRODUCTION

Taiwan's economic miracle is a remarkable story, almost without parallel in the post-war world. A defeated, corrupt government imposed itself brutally on an island whose economy had been severely disrupted by years of war. But through four decades of a combination of state interventionism, private initiative, external financial assistance, and the exploitation of the positive elements of the legacy of Japanese colonialism, the island was transformed. By the 1980s, it was already one of the most prosperous of all developing countries, and in the 1990s will take its place in the ranks of the industrialised nations.

The history of this rapid economic development can be divided into three stages. In the first, in the 1950s, rapid agricultural expansion provided the basis for the development of highly protected import-substituting industries. In the second, in the 1960s, Taiwan experienced rapid industrialisation spurred by the growth in manufactured exports. The third phase, beginning in the 1970s, saw a second wave of import-substituting industrialisation, as Taiwan responded to the erosion of its competitive advantages as a low-cost producer by promoting higher value-added industries.

THE FIRST STAGE: AGRICULTURAL DEVELOPMENT

Apart from its agricultural surplus, Taiwan had little to offer the KMT in terms of natural bounty. Even in the mid-1950s, it needed to import nearly a quarter of the energy it used, in the form of US crude oil. When, in the early 1950s, the Kuomintang set about rehabilitating and reconstructing Taiwan, the one Chinese province it controlled, it inherited a

75

battered economy. The anti-Japanese war and the civil war on the mainland had exacted a heavy toll on the island. Infrastructure was crumbling; inflation was rampant, as it had been on the mainland; foreign trade and investment had dried up; and industrial and agricultural production were stagnant. The economy had suffered severe dislocation from the KMT's frantic attempt to turn it, in the late 1940s, from a basically monocultural plantation colony servicing Japanese require-ments to a key logistical support in the civil war with the communists. Invasion was expected imminently; defence and expenditure soaked up most of the government's income.

Of the population of about 8 million, roughly 25 per cent were refugees from the mainland, and many of those were soldiers and bureaucrats who had somehow to be absorbed into the economy. The indigenous population was young, growing fast, undereducated and poor. In 1954, 42 per cent of the population were under 15, and the rate of natural increase was 3.7 per cent. Forty-two per cent of the population over the age of six were illiterate. Living standards were low – per caput GDP was US$186 in 1952, and expenditure on food took up 58 per cent of private consumption. Life expectancy at birth was 58. Already, Taiwan was quite crowded, with the population density in 1952 at 235 persons per square kilo-metre. Moreover, Taiwan's arable land, about a quarter of the land area of the island, was virtually fully cultivated. The total area of planted land remained more or less constant throughout the 1950s.

Taiwan was predominantly agrarian. In 1952, the earliest year for which data are available, the agricultural population made up 52 per cent of the total (as opposed to 22 per cent in 1986), and agriculture provided work for 54 per cent of the workforce. The main crops were rice and sugar, though sweet potatoes, peanuts, soybeans, fruits and tea were also grown. Sugar, sold, as in the colonial days, almost exclusively to Japan, made up 59 per cent of the value of Taiwan's exports in 1952, when rice (15 per cent) was the only other product to make a significant contribution. That Taiwan's potential farm-land was almost entirely cultivated is testimony to the suc-cesses of Japanese investment. The colonial government had introduced improved crop varieties, and chemical fertilisers, and had formed a network of government-controlled farmers' associations, which disseminated information about farming techniques, as well as marketing and credit assistance. The KMT was to copy this sytem with great success.

Japan had also left behind a relatively developed infrastructure in other areas, although it was generally in poor repair after the neglect of the war years. By 1952, there were 6000 km of railway track, and nearly 16 000 km of road, although most were only gravel, and only 7 per cent were paved. Keelung and Kaohsiung harbours, in the north and south of the island respectively, were both capable of handling close to two million tons of freight. The growth of Kaohsiung was soon far to outpace that of Keelung, which had been better placed for the Japan-dominated traffic of the 1920s and 1930s. The Japanese also left behind an electric power and generation system, relying heavily on hydroelectric energy.

Manufacturing industry was in its infancy. In 1952, it accounted for only 15 per cent of current price GDP, and 12 per cent of employment. Industrial development had been concentrated in agricultural processing – of the nearly 10 000 factories registered in 1952 more than two-fifths were in the food processing industries. There were also just under 1000 textile factories, producing cotton yarn and fabrics. The Japanese war effort left behind a few heavy industrial investments in areas such as metal smelting, which were on the whole uneconomic.

But agriculture was still the economic kingpin. As they cast around for reasons for the collapse of their regime on the mainland, the KMT ascribed it to two factors. The first was the runaway inflation of the late 1940s; the second was their failure to instigate a proper land reform in the mainland areas they had controlled. There was little doubt that the communists' success in winning popular support in China, whose population was overwhelmingly dominated by landless peasants, was in large measure due to their concerted efforts to redistribute land. The KMT, on the other hand, in so far as it had a class base in the countryside at all, represented the interests of the landlord–gentry class. This had obstructed them from putting into effect one of Sun Yat-sen's more concrete ideological aphorisms – 'land to the tiller'.

On Taiwan, the KMT were anxious not to make the same mistake. Here, they did not face the same impediment of landlord influence on policy. The KMT had very few links with the indigenous Taiwanese gentry; as outsiders anyway, they had no inhibitions about dispossessing Taiwan residents, and they had no land to lose themselves. In April 1948, Ch'en Ch'eng started the process of land reform. This was not so much in the interests of social justice, as to prevent upheaval from undermining the KMT on Taiwan as it had on the mainland.

The reform was effected in three stages. In April 1948, farm rents were fixed at a maximum of 37.5 per cent of the total annual yield of the main crop. Then, over the next three years, public farmland was leased or sold to tenant farmers. This was public land confiscated by the KMT, either from the Japanese, or from individual land-owners. By 1953, about 61 000 ha of this land had been distributed. Finally, in 1953 the 'Land to the Tiller' Act codified the redistribution of privately held farmlands. First, land was graded for quality and classified by owner. A retention limit was set at three 'jia' (one jia is slightly less than one hectare) of seventh- to twelfth-grade land. There were 26 grades of land in all, with four jia of the poorest quality equivalent to one jia of seventh-to-twelfth grade, which was in turn regarded as equivalent to 0.5 jia of the finest land. All land in excess of the retention limit was compulsorily purchased by the government for resale to its incumbent cultivators.

One of the most successful features of the land reform was the method of landlord compensation adopted. Landowners were paid 70 per cent of the purchase price in 'land bonds in kind'. These were ten-year bearer government bonds, repayable in either rice or sweet potato, depending on whether the land was paddyfield or dry. The balance of 30 per cent was paid in shares in four government enterprises shortly to be transferred to the private sector (Taiwan Cement, Taiwan Paper and Pulp, Taiwan Agriculture and Fishery, and Taiwan Industry and Mining). These methods of compensation proved relatively cheap, since the government controlled and kept down the price of rice over the next decade. They were also a useful stimulus to domestic investment, as the government began to divest itself of its commanding role in the industrial economy.

The purchaser was extended credit to pay for his land. The credit matched the terms of the government's own 'land bonds in kind'. That is, the former tenant farmer was given ten years to pay for his newly acquired land, and payment would be made in kind, with interest calculated at four per cent per annum.

Taiwan's land reform is often cited as a model for developing countries, and has attracted much interest in recent years in, for example, the Philippines. It was remarkably successful both in increasing agricultural productivity, and in creating the conditions for a comparatively equitable distribution of rural wealth. It was also effected without notable outbreaks of violence, Taiwanese resistance by this stage having been largely cowed into submission, and the KMT now enjoying unchallenged military dominance. The land reform affected more than a quarter of the arable land in Taiwan. Between 1949 and 1953 the percentage of land under owner cultivation grew from 51 to 79 per cent, while tenant-farmed land dropped from 42 to 21 per cent. One estimate is that as much as 13 per cent of Taiwan's 1952 GDP was redistributed. Small land-owning families came to dominate agricultural production. The average area of cultivated land available to each farm family in 1954 was just 1.24 ha. Although this had some negative impact on the pace of mechanisation, it did not prove a major disincentive to agricultural investment, nor to have contributed to the degradation of land seen in other land reforms where individual plots are small – such as mainland China's 1980s experiment with the household responsibility system.

Stimulated by the reforms, agricultural production flourished. The index of agricultural production rose from a base of 100 in 1952 to 143 in 1960, while planted land remained constant in area. Rice yields had increased by 25 per cent per hectare in that period, under the technical guidance of the KMT's farmers' associations, and with the more widespread use of fertilisers. There was some crop diversification, especially when the late 1950s witnessed a major but temporary boom in cotton-growing, as a domestic cotton textile industry took off.

The government was efficient in exploiting the agricultural surplus to finance its early industrialisation. Low rice prices, set by the government, meant that land taxes, paid in kind, were in effect high. The state fertiliser monopoly operated on a barter basis, receiving payment for the highly priced fertilisers in cheap rice. Hence, on a national level, resources were transferred from the countryside to the cities.

THE DRIVING FORCES OF EARLY ECONOMIC GROWTH

In the 1950s, following its full-blooded commitment to the KMT following the outbreak of the Korean War in June 1950, the United States became a major player in Taiwan's economy. Between 1951 and 1968, the US provided Taiwan with US$1.5 billion of what was misleadingly called 'non-military aid'. More than half of this was designated 'defence support'. It was meant to enable the KMT to defend the island without undue strain on the economy. Defence expenditure took up more than 60 per cent of the government's budget for most of the 1950s. A further 10 per cent of the US aid went on direct support for Republic of China troops, to maintain forces 'necessary to carry out mutual US–ROC obligations'. Finally, 28 per cent of the aid was in the form of surplus agricultural commodities, a programme known as PL 480, after the relevant US public law. The most important commodities supplied by US aid by value were fertiliser, cotton, wheat and soybeans.

This financial support was backed up by a substantial cadre of US advisors and experts. By the end of the Korean War in 1953, there were 1200 operational US personnel in Taiwan. The Joint Commission for Rural Reconstruction (JCRR), a co-operative body set up in 1948 by the US and the KMT, was extremely influential both in encouraging the land reform programme, and in channelling advice, funds and trained personnel for the agricultural reform effort.

The US also played a key part in early industrialisation. Under the KMT's first 'Four Year Plan', which started in 1953, entrepreneurs, primarily drawn from the underemployed mainland immigrants, were given incentives to establish themselves in textiles and flour milling, and received state allocations of US aid-financed imports of wheat and cotton. In 1953, the US was financing a staggering 43 per cent of Taiwan's imports. That proportion shrank as the decade wore on, but even in 1960 the US funded 36 per cent of Taiwan's imports.

US aid was crucial in helping the KMT stabilise the economy, contain inflation and arm itself. Its importance to the government's finances gave the US an effective veto over many aspects of economic policy. Taiwan finally graduated from aid recipient status in 1969. That was also the year when, for the first time, its trade with the US moved into surplus, a position it has retained ever since.

The government itself was another key participant in economic life. Despite its enthusiastic espousal of capitalist principles, the KMT on Taiwan has never been averse to intervening in the market. In the 1950s and 1960s, the debate over the emphasis of government policy between the 'reunification first' school and the 'developers' was mirrored in different approaches to economic policy itself. On the one side were the more 'socialist' KMT technocrats, who wanted to see the government retain the control of the commanding heights of the economy it had inherited after the Japanese surrender, partly as a security measure to ensure effective resource mobilisation against mainland disruption. On the other side were those who wanted to see the government step back faster from ownership and control of many important industries, and stimulate private investment. For most of the 1950s, the 'socialists' had their way. The proportion of industrial production contributed by the public sector declined only from 57 per cent in 1952, to 48 per cent in 1960, during a period when industrial production as a whole rose by 240 per cent. The state held on to the Japanese-built enterprises it confiscated at the end of the war. It owned all major industrial concerns, retaining a virtual monopoly in heavy industry, as well as in banking.

Exports were dominated by sugar and rice. The reorientation of Taiwan's trade towards mainland China in the late 1940s inevitably led to quite serious dislocation in the early 1950s, when legal commerce across the Taiwan Strait stopped altogether. External trade was at a very low level, and, as before the war, dominated by Japan, which in 1952 took half of Taiwan's exports, and provided a third of its imports. Nearly half Taiwan's imports came from the US, largely paid for out of aid.

The government adopted an import substitution strategy, and established a protective cordon around Taiwan's new industries. Multiple exchange rates, tariffs and import quotas were all used to shelter new factories. In 1956, 46 per cent of Taiwan's imports were in what was called a 'controlled' category, meaning that they were only granted import licences if comparable goods were not produced domestically. The average tariff rate on imports was 47 per cent. By the middle of the 1950s, these highly effective protectionist policies were having some unwanted side-effects. The domestic market was saturated for textiles, wood products and rubber goods. Meanwhile, rigid exchange controls requiring the immediate surrender of all foreign exchange receipts to the Central Bank discouraged exports. The multiple exchange rate system, which favoured imports of essential raw materials and capital goods, made export competitiveness hard to achieve.

By the end of the 1950s, Taiwan had a population of 10.4 million. The government had achieved stability and steady economic growth under siege conditions – perceived military siege by the communists, and a self-imposed economic siege. The two forms of 'economic martial law' – restricting the outflow of foreign exchange, and the inflow of foreign goods – served Taiwan well, but contained the germs of many of the problems as well as opportunities the economy faced as it entered the 1990s. From 1953 to 1960, GDP growth averaged 7.3 per cent, although it was slowing down at the end of the decade from the double digit growth of the early 1950s. The growth was based on agricultural consolidation, which was increasingly able to support import-substituting industrialisation. Agriculture's share of GDP shrank from 38 to 33 per cent, while industry's grew from 18 to 35 per cent. But this phase of economic development had achieved all it could. Agricultural growth had made unrepeatable, 'once off' gains, and agricultural exports could not be relied on to finance continued import-substituting industrialisation. A change of tack was called for, and forthcoming.

THE SECOND STAGE: EXPORTS FOR GROWTH

The government's response to the economic stormclouds of the late 1950s was to introduce a radical set of economic reforms,

with two central planks: the encouragement of private investment and the promotion of exports. These two strategies were
to prove highly effective in achieving the target of rapid
industrialisation. The reform programme was enumerated as a
'19 Point Programme of Economic and Financial Reform'. Its
private sector bias encountered opposition from some of the
KMT leadership, who feared that the expansionary plans
might revive the spectre of inflation, which had been brought
under control in the 1950s, but was a vivid memory to the
mainland élite from the chaos of post-war Shanghai. US
pressure, however, helped push the reforms through. The US,
whose aid was still regarded as 'defence support', made known
that it intended to graduate Taiwan from its aid programme
by the end of the 1960s. This made alternative sources of
foreign exchange income essential. The threat of an earlier
cut-back was used to encourage Taiwan to implement the 19
Point Plan, which was incorporated in Taiwan's third Four
Year Plan (1961–4).

The most important of the financial reforms had already
been introduced in advance of the third plan. That was the
abolition of the complex multiple exchange rate system. The
NT dollar rate applicable to most traded goods and services
was devalued in 1958 from US$1 : NT$15.55 to US$1 :
NT$24.68. Then in 1960, it was further devalued, and a
unified exchange rate of US$1 : NT$40 introduced. The local
currency was pegged at this rate to the US dollar until 1973,
and only after September 1985 did it rise appreciably from
what was by then this artificially low level.

The '19 Points' covered a range of further liberalisation
measures. Import duties were slashed. By 1965, the average
import tariff rate had fallen to 35 per cent, from 47 per cent
ten years earlier. Tariffs on inputs for manufactured exports
saw the biggest cuts, and rebates were available for some
materials re-exported in the form of manufactured products.
Income taxes were reduced to encourage capital formation.
Relatively easy credit at low interest rates was made available
to exporters from the public sector banks.

The '19 Points' were accompanied by the 1960 'Statute for
the Encouragement of Investment'. This offered what has
since become a standard package of investment incentives
offered by developing countries. A five-year tax holiday was

Is it still going on?

available to new enterprises in target industries ('productive enterprises'), which would also benefit from a reduced top rate of corporate income tax, of 15 per cent. Re-invested profits were allowable against tax, as were two per cent of annual export proceeds. Productive enterprises with foreign currency debt were allowed to set aside a proportion of pre-tax profits as a reserve against foreign exchange rate fluctuation.

Even with what was, for 1960, a relatively pioneering liberal foreign investment code, Taiwan clearly had an uphill struggle in trying to attract foreign capital. It could offer no outstanding natural resource base; no sizeable domestic market; no long-term guarantee of political stability. What it did have by this time was a capable, educated and cheap workforce, a relatively developed infrastructure, and a US aid-sponsored investment marketing strategy of some sophistication. The consultants, the Stanford Research Institute, had been engaged to study the industries that Taiwan should foster. It selected petrochemical intermediaries, plastic resins, synthetic fibres, transistor radios, and clocks and watches. Even so, investor response was slow. In 1965, a further investment promotion scheme was launched with the establishment of an Export Processing Zone (EPZ) at Kaohsiung. This offered complete duty exemption and other tax incentives for export businesses set up in the zone.

EPZ

By 1965, however, already there were signs of investor response. General Instruments of the US became in 1964 the first major electronics concern to establish an assembly operation in Taiwan. That year, Taiwan produced its first television sets, and the output of locally made radios jumped from just under 25000 to 0.5 million, and in 1965, to 1.2 million. US investment raised a head of steam. As one US multinational gained a competitive advantage through a low-cost assembly operation in Taiwan, its competitors felt compelled to follow suit. US electronics, textiles and other industries were also being squeezed by Japanese imports in their own market, and forced to invest overseas on grounds of production costs. Similarly, this then forced the Japanese to begin investing in Taiwan, with the additional spur of US import quotas on their domestic production. Japanese investment also concentrated in electronics, and, to a lesser extent, in textiles and garments.

The third major category of foreign investor was the overseas Chinese, primarily from Hong Kong. It was the network of overseas Chinese in South-east Asia to which Taiwan first turned when it began to market overseas to boost exports. This alerted many to Taiwan's comparative advantages, particularly its privileged relationship with the US, and continued flow of aid-financed imports.

The results of the foreign investment drive were impressive. In 1960, there were 14 individual cases of approved foreign investment, worth a total of US$19.9 million. In 1968, there were 325, to a value of US$89.9 million. Of these, 47 per cent by number (but only 20 per cent by value) were by Hong Kong Chinese. Seventeen investments, making up 41 per cent of the total value, were by US concerns. Japanese investors (including those classified by Taiwan as Overseas Chinese) made 46 separate investments, accounting for 12 per cent of the total value.

Investors were attracted by the mixture of a liberal investment climate with an authoritarian political framework which helped ensure a docile labour force. Taiwan's bid to attract foreign investment was also helped by a number of favourable international developments. The Cultural Revolution in mainland China put paid to any residual hopes of imminent rapprochement between Peking and Washington. It also slammed shut the economic door to mainland China, which closed itself off in ten years of economic isolation. The US, however, was forced to take a more active interest in the region as the Vietnam War intensified in the second half of the decade. Like Thailand and Singapore, Taiwan profited from US investment in military support and 'R & R' facilities. Furthermore, Taiwan's aggressive and well thought-out marketing strategy towards foreign investors came at a time when many potential competitors were adopting less friendly stances. The tide of economic nationalism was running especially high in some Latin American countries, which in terms of labour cost alone should have been well placed to attract far larger amounts of export-oriented overseas investment. Despite these various contributory factors, however, it was above all because of its cheap labour that Taiwan attracted foreign investment. Even in 1972, according to a report by the consultants Arthur D. Little, skilled labour in Taiwan earned an average of US$72 per month, compared with US$102 in South Korea, US$122 in Hong Kong, and US$183 in Singapore.

The policy changes of the early 1960s stimulated local entrepreneurs into exporting, first in the areas of domestic dominance – textiles and processed food. The large-scale assembly and manufacturing enterprises set up by US and Japanese investors also spawned a plethora of small-scale local operations to supply them. The upshot was an enormous upsurge in industrial output and in exports. The index of exports by value rose an average of 26 per cent during the 1960s, after the comparative stagnation of the 1950s. The composition and destination of Taiwan's exports also changed dramatically over that period. As a percentage of total exports, industrial products rose from 32 per cent in 1960 to 79 per cent in 1970. Exports to the US grew as a proportion of the total from 12 to 38 per cent, an apparently inexorable trend that was not to be reversed until 1985. Meanwhile exports to Japan, which had made up 53 per cent of the total in 1952, and 38 per cent in 1960, dropped to a mere 15 per cent in 1970.

Textile products became the most important export, over-taking sugar in 1965, and increasing their share of total exports from 14 per cent in 1960 to 32 per cent in 1970, while sugar declined from 44 per cent in 1960 to 3 per cent in 1970. By the end of the decade rice exports were almost negligible, and the only other significant commodity exports were basic metals (4 per cent) and bananas (2 per cent). The other major exports were, first, electrical machinery and apparatus, which had expanded from next to nothing in 1960 to 12 per cent in 1970, second, canned food (6 per cent in both 1960 and 1970), and third, plywood and other wood products (1.5 per cent in 1960, 8.5 per cent in 1970).

THE RESTRUCTURING OF TAIWAN'S ECONOMY IN THE 1960s

This surge in exports brought about a radical transformation of the structure of Taiwan's economy. From a country that in 1960 still relied for such prosperity as it enjoyed on its agricultural fertility, it had become by 1970 one where manufacturing contributed a greater share of Net Domestic Product than agriculture and where economic growth was driven by a rapid rise in exports. Agriculture's share of Net Domestic Product shrank from 32.8 per cent in 1960 to 17.9 per cent in 1970. Over the same period, industry increased its share from 24.9 per cent (of which manufacturing accounted for 16.8 per cent) to 34.6 per cent in 1970 (manufacturing, 26.4 per cent). Meanwhile, the agricultural population had shrunk from 49.8 per cent of the total to 40.9 per cent. The percentage of the workforce employed in manufacturing increased from 14.8 per cent in 1960 to 20.9 per cent in 1970.

This transformation of the sources of national wealth was accompanied by the development of one of the characteristics of Taiwan's economy: the proliferation of small- and medium-scale export-oriented manufacturing entities. In part this can be attributed to the congruence of Taiwanese cultural traditions with the rapid rates of economic growth known since the 1950s. As opportunities expanded for manufacturing industry, everyone with a modicum of capital wanted to form his or her own business, rather than 'grow with the company' in the more timid traditions of mature capitalism. But the predominance of the small-scale manufacturer in Taiwan was also in part a consequence of the type of investment sought by the government. Typically, a multinational company would be induced to invest in Taiwan, would establish a large manufacturing plant, and would generate a market for a host of small local suppliers and assembly operations, to whose products the foreign investor would be committed by the terms of his investment licence.

This pattern – of the substantial foreign investor spawning a profitable brood of local upstream suppliers – took hold. The number of local competitors for the business, and the peculiar ethos of Taiwan's commercial world, however, meant that despite the Japanese influence, the Japanese model of long-term arrangements with local suppliers never took hold, and the local subcontractors were constantly competing again for their orders. By 1978, there were still only 175 companies registered in Taiwan defined as 'large', meaning either having paid-up capital of more than NT$20 million, or with assets in excess of NT$60 million, or employing more than 300 workers. Eighty-seven per cent of the factories were locally owned. But

57 per cent of the large factories were wholly or partly foreign owned, including 27 American firms, and 30 Japanese.

Taiwan's export industry remained, throughout the 1960s, dominated by the labour-intensive textile sector. Over the decade, textile exports increased 20-fold, so that by 1970, textile product exports were running at about US$470 million, or 31.7 per cent of total exports, up from 14.2 per cent in 1960, when sugar was still the major single export earner. Already, however, the government could foresee that textiles were not a sound basis for continued export-led growth. The markets, largely in the developed world, were increasingly protected by import quotas and tariffs, and competition was becoming fiercer. Although, as we have seen, Taiwan still offered healthy labour-cost advantages over its most immediate competitors, the Asian 'tigers' (Hong Kong, Singapore and South Korea), who were at that stage still cubs, new, even lower-cost producers like Sri Lanka, Thailand and Pakistan, were eager to emulate Taiwan's example and enter the market.

In this context, the spectacular growth of the Taiwanese electronics industry seemed to offer the best hope. In 1960, electronics production was nugatory. Exports of 'electrical machinery and apparatus' were less than US$2 million, or under one per cent of total exports. By 1970, they were close to US$200 million, or 12.3 per cent of the total. This, the most dynamic sector of industry and of the economy as a whole, was also vulnerable. The electronics industry is notoriously cyclical. Taiwan's strength was in labour-intensive, relatively low-technology assembly work. Taiwan's technological edge over its competitors was still marginal.

By the early 1970s, therefore, Taiwan was again confronted with an apparent dead-end in the road it had chosen to continued rapid growth. The situation was strikingly reminiscent of that prevailing at the end of the 1950s. As before, a decade of remarkably high, consistent economic growth had been achieved. During the 1960s, real GDP growth averaged 9.6 per cent annually, as against 7.3 per cent for the period from 1953 to 1960.

But this rapid development no longer appeared sustainable without radical change in policy. Protectionism internationally and competition from new low-cost entrants to the market threatened the exports which had been the major contributor to economic growth. Manufacturing industry had grown too fast for the island's infrastructure to support it. Communications by road, rail, and especially by sea had become a serious bottleneck on industrial output.

The international outlook was further clouded in the early 1970s by the emergence of China from its self-imposed isolation, and the co-incidence of geopolitical strategies in Washington and Peking that led the Nixon administration to start playing 'the China card' against the Soviet Union, at the same time as China grew more convinced that Soviet expansionism constituted the major threat to its own security. Taiwan could see diplomatic isolation looming. It withdrew from the United Nations in 1971, and the next year President Nixon visited Peking, and Japan switched recognition from Taipei to Peking. The dependence on cheap exports to Western countries began to appear politically as well as economically vulnerable.

In another echo of the switch a decade earlier to export promotion, the government again appointed an American firm of management consultants to formulate a strategy. This time it was Arthur D. Little. Their recommendations were to be incorporated in 1972 into the sixth Four Year Plan, which marked a new direction in policy. The export dependence would remain, but Taiwan would develop a new tier of import substituting industries in spheres like petrochemicals, machine tools and electrical machinery. The government would launch a major programme of infrastructure improvement. Taiwan would move up-market, from the bargain basement to the white-goods counter.

THE THIRD PHASE: THE 1970s AND 1980s

All of these inherent structural problems in Taiwan's internal economic organisation and international standing came to a head with the first oil price shock of 1973–4. The crisis had the effect of accelerating the implementation of the new policy direction: one of heavy government investment in infrastructure, of industrial up-grading and of secondary import substitution. In broad terms, that phase of Taiwan's economic development still obtains. After weathering the 1973–4 world slump through counter-cyclical government spending, and the 1982 recession through export growth and diversification, Taiwan is facing the threats of the late 1980s and early 1990s with the same weapons.

The November 1973 announcement by OPEC of a quadrupling of oil prices had a dramatic effect on Taiwan's balance of payments and economic growth. A 1973 surplus in merchandise trade of US$734 million, became a deficit in 1974 of US$830 million, as the import bill leaped from US$3.8 billion in 1973 to US$7 billion in 1974. The enormous rise was partly accounted for by huge price increases in oil and other raw material imports. Oil imports rose from US$98.9 million in 1973, 2.6 per cent of the total import bill, to US$715.4 million in 1974, 10.3 per cent of total imports. Wheat, corn, and soybeans imports meanwhile grew from US$354.2 million, 9.3 per cent of the total, by 38 per cent to US$489.9 million, 7 per cent of total imports. But there were also huge rises in the dollar cost of imports of iron and steel, machinery and transportation equipment. In part this reflected the inflation afflicting the Western producers of capital goods. In part it represented a large volume increase, as the government's programme of increased public spending gathered momentum, and as inflationary expectations led to large-scale stock-building in industrial inputs.

By 1974–5, the West was in serious recession. At one point in late 1974, industrial production in the developed Western economies had fallen 13 per cent. In real terms, the loss of purchasing power in the OECD countries has been calculated at double that which was transferred to the oil-exporting countries in the shift of global wealth taking place so suddenly. The phenomenon of stagflation in the developed world thus effectively blocked Taiwan's economic growth in two ways – it attacked the markets for Taiwan's products, and it made imports much more expensive. In the early 1970s, economic growth rates had been consistently high. This was in large measure due to exports, which were growing at about 30 per cent a year in local currency terms with import growth at about 22 per cent. When the trend was reversed in 1974, real GDP growth slumped to 1.1 per cent, followed by a recovery to 4.8 per cent in 1975. That it was positive at all in these years was due in 1974 to massive increases in stocks and to government-led capital formation, and in 1975 to a large rise in government consumption expenditure, a modest export revival, and a fall in the import bill which had been inflated by the inventory build-up of the previous year.

As mentioned above, by the end of the 1960s, infrastructural shortcomings were already acting as a bottleneck in Taiwan's race for growth. The government had largely relied on its existing communications network, the road, rail and harbour facilities developed by the Japanese, and highways, railways and ports were by now all chronically congested. Although there had been significant public investment in power generation, there had been sporadic electricity shortages ever since 1957. Now, the need to unplug the bottlenecks coincided with the demands of Keynesian counter-cyclical investment, and the government launched a big spending programme to improve Taiwan's infrastructure.

As so often in Taiwan, the spending programme was listed and numbered. A key part of the plan became the 'Nine Major Development Projects', announced in November 1973, and increased to Ten in 1974. Six of the ten projects tackled the communications and transportation bottlenecks: the construction of a north–south highway down the west coast of the island; an expansion of the railway network in the north, and electrification of both east and west coast railway lines; a new airport, outside Taipei, now known as Chiang Kai-shek International Airport; and new harbour facilities. Three others gave the state a guiding role in strategic heavy industries: the Kaohsiung Shipyard, China Steel's Integrated Cold-Rolling Mill, and China Petroleum's petrochemical project, including both upstream naphtha cracking facilities and downstream petrochemical production. The tenth project was the construction of the first nuclear power plants, a direct response to the oil shock.

The Ten Major Projects accounted for about a fifth of government investment in 1974 and 1975. All the projects were completed by the end of 1979, with the exception of all three nuclear power plants which came on-stream in 1977, 1981 and 1984. The Ten Projects were counted such a success that the strategy was immediately followed again, with the announcement in 1979 of 'Twelve Key infrastructural

Projects', increased to Fourteen in 1984. Again these projects emphasised improvement in communications and transport systems. They included three new east–west highways, completion of the railway network round the island by adding east–west links, the second and third nuclear power plants, more harbours, a mass rapid transit system for Taipei, modernisation of the telecommunications network and more naphtha cracking facilities. In 1987, the government's economic think-tank, the Council for Economic Planning and Development, began preliminary evaluation of a further 16 projects.

Taiwan's highly successful export-oriented industries underwent a gradual transformation in the 1970s. The textile industry continued to play an important role, but the other mainstay of Taiwan's early exporting success – the agricultural processing industries – although maintaining a healthy growth, declined in importance in favour of electronics, electrical goods, and as some heavy industries like iron and steel and petrochemicals.

Partly this was a response to a deliberate policy of upgrading into more capital- and technology-intensive industries. Partly it reflected a process of vertical integration of existing industries through a second wave of import-substituting capital investment. Industry in the 1960s was heavily dependent on imported inputs. In fact the imported content of exports was actually increasing, because in most cases domestic production of industrial inputs could not keep pace with exports of the finished products. Gradually, the manufacturing sectors began replacing imported intermediates and capital goods with domestic substitutes. Thus the 1970s saw huge rises in the domestic production of pig iron, of steel bars, of machine tools, of man-made fibres, of integrated circuits, and of downstream petrochemicals, and polyethylene.

It is noteworthy that in two of these industries – petrochemicals, and iron and steel production – the government played a major role as investor. The same is true of a third, shipbuilding, where, through the China Shipbuilding Corporation, again the government kept control of what was seen as a key strategic industry. Despite the chronic global oversupply in shipbuilding that appeared in the late 1970s, Taiwan's industry has been kept afloat through a mixture of domestic demand and government subsidy. Taiwan's ship-building industry is undoubtedly competitive in world terms, but the other government-run import-substituting industries, petrochemicals and iron and steel, have not consistently been efficient in international terms, so sometimes domestic prices have been higher than those available on international spot markets. However, the goal of vertical integration and self-sufficiency in important industrial inputs has meant that these industries have never been seriously under threat. In the 1980s they achieved efficiency levels comparable with their international rivals.

heavy indus.

A similar *dirigiste* strain in KMT economic policy can be detected in the move – still in process – into first more capital-intensive, and second more technology-intensive industries. This trend gathered momentum in the early 1970s, as a result of the slow waning of Taiwan's comparative advantage as a low labour-cost producer. In the 1950s and 1960s there had been a substantial pool of cheap unskilled labour freed from the land by improvements in agricultural productivity. Redeployed in the export industries, labour remained cheap by international standards, and productivity grew much faster than wages. In the 1970s, the rate of migration from the farms to the cities continued to be substantial, with the agricultural population falling from 6 million in 1970 (40.9 per cent of the total) to 5.3 million in 1980 (29.7 per cent of the total). But educational standards were rising rapidly across the country. In 1980, 45.8 per cent of the population aged 6 and over had completed at least secondary education, as opposed to 30.2 per cent in 1970.

Inevitably, wage rates, especially for unskilled labour, began to rise much faster. Although productivity increases did keep pace, no longer were they greatly in excess of wage rises. The higher wage trend was accentuated when the continuing buoyancy of the economy brought the virtual disappearance of unemployment. By 1968, it had already fallen to an average rate of 1.6 per cent, compared with 4.0 per cent in 1968.

The government directed its attention to the 'sunrise' indus-tries. It was felt that eventually the old bulwarks of export performance like textiles, garments and footwear would have to die out. The electronics and information industries, already the most dynamic in Taiwan, were targeted in the late 1970s for promotion. They were not only more suited to the new shape of Taiwan's labour force – better educated and more expensive – but also less energy-intensive, again a major consideration after the second oil price shock of 1979, and, of growing concern following the rape of many of Taiwan's natural resources and innate beauties in the cause of industrial growth, they were less noxious to the environment.

As in its single-minded attraction of earlier generations of electrical machinery industry the Taiwan government relied in the late 1970s again on a mixture of foreign investment promotion, direct involvement and incentives to the indigenous private sector to help it complete this transformation. Government R & D expenditure rose sharply, and in 1980, it established the Hsinchu Science-based Industrial Park. This offers the usual package of investment incentives, with the added bonus for Taiwan of a relatively pleasant working environment, and the proximity of the government's most prestigious technology institute and university.

Taiwan's economy weathered the 1973–4 oil price shock remarkably well. Growth rates remained positive, and by the late 1970s, the double digit real GDP growth rates of the beginning of the decade had been recaptured (13.7 per cent in 1976, 10.0 per cent in 1977 and 13.5 per cent in 1978). Thereafter, they tapered off somewhat (8.2 per cent in 1979, 7.3 per cent in 1980, 6.1 per cent in 1981 and 2.8 per cent in 1982). However, from this it will be seen that Taiwan proved even more resilient to the world recession of 1981–2 that followed the second oil price shock of 1979. Once again, the recovery was rapid and impressive. In 1983 and 1984 real GDP growth was 7.7 and 9.6 per cent respectively. 1985 was a bad year in Taiwan terms (growth of 4.3 per cent).

The 1985 slow-down was in part due to specific domestic problems and scandals surrounding the economy's inadequate financial infrastructure. However, the stagnant demand for its products in the early 1980s, combined with the growing strength of the US dollar, to which the NT dollar remained loosely pegged, had had a major long-term impact on Taiwan. Unlike a decade earlier, when Taiwan fought its way through recession by stimulating government consumption and investment, now recovery was firmly tied to exports – which rose about 16.8 per cent in national account terms in each of 1983 and 1984, and 27.0 per cent in 1986. But since the currency appreciation made Taiwan's exports less competitive in many markets, its dependence on the US market grew, after declining in the 1970s. This dual dependence – on exports for growth, and on the US for exports – made up, crudely put, Taiwan's economic dilemma in the late 1980s.

PRESENT ECONOMIC STRUCTURE: ASSETS

The structural worries which beset Taiwan's economy at the end of the 1980s should not muddy a picture of remarkable economic achievement. Per caput gross domestic product reached US$6000 in 1988, and the previous year, Taiwan had overtaken South Korea to become the world's thirteenth largest trading nation. Foreign exchange reserves had peaked at US$76 billion at the end of 1987, and did not decline significantly in the following year. In 1986 and 1987, inflation had been negligible or negative, while in both years the economy achieved double digit growth. This rapid growth naturally also entailed a structural transformation of the economy – the worry of Taiwan's planners was that this transformation lagged too far behind the pace of growth. Taiwan's very success in its traditional areas of excellence – primarily the production of low-cost manufactures for export to the United States – acted as a brake on the long-term plan to up-grade and prepare for the inevitable downturn in this business. However, by the late 1980s, Taiwan had in place an economic structure that should allow a relatively smooth adaptation to the new requirements of an industrialised economy relying on domestic demand to withstand any new shocks to the international system. The model is far more the neo-Keynesian response to the first oil price hike than the export-led resilience to the 1982 recession.

One of its great assets is its population, which reached 20 million in 1989. Like so many crucial aspects of economic policy in Taiwan, population policy faces a political constraint. The 'siege' conditions which justified the closing off of many aspects of the economy until the wave of import promotion measures of the late 1980s and the lifting of exchange controls in July 1987 had their mirror image in the debate on population. Since the eventual goal of national reunification was a constitutional axiom, it was difficult to argue that Taiwan is a small and overcrowded island where population growth should be carefully constrained. Reunification would imply the possibility of internal migration, and the size of Taiwan itself should not be a factor in population targets. Indeed, population growth should be promoted to build a strong army. One strange feature of this belief in the return to the mainland is that until 1969, Taiwan's sizeable armed forces did not even figure in the population totals. The argument about population and reunification was almost forgotten, until the reunification issue began to undergo a renewed and lively debate after the reforms beginning in 1986, and this coincided with growing evidence of a labour shortage.

Despite this political constraint, population policy has been pragmatic. From the 1960s on, the government began a vigorous promotion of family planning. As in many cultures with its roots only a generation or two away from the land, this bid to limit family size encountered some opposition. Mainland China has in the late 1980s had to abandon its 'one child family' policy in most rural areas in the face of a continued peasant determination to keep breeding until a boy-child is produced. In Taiwan, there was another problem: some businesses set wage rates according not just to work done, but to size of family. But the family planning drive, accompanied as it was by rapid industrialisation, proved remarkably successful. Today, population growth is extremely low by developing country standards. For the ten years up to 1987, it averaged 1.7 per cent a year. That is below less developed regional economies, such as Thailand (2.1 per cent) and Malaysia (2.6 per cent). It is still, however, much faster than fully industrialised economies, like Japan (0.7 per cent) or the United States (1.0 per cent). The four Asian 'tigers', with the exception of Hong Kong, are in this respect all more or less on a par (Singapore: 1.3 per cent; South Korea: 1.9 per cent; Hong Kong: 2.5 per cent). Population growth relies almost entirely on births; immigration remains negligible, since even the few tens of thousands of immigrant workers who slipped in during the years 1986–8 to take up the slack in the job market did so largely on tourist visas, and do not appear in the figures.

However, one worrying feature is that the composition of the dependent population is undergoing a steady and relentless shift, and in the 1990s, Taiwan will have to cope with the problems of a far larger proportion of its population out of the labour force. The under-15 age group has also declined as a proportion every year since 1962, numbering in 1986 29 per cent of the total population. Similarly, the population aged 65 and over has grown as a precentage of the total every year since 1962, from 2.5 per cent to 5.3 per cent in 1986. Health care standards are high, with one doctor per thousand of population, and, in 1986, a hospital bed for each 238. So life expectancy at birth is also on an apparently remorseless upward trend, to the very high ages in 1986 of 76 for women, and 71 for men. Notwithstanding this gradual ageing, Taiwan's population structure still represents one of its most important resources. It is relatively young, and highly educated. In 1986, 52 per cent of the population had enjoyed at least a secondary education, and illiteracy rates had fallen to 8 per cent, from the figure of over 40 per cent inherited by the Kuomintang in the 1940s.

Despite its poverty of natural resources, and the small proportion of farmland, Taiwan's geography must be counted an asset. The compactness of the island, its possession of fine natural harbours and its fertile climate and soil all have played important parts in the 'Taiwan miracle'. It is well-located at the hub of the booming trans-Pacific trade, well-placed both to sell across the Pacific into the Americas, and to profit from trans-shipment and other business stemming from Japan's growing commitment to eastern and South-east Asia. Only the political anomalies of the mainland relationship inhibit Taiwan from playing a full part in the Pacific boom, and its trade shows few signs of suffering as yet from its diplomatic isolation.

Although the Kuomintang controls some 86 islands, only Taiwan itself is of any economic significance. The population is concentrated on the western and northern coastal areas of Taiwan island, between the capital, Taipei (population 2.6 million) and the third city, Taichung (0.7 million). The second city is Kaohsiung in the south (1.3 million). The population is now mainly urban. In 1986, 94.4 per cent lived in towns or cities of more than 20 000 inhabitants, and more than 50 per cent in towns of more than 100 000. This proportion grows every year as agricultural employment drops in favour of industry.

Ever since the land reform of the 1950s, agricultural production has been concentrated in small family farms. The average holding is still about 1.1 ha per farm, and is only increasing marginally (i.e. not much above the three jia retention limit set in the land reform of the 1950s). Moreover, as noted, the small size of the plots does not seem to have caused problems of underinvestment or land degradation. Productivity of land, labour and capital are all high by regional standards. Paddy rice production at 4696 kg per ha in 1986, for example, is double that of Thailand and the Philippines.

Taiwan in fact suffers from a chronic oversupply of rice. This is partly a direct result of a deliberate government policy in the early 1970s to promote rice production, at a time when there was a small shortfall between production and domestic demand. The government subsidised prices, and brown rice production increased from 2.32 million tons in 1969 to 2.71 million tons in 1976. This backfired a decade later, however. The government was forced to store large amounts of rice because production now outstripped consumption, which was actually falling as rising living standards brought a change in eating habits. By 1988, consumption was just below 2 million tons per year. The government sought to encourage a new wave of crop diversification. More paddy was taken out of production altogether, and production fell to 1.97 million tons in 1986. By the end of 1987, however, the government still had stocks of about 1.3 million tons of rice. Exports of rice are restricted under a rolling series of five-year agreements with the United States, which sets quotas on rice exports (in 1987, 225 000 tons) and bans the sale of rice to countries with a per caput GNP of over US$795.

Sugar cane, the other traditional mainstay of Taiwan's agricultural production, and of the country's exports in the 1950s, is also in decline as a domestically produced commodity. Sugar production fell an average of 3.7 per cent a year from 1977 to 1986, to just over 6 million tons. Sugar exports are now insignificant.

Even now, Taiwan is close to self-sufficiency in food production. It produces all it needs of rice, fruit and vegetables, fishery products, eggs, poultry and pork but has to import more than half the beef consumed, and almost all the non-rice grains. Agriculture became in the late 1980s the scene of one of the most bruising battles with the United States over market opening measures. The US already supplied most of Taiwan's imported grain and beef requirements, but then, in 1986–7, gained access to the domestic poultry and citrus fruit market. Accused by local farmers of allowing dumping of these products, the government faced some of its most bitter public protests from the farmers' lobby. The most serious riot in Taiwan since 1947, on 20 May 1988, had its origins in a farmers' protest.

The agricultural sector can with some justification feel aggrieved at the way it has been used as a tool of government policy in Taiwan, but has reaped inadequate reward for its achievements. It was, as we have seen, the creation of a substantial agricultural surplus in the 1950s that provided the base for Taiwan's economic dynamism. At the time, farmers were exploited through the government's preferential pricing system between rice and fertiliser. Ever since, similarly crude mechanisms have been used to control agricultural production, and the diversification into non-rice crops in the late 1970s has left a legacy of distrust now that farmers are confronted with what they see as unfair competition in precisely these products. Although living standards have risen enormously for farmers as for everyone, the agricultural population appears increasingly alienated from the Kuomintang.

The government's spending spree starting in the early 1970s on infrastructural development unplugged most of the bottlenecks that threatened to impede economic growth. Communications facilities have proved able to keep pace with most of the rapid increases in economic activity. There is still a major emphasis on port expansion, however, to keep up with the growth in trade, and on mass transit systems to unclog the congested streets of Taipei, and, to a lesser extent, of Kaohsiung. The other major developmental goal of government investment in the communications network is to bring the less advanced east coast up to the levels of the west.

National communications are almost all controlled by the government, and have enjoyed considerable protection from international competition. The railways are a government monopoly. A fine, though decaying, system was left behind by the Japanese, and has actually shrunk under the Kuomintang as stations and uneconomic small lines have been closed. There were 4800 km of track in 1986, down from 6100 km in 1952. The number of stations had dwindled from 592 to 271. All of the network has been electrified since 1979. However, the rail network is still incomplete. In 1983, the government approved a project to build the South Link Railway, which will complete a circuit of the island. The east and west coast lines still use different gauges, however. The rail network is losing passengers and freight to the roads.

The length of paved road has increased by an average of 450 km a year since 1952, to a total in 1986 of 16 781 km. Taiwan is a motorcycle, or moped, culture. There are more than 7 million on the roads, and just under a million private cars. Inland freight transportation is one of the contentious issues that continually dogs trade talks with the US. It is closed to foreign competition, causing frustration not just to would-be participants in the inland freight market, but to many exporters to Taiwan who feel the domestic cartel discriminates against them.

The docks were, until 1987, similarly protected. Until then, only domestic firms were able to own and operate their own dockside equipment. The US claimed that this was being used as a form of discreet government subsidy to Taiwan's big shipping lines, Yangming and Evergreen, who could use their own loading and unloading machinery while foreigners had to pay rental to the Harbour Board for use of their equipment, and then an additional fee to the monopoly operator of the equipment. Certainly, Taiwan's shippers have fared comparatively well in the ailing industry. In 1986, Taiwan-flagged vessels carried 53.7 million tons, and Taiwan had the third largest cargo container fleet in the world.

Much the largest harbour is Kaohsiung, which in 1986 handled 144 million metric tonnes of freight, 63.4 per cent of Taiwan's total. This was twice what Kaohsiung had handled in 1980. It is now the world's tenth largest port, and fifth largest container terminal. It currently houses three container terminals with eleven berths, and a fourth is under construction. Its capacity has made it an important trans-shipment centre, in competition with Hong Kong and Singapore, and enjoying a favourable location on Pacific shipping routes.

International air traffic is also a government monopoly. Although China Airlines had several loss-making years before returning a profit in 1987, its prospects now look good, as lower fuel prices come at a time of considerably increased traffic. Because of sensitivities about their relations with Peking, many countries do not fly direct to Taiwan, giving CAL a significant advantage. Apart from CAL, for example, only KLM flies direct from Taiwan to Europe. The boom in travel to the mainland has made the Hong Kong and Tokyo routes real money spinners. The two international airports, at Taoyuan, serving Taipei, and Kaohsiung in the south, are both being expanded, with a target of 10 million passengers and 500 000 tons of freight by 1990.

Telephone and telecommunications systems are also well prepared to keep up with the pace of economic growth. The government is taking an interventionist approach here as well. It has an ambitious plan for Taiwan to launch its own communications satellites by 2005. A ground station is already close to completion. Taiwan then intends to invest in the Pacific Regional Satellite System, with the avowed aim of eventually gaining a controlling stake. Finally, Taiwan will design and manufacture its own launch vehicles and satellites. It must be debatable whether these schemes can survive against the presumed obstacles that mainland China will erect. In the meantime, Taiwan already has an internal communications network of industrialised country scope – almost one in four people subscribes to a telephone.

PRESENT ECONOMIC STRUCTURE: LIABILITIES

Still, Taiwan's economic structure has at least three chronic problems: its dependence on imported energy, its rising cost base, and its underdeveloped financial sector. Throughout the 1970s, Taiwan grew more and more reliant on imported oil, notwithstanding the first oil price shock. Oil gained importance both as a source of energy, and as a component of the import bill. Having leapt from 2.6 per cent to 10.3 per cent of total imports by value between 1973 and 1974, oil imports made another quantum leap between 1979 and 1980, from 14.7 per cent to 20.6 per cent. It stayed at this level for four years, before the soft oil prices of the mid-1980s brought a sharp drop in oil's importance as an import, sharpened by a drive to convert from oil use to coal. In 1986, oil accounted for only 8.4 per cent of the total import bill, followed by a further fall to 7.3 per cent in 1987, and just 4.9 per cent in the first half of 1988.

Taiwan's sources of crude oil are rather limited. In 1986, almost 35 per cent of imported oil came from Saudi Arabia, and 19 per cent from Kuwait. Saudi Arabia maintains full diplomatic relations with Taipei, and even Kuwait, which recognises the Peking government, allows a trade office on its soil in the name of the Republic of China. However, these sources of oil are clearly not politically secure. There is a good chance that as Peking tries to extend its influence in the Middle East, it will find some inducement to offer Saudi Arabia sufficient to entice Riyadh to switch recognition. Even if that happened, of course, there is no reason to suppose that Peking would seek any change in the commercial, as opposed to political, relations between Saudi Arabia and Taiwan. But in the event of a crisis in mainland–Taiwan relations, the relatively few numbers of major crude suppliers strengthens Peking's hand in trying to enforce commercial sanctions.

It is, paradoxically, precisely this fear which has led to the concentration of suppliers. Taiwan's oil monopoly, the China Petroleum Corporation, buys only on long-term contracts, never on the spot market. Even in the event of an unanticipated additional requirement, their policy is to negotiate incremental supply under existing contracts, rather than turn to the spot market. CPC argues that this policy was vindicated by the 1979 oil crisis, when its major supplies kept up deliveries, and in some cases increased them, while other, more fickle, customers than Taiwan suffered cancellations. Taiwan's attempt to extricate itself from this awkward reliance on a volatile oil market has two dimensions: the development of other sources of energy, and the attempt to diversify sources of hydrocarbon supply to other countries, and to Taiwan itself. Neither fork of this two-pronged approach has been entirely successful. Demand for oil has actually increased since 1979, though at a very slow rate. Meanwhile, the ratio of imported to domestically produced energy has increased from 83 per cent to 91 per cent.

The environmental lobby poses a serious threat to the other main plank of Taiwan's energy diversification strategy – the conversion to nuclear power. Nuclear power plants came into operation in 1977, 1981 and 1984. By 1987, they accounted for 31 per cent of installed power station capacity, and 49 per cent of power generation. In 1985, a fire damaged one of the nuclear power generators. A dispute with the contractor, General Electric of the US, was resolved, but the accident gave new strength to the anti-nuclear movement, which in 1988 secured the indefinite postponement of the planned fourth nuclear power plant. There is now a real potential problem of a looming shortfall in power generation.

A more fundamental problem than the energy shortage, however, is the erosion of Taiwan's traditional comparative advantage as a low-cost assembler. One of the foundations of Taiwan's economic success has been its labour force. It has proved flexible, cheap, productive and, by and large, docile. Under martial law, lifted only in July 1987, strikes were effectively illegal. The unions were tame, dominated by KMT cadres, and restricted to individual firms rather than allowed to forge craft-wide links. With the lifting of martial law, a new package of more liberal labour legislation was drafted. This still heavily restricted the right to strike, which remains technically illegal when a dispute is in course of mediation. The Labour Standards law was revised in 1987, partly under pressure from the US union, the AFL-CIO, who threatened to use their influence to persuade the US administration to impose trade sanctions if employment laws were not tightened up in favour of the worker. The new law sets minimum ages, hours, annual leave and pension arrangements. In 1988, unions began to organise into their own national grouping, in competition with the government-sponsored Chinese Federation of Labour.

The improvements in labour legislation were a political necessity once a degree of pluralism became tolerated. With about 7 million members in 1988, the industrial labour force was too potent an interest group to be ignored. The infant opposition parties faced their most critical debate over how this group should be represented. By forsaking a class-based politics in favour of Taiwanese Nationalism, the first and largest opposition party, the DPP, left some of its members dissatisfied.

However, this political liberalisation coincided with a period of considerable strain on labour relations anyway. The massive appreciation of the NT dollar after autumn 1985 placed new pressure on costs in the labour-intensive industries. Through most of 1987, manufacturing wages lagged behind other sectors. By the Chinese New Year festival of February 1988, labour unrest had become, by Taiwan standards, epidemic. The size of the traditional 'thirteenth month', (new year) bonus, due in January, provided the trigger for a whole series of labour disputes affecting domestic industry, especially textiles, but also foreign joint ventures and the state-owned railway network. For most of the 1970s, wage rises in manufacturing had been accompanied by much higher rises in productivity. Now the process was reversed, as a result of real wage rises in excess of the stable cost of living, and the exhaustion of the scope for productivity rises in the traditional labour-intensive industries. These social and political pressures on wages combined in 1987 and 1988 with the emergence of a labour shortage. Unemployment has been at or near its frictional level since the 1986 recovery from the setbacks of the previous year. In 1988, this resulted in quite an acute labour shortage in some sectors, especially in the low paid textiles and electronic assembly industries. The government refused to recognise this as a problem, arguing that it would force mechanisation and increase the intensity of capital. The influence of Singapore's deliberate high-cost policy of the early 1980s led some in government to believe that only this type of pressure would force the modernisation of Taiwan's industrial base, and attract the higher-technology investment seen as the country's potential salvation.

The immediate response of the threatened export industries was not always, however, what was sought. The labour shortage led to an increase in both low-level foreign investment, and in some cases, of subcontracting out to cheaper labour environments like the Philippines, Malaysia, Indonesia, Thailand and the mainland of China. It also led to an influx of foreign workers, mainly from Malaysia and the Philippines. By mid-1988, 10 000 such workers were legally employed in Taiwan, and a further 50 000–80 000 were guessed to be working illegally. Average wage rates for the illegal immigrants were reported to be around US$250 per month, less than half the average monthly earnings in manufacturing, calculated as NT$15 526 in April 1988.

Taiwan may have been dubbed 'Formosa', the beautiful island, by romantic Portuguese sailors in the sixteenth century, but in the second half of the twentieth century, it has been doing its best to live down this reputation. In its breakneck rush for industrial growth, the government paid little heed to the damage it was wreaking on the natural environment. Now, Taiwan suffers severe pollution of just about every type, and expressions of concern about the long-term dangers of this environmental carelessness have moved from being pious regrets into the realm of government policy and major political battlefield. Environmental control measures are forcing extra costs on a wide range of industries, forced to invest in non-productive pollution control equipment. The government is helping out. Its own plans envisage NT$67 billion expenditure of government funds on pollution control in the decade to 1997. There are also funds available direct from the Executive Yuan, and from the state-owned commercial banks to subsidise environmental protection investment.

Much of the new stringency might be dismissed as lip-service to the newly vocal opposition. Taiwan's planning laws are still lax by developed country standards. However, the strength of feeling aroused on many of these issues is such that environmental concerns cannot now be ignored; and, indeed, the government does seem to have recognised that continued prosperity also relies to a certain extent on refraining from further despoliation of Taiwan's natural bounty.

We have seen how Taiwan's resilient response to the 1982 recession was founded on the growth in exports, and that was in turn founded on buoyant US demand, at a time of rising US dollar strength. The NT dollar had been loosely pegged to the US dollar since 1960, at a rate of US$1 : NT$40. It had risen to 1 : 36 after 1973, but had fallen back to 1 : 40 by 1983. Even this depreciation of the NT dollar did not match the rise of the US currency, making it harder for Taiwan's exporters to compete in other markets, while healthy US growth in the Reagan years led to the development of an ever larger surplus in bilateral Taiwan–US trade. Since September 1985, however, the NT dollar has appreciated sharply. This realignment of the US$/NT$ rate had three main causes. First was the concerted international action to allow the US dollar to fall. This followed the September 1985 meeting in New York's Plaza Hotel of the 'G7' leaders of the industrial world. The 'Plaza Accord' set in motion a process of rapid US dollar devaluation against the yen and the Deutschmark. There was little reason for the NT dollar to follow the US dollar down, and the peg was snapped. Second, the NT dollar appreciation resulted from explicit bilateral US pressure. The deemed undervaluation of the currency was blamed for the persistence of the United States' deficit in bilateral trade, and Taiwan, along with its Asian 'tiger' partners, was the target of bitter US criticism for keeping its currency at an artificially low level. Third, the public talking up of the exchange rate created a climate of expectation that, with the lifting of exchange controls in 1987, encouraged Taiwanese with NT dollars to hold on to them, and indeed large amounts of 'hot money' flowed into the economy, inflating the stock market and putting further upward pressure on the local currency. Unlike rising labour costs, exchange rate rises are something that few government spokesmen find admirable, at least in public. Although the new parities have clear advantages – in stemming inflation, and in encouraging the import boom which is keeping up domestic demand, for example – there has been alarm at the sheer speed of the appreciation.

The other major difficulty facing Taiwan's economic restructuring is the inadequacy of its financial system. There is a convincing school of thought that what persuaded Chiang Ching-kuo to open the floodgates of political and economic reform was not so much any broad perception of historical necessity as a rather murky financial scandal that erupted in 1985, with dire consequences for the whole economy. It involved the Tenth Credit Co-operative, part of the extensive empire controlled by the Cathay group. Tenth Credit was found to have extended loans in excess of the legal limit of 78 per cent of total assets. It was closed for three days, during which it emerged that some of these loans were clandestine intra-company lending operations. A run on Tenth Credit ensued, which extended to another Cathay group finance company, Cathay Investment and Trust (CIT). Both Tenth and CIT had to be bailed out by a government takeover.

Several Cathay companies ceased trading, unable to service their mounting debts.

This was the culmination of a string of corporate failures that followed the 1982 downturn. Many banks suffered huge losses on their loan portfolios. Foreign banks, relying more on the formalities of credit analysis than on the word of mouth and personal guarantees that probably offered better security in many cases, were especially hard hit. The bankruptcies drew attention to the inadequacies of the financial system as a whole. Not only were accounting standards unevenly applied, with a myriad of small- to medium-sized companies habitually producing different balance sheets and profit and loss accounts for the different requirements of bank, taxman and share-holder, but also the structure of the banking industry encouraged abuse.

The structural problem in the credit industry is the predominance of state ownership combined with the lax enforcement of legal requirements. The large domestic banks are tied up by a plethora of knotty requirements inhibiting them from all but the most unadventurous forms of lending, almost all secured. This creates an environment where the 'kerb' market of illegal financing companies can flourish. Some 30 per cent of corporate credit has been estimated to come from these sources as late as the mid-1980s. In 1989, a reform of the banking system was finally voted through the Legislative Yuan. It had been a political football. KMT conservatives were frightened by one of its key provisions – the granting of new banking licences, and the privatisation of some of the 16 state-controlled commercial banks. Control of the banking system had been seen as a key economic safeguard.

The commitment to privatisation was both a victory for the 'liberal' strain in the Taiwan policy debate, and an effort to add more stock to the very limited number of companies listed on the Taipei Stock Exchange (TSE). In the late 1980s, the TSE enjoyed a boom of phenomenal proportions, which saw market capitalisation reach double the size of Taiwan's GDP, and daily trading volumes regularly surpass those on all the world's exchanges other than Tokyo and New York. The scale of investment in the Taipei Stock Exchange (TSE) owed far more to extraneous considerations than to the underlying health of the listed stocks. The expectation of NT dollar appreciation took the shine off the ease of investment abroad that had appeared since the lifting of exchange controls in July 1987. Meanwhile, the stock exchange represents one of the very few legal outlets for a national passion for gambling. In 1986–7, an idiotic game called 'Ta Chia Le', or 'Everybody Happy', involving a kind of secondary market in gambling on the national lottery, became a countrywide craze, before being stamped out. The stock exchange has, to a certain extent, taken its place. By 1989, there were four million registered investors in the TSE.

The most important reason for the balloon-like expansion of stock-market capitalisation is the extraordinary degree of liquidity slopping around the financial system in 1986–8. This is a result of two of the most striking characteristics of the Taiwan economy: one is the level of current account surplus achieved from 1986 on; the other is the remarkable propensity of Taiwanese residents to save. Until the modification of exchange controls in July 1987, the current account surplus fed almost directly through into money supply growth. Exporters were obliged to surrender their foreign currency receipts immediately to the Central Bank. Foreign exchange reserves thus ballooned, and the amount of NT dollars in circulation was only restrained by government sterilisation measures. Since in these years, government revenues were in any event exceeding forecasts, the scope for sterilisation through government bond issues was limited.

Even the removal of restrictions on the holding of foreign currency by individuals and banks had a very limited effect in reining in money supply growth. Much of the potential of this measure had been exploited by the evasion of exchange controls for many years by traders and exporters. In fact, the lifting of controls on the outflow of foreign capital was preceded, in March 1987, by tough restrictions on its inflow. Individuals are only allowed to bring in US$50 000 of foreign capital a year without individual approval. This attempt to quell the rise in so-called 'hot money' seems to have been almost as ineffective as the long years of limitation on capital outflow. Indeed, having devoted much energy over the years to salting away their foreign currency profits overseas, Taiwan's business community now seems to have become adept at bringing it back. All of this has led to a swelling of the money supply. Added to the cost-push pressures outlined above, this in turn fuelled inflationary expectations. Taiwan has enjoyed negligible inflation for most of the 1980s. Its reappearance in 1989, although at a modest level of around 5 per cent, was deeply worrying for a government which, like its counterpart on the mainland, had prided itself on overcoming the hyper-inflation of the late 1940s.

5 Relations with China 1945–76

THE LINES ARE DRAWN: 1945–54

It is strange to think that the Kuomintang's right-wing dictatorship owed much of its international credibility, and even its survival, to North Korea's Kim Il-sung, most extreme of all the Stalinist leaders thrown up by the People's Democratic Republics formed in the wake of the Second World War. Yet until the outbreak of the Korean War in June 1950, the KMT's future, even on Taiwan, seemed doomed. US support in the 1943 Cairo Declaration and the 1945 Potsdam agreement for the ceding of Taiwan by Japan to China had been based on the assumption that the Kuomintang would, after the Japanese defeat, become the rulers of a strong, united, Western-aligned China. In the meantime, the priority was to placate Chiang Kai-shek and pre-empt any thought he may have had of seeking a separate peace with Japan.

During the humiliation of the KMT, and, by extension of their US allies, during the civil war on the mainland, the US attitude to the KMT underwent a transformation. Disillusioned by their incompetence and corruption, it became plain that even massive US assistance could not win the KMT the civil war. In August 1949, the US State Department published its 'White Paper' on China policy. In his letter of transmittal to the President, Secretary of State Dean Acheson concluded that if the US was to prop up the KMT 'full-scale intervention in behalf of a government which had lost the confidence of its own troops and its own people' would be needed. This, he said, would have been 'resented by the mass of the Chinese people, would have diametrically reversed our historic policy, and would have been condemned by the American people'.[1] Acheson concluded that China was temporarily controlled by Soviet imperialism, but that the Chinese people would ultimately 'reassert themselves and throw off the foreign yoke'. After the Soviet–Yugoslav split of 1948, the State

110

Department harboured the hope – astutely as it was to unfold – that China's communists might also turn out to be 'Titoist'.

In this context, the question of the future of Taiwan came up again. The Cairo declaration had pledged that Taiwan would be returned to China. But which China? At a press conference in October 1949, Acheson listed three criteria a government must meet before receiving US recognition: (1) it must exercise effective control in the country it purports to govern; (2) it must recognise its international obligations; and (3) it must govern with the consent of the people. Clearly, the KMT failed on all three counts. The press conference followed a three-day conference on US Far Eastern policy at the State Department, attended by 24 leading scholars, academics and businessmen. A majority concluded that the US should recognise the newly founded, communist, People's Republic of China. But in his press conference, Acheson doubted that the communists met the second of his criteria – recognition of their international obligations. The issue bcame crucial to the gathering McCarthyite witch-hunt, in which finding the men in the US administration who had 'lost China', was a central feature. Recognition of the communists so soon was not on the cards.

For US policy over Taiwan, this debate was further complicated by the evidence of KMT atrocities when they took over the island, coupled with a general recognition that US strategic interests would be well served by a friendly government on Taiwan. On a mission to China in August 1947, US envoy General Wedemeyer had described how 'Chen Yi and his henchmen ruthlessly, corruptly and avariciously imposed their regime on a happy and amenable population'.[2] Handing Taiwan formally to such a government seemed in violation of all the avowed principles of the US. Consequently, a number of other options were considered. Taiwanese nationalists appealed directly to the US, and found some supporters for their claim to home-rule and self-determination. In late 1949, the American diplomatic mission in Taiwan was asked, discreetly, to name local, Taiwanese, leaders, who might be 'cultivated in the US interest'.

One idea that gained currency, and support among Taiwanese nationalist leaders, was that Taiwan be made a US or Allied trustee, under UN auspices, like the Marshall Islands and Palau, until such time as the civil war was resolved, and until a self-determining plebiscite could be held. In June 1945, 51 nations had signed the United Nations Treaty, one of whose provisions was that 'no territorial changes will take place except through the freely expressed wishes of the people concerned'. The transfer of Taiwan from Japan to the KMT had manifestly not met this condition, and there was a residual hope in Taiwan that, even at this late stage, the United Nations might live up to its promises. But, with the rising tide of anti-communism in Washington, the 'China lobby' of KMT supporters was able to block any such move. The US also toyed with the idea of backing an 'alternative KMT' under elected President Li Ts'ung-jen, who had been in the US since December 1949, and was growing ever more outspoken in his criticism of Chiang Kai-shek.

The China lobby was not able, however, to secure continued massive financial and military backing for the KMT. The continuation of a modest aid programme was approved, but President Truman decided against resuming military aid. In January 1950, President Truman announced that the US

> has no desire to obtain special rights or privileges or to establish military bases in Formosa at this time. Nor does it have any intention of utilizing its armed forces to intervene in the present situation. The US will not pursue a course which will lead to involvement in the civil conflict in China. Similarly, the US will not provide military aid or advice to Formosa.

In the same month, the KMT nearly lost its seat on the United Nations Security Council on a Soviet initiative. They clung on, since the Republic of China was at the time Chairman of the Security Council, and the Soviet Union walked out. The next day, 12 January, Dean Acheson made a speech defining US security interests in the Western Pacific. He described a perimeter running south from the Aleutians, through Japan and the Ryu-kyu Islands to the Philippines. Both Korea and Taiwan lay beyond the perimeter, as part of continental Asia. The KMT, in other words, were to be left to fend for themselves.

On the battlefield, the KMT were still being routed. Driven out of the mainland, their forces grouped on Taiwan and on

Hainan island. In January, the KMT announced that their planes had destroyed 2000 communist landing craft assembled for the assault on Hainan. Meanwhile, at the end of the month Tibetan radio broadcast a forlorn appeal for aid against impending communist invasion. In March, large-scale damage resulted from KMT bombing of Canton and Shanghai. By now, widespread famine was afflicting China, and Chiang tried to capitalise on this with a call for aid to be air-dropped by KMT planes. But in April, Hainan fell, with 125 000 KMT troops evacuated in the nick of time. Chiang appealed again to the US for a resumption of military aid. In May, a further 125 000 KMT troops were withdrawn from the Zhoushan Islands, about 75 miles south-east of Shanghai, and the islands were taken without a fight. On the mainland, preparations were in full swing for an invasion of Taiwan. Between 150 000 and 300 000 assault forces were massed in Fujian province. New airfields were constructed, with 400 aircraft deployed and a fleet of invasion barges was built, together with thousands of junks and sampans commandeered for the amphibious operation. The success in taking Hainan encouraged the People's Liberation Army to believe that it could also capture Taiwan without undue difficulty. But Hainan was only 15 miles off the mainland, and was not the very last redoubt of the KMT. A bitter and drawn-out battle could have been expected. By now 800 000 troops had been withdrawn to Taiwan. Meanwhile, in Washington, the McCarthy onslaught on alleged communist spies in the State Department and other bodies with an influence on China policy was reaching a crescendo. But still, the US administration resisted both pressure in the United Nations to unseat the KMT and recognise the People's Republic, and the China lobby's call for a last-ditch commitment to Chiang's apparently collapsed regime.

Meanwhile, China had moved firmly into the Soviet camp. In July 1949, Mao Zedong had asserted that China must ally itself with 'the Soviet Union, with every new democratic country, and with the proletariat and broad masses in all other countries.'[3] With US–KMT relations at their lowest ebb, Peking resisted tentative overtures from Washington on the possibility of diplomatic relations. This was to be expected of an emergent communist party, but the history of the CCP's, and Mao's in particular, relationship with Moscow was not a happy one. Misled by Soviet strategy in the 1920s, effectively abandoned in the years in rural hideaways, the Chinese communists had then seen Stalin deal with the KMT as China's government at the outset of the civil war, and sign a treaty with the Nationalists in 1945. Worse, the Soviet Union had plundered the Japanese legacy of industrial plant in Manchuria. Only when it became clear that the CCP was going to win, without total reliance on Soviet assistance, did the Soviet Union start backing it internationally with the full weight of its post-war influence.

The history of US backing for Chiang Kai-shek, however, was such that there was never any possibility of non-alignment, let alone of a pro-Western slant, for the new communist Chinese state. The world as seen by Mao Zedong, sustained by his reading of Marxist-Leninist political philosophy, seemed irretrievably split into two opposing camps: the imperialist, led by the US, and the socialist, led by the Soviet Union. Mao decided to 'lean to one side', the side of the Soviet Union. In February 1950, the Soviet Union and China signed a 30-year 'Treaty of Friendship, Alliance and Mutual Assistance'. The treaty guaranteed the independence of Outer Mongolia, effectively perpetuating the Mongolian People's Republic's status as a Soviet client, and relinquishing China's claim to sovereignty. The Soviet Union handed back its acquisitions from the Japanese in Manchuria, and the two countries pledged mutual assistance against any resurgence of Japanese or other imperialist aggression. After signing the treaty, China's Foreign Minister Zhou Enlai declared that the two countries were welded into a force of 700 million people 'which it is impossible to defeat'.

The Korean War was the first test of this new, enlarged Soviet bloc. On the Korean peninsula, the Japanese surrender had been accepted by communists backed by the Soviet Union in the north, and an American-backed regime in the south. On 25 June 1950, the Korean War broke out, as North Korean troops poured across the dividing line at the 38th parallel, pursuing what they called a 'defensive' action against aggression from the South. Suddenly an aggressive, expansionist Soviet-dominated communism seemed on the march in eastern Asia. The United Nations called for an immediate ceasefire, and asked member states to 'render every assistance to the UN' in carrying out this resolution. This provided the basis for extending US military assistance to South Korea. A Soviet veto was avoided because the Soviet Union was boycotting the UN Security Council over the issue of China's representation. On 27 June, President Truman announced that he had ordered US air and naval forces to go to the aid of South Korea, notionally under UN auspices.

Overnight, Chiang Kai-shek had been rescued. Not only did the perception of the communist threat suddenly shift; also, it was hard for President Truman to argue for a huge commitment of men and resources to Korea, while appearing to abandon an old American ally to its apparently inevitable absorption into a communist state. Accordingly, in his troop mobilisation announcement on 27 June, Truman ordered the Seventh Fleet into the Taiwan Strait to deter communist invasion. The quid pro quo was agreement from Chiang Kai-shek to halt provocative raids on the mainland from across the straits, and to adopt a defensive posture maintained by the US navy. Truman explained: 'The occupation of Formosa by Communist forces would be a direct threat to the security of the Pacific area and to US forces performing their lawful and necessary functions in that area.' But Truman still stopped short of whole-hearted diplomatic support for Chiang: 'The determination of the future status of Formosa must await the restoration of security in the Pacific, a peace settlement with Japan, or consideration by the United Nations.'[4]

Chiang Kai-shek offered to send more than 30 000 of his crack troops to Korea. It seemed a grand opportunity, both to secure US friendship, and also to open a second, Manchurian, front against China in alliance with the world's most powerful army. Chiang's offer was rejected, but his sulkiness about this helped win further US concessions on aid and other demands. His offer uncovered a split in the US command between President Truman, anxious to avoid escalation into a global conflict, and UN commander General Douglas MacArthur, who thought the war should be won at any cost, and that the US should both welcome Chiang's offer and back an invasion of the mainland from Taiwan.

The US measures appeared deeply unsettling to Peking. Here was the United States putting its full military weight behind the defeated remnants of a regime with whom the communists had been engaged in an intermittent civil war for more than two decades. At the same time, American fire-power, including perhaps nuclear weapons, were to be deployed against North Korea, the country bordering China's industrial heartland, Manchuria. So, in October 1950, the first of what were to be as many as a million 'volunteers' from China joined the Korean War on the North's side. From Washington's perspective, China had shown itself to be a fully integrated and aggressive member of an expansionist Soviet bloc, seeking to capitalise on the instability of the newly emerging nations in eastern Asia to extend a Marxist–Leninist dominion. The US was thrown, regardless of its reservations, behind the discredited Chiang Kai-shek. To have recognised the Peking government would have implied following the precepts of the Cairo Declaration and turning Taiwan over to Peking. But now Taiwan was seen as of vital strategic significance. The US Supreme Commander in the Pacific and commander of the UN forces in Korea, General Douglas MacArthur visited Taiwan and stressed the importance of defending it as an 'unsinkable aircraft carrier'. President Truman ordered the withdrawal of the statement, seen at the time as hinting at US territorial designs on Taiwan, and hence in danger of precipitating China's entry into the Korean War. Meanwhile, viewed from Peking, the United States, having seen its client Chiang Kai-shek defeated, was now engaged in not just salvaging a portion of Chinese territory – Taiwan – but in a menacing strategic encirclement of China, with its forces deployed in Japan, South Korea, Taiwan and the Philippines. For the US, Mao Zedong had become a dangerous protagonist on Moscow's side in a global cold war. For China, Chiang Kai-shek had become a puppet of US imperialism, all the more antagonising because his strings were being pulled on what became more and more emo-tionally perceived as Chinese sovereign territory.

HOSTILITY IN THE 1950s

This had not always been the Chinese communists' attitude. Indeed, in their early days, they seem to have regarded

Taiwan with the same distant reserve as did the old emperors. We have seen how, in 1928, a small and distinct 'Taiwan Communist Party' (TCP) was founded in Shanghai, apparently acknowledging that Taiwan had a separate nationalist struggle allied to its revolution. The TCP was crushed on Taiwan by the Japanese in 1931. In July 1936, Mao Zedong had spoken to the US journalist Edgar Show about the extent of the CCP's ambitions for 'national reunification':

> It is the immediate task of China to regain all our lost territories, not merely to defend our sovereignty south of the Great Wall. This means that Manchuria must be regained. We do not, however, include Korea, formerly a Chinese colony, but when we have re-established the independence of the lost territories of China, and if the Koreans wish to break away from the chains of Japanese imperialism, we will extend to them our enthusiastic help in their struggle for independence. The same thing applies for Taiwan.[5]

Mao's remark seems an unambiguous assertion of Taiwan's right to independence. He did not even cite it as a candidate for 'autonomy' under Chinese sovereignty, as he did, in conversation with the same author, for Inner and Outer Mongolia, Tibet, and China's Muslim peoples.

However, after the KMT acquisition of Taiwan under the Cairo Declaration, the communists saw Taiwan, too, as part of the China whose sovereignty they were contesting with the KMT. On 15 March 1949, the CCP announced that it intended to 'liberate' Taiwan, because the US wanted to use it as a 'springboard for future action against China proper'. Ever since, reunification with Taiwan has been a central article of the CCP's creed, and there is no sign that it will lose that status.

However, the interposition of the US Seventh Fleet into the Taiwan Strait in June 1950 put invasion plans into cold storage. The PRC moved to a more defensive strategy along the coast, especially after its intervention in the Korean War. That its troops were now engaged in direct combat with those of the US made it more likely that the US would support a KMT military operation against the mainland. Indeed, during the Korean War, both American military men and the Chiang regime frequently made bellicose statements. In April 1951,

Truman dismissed MacArthur, for persistent flouting of presidential orders not to make warmongering statements against China. Seeing that the Korean War was becoming hopelessly bogged down in a bloody stalemate, MacArthur urged the atomic bombing of Manchuria, a naval blockade of China, and the equipping of the KMT on Taiwan for a full-scale invasion of the mainland. The administration held back from extending the war to China proper, fearing the prospect of escalation into a new world war with the Soviet bloc. But the supply of arms to Taiwan was stepped up. In February 1952, President Eisenhower announced that the Seventh Fleet would no longer be used to 'shield' mainland China from possible KMT invasion. The same month, Chiang Kai-shek claimed his forces could invade China whenever they chose, but conceded they were not yet 'adequately' equipped for a full invasion.

With the end of the Korean War in 1953, it seemed probable that Taiwan would become the next focus of the battle for strategic influence between Peking and Washington. At this time, the ROC actually controlled not just Taiwan and the Pescadores, but many more tiny islands as well. These 'offshore islands' became the site of two crises in the 1950s. The two closest to the mainland are Quemoy and Matsu, from where KMT forces had driven back an invading communist army in 1949, and which were important to KMT invasion and defence plans as a base for blockading the Fujian ports of Xiamen and Fuzhou. In September 1954, as Soviet leader Khrushchev visited China in a display of Sino-Soviet amity, the communists bombarded Quemoy, and the KMT retaliated by bombing the mainland. In November, the communists bombed the Ta Chen and other islands off the coast of Fujian and Zhejiang. In January the following year, the KMT was forced to withdraw its troops from the Ta Chens with the help of the Seventh Fleet. The question of the offshore islands became a matter of heated debate in Washington. The argument was over whether the US should go to the KMT's aid on behalf of islands which, as Democrat leader Adlai Stevenson put it, were almost as close to the mainland as Staten Island is to New York. The conclusion was to be that the KMT's self-defence, and the US security interest in the region, was to extend no further than the Pescadores.

In December 1954, the Republic of China and the United States signed a mutual defence pact. Each government promised to help the other defend the territory it controlled. In the United States' case, this referred to the various small islands in the Western Pacific under US jurisdiction. In the ROC's case, it mentioned explicitly only Taiwan and the Pescadores. The implication was that the US would not be drawn into a war over the offshore islands. The US–ROC Defence Pact in fact led to some defusing of tension. An exchange of letters had accompanied it, obliging mutual consultation before committing the use of force. Any adventurist notions of launching an invasion from Taiwan were thus tempered by US caution. Similarly, the communists were deterred from resuscitating their own invasion plans. The Peking government, however, continued its blood-curdling calls for the 'liberation' of Taiwan. At the height of the first Taiwan Strait crisis, in December 1954 and January 1955, China's Foreign Minister Zhou Enlai reiterated China's intention to invade Taiwan, and warned the US that it would face 'grave consequences' if it did not withdraw all its armed forces from the island.

Later in 1955, however, Zhou Enlai was to adopt a softer line. In April, he offered talks with the US on relaxing tension in the Far East, and especially the Taiwan area. In July, he elaborated the offer, and said that China was ready to enter into talks with the 'responsible local authorities' in Taiwan, provided the framework of the talks made clear that they were between a central government and one of its 'local' authorities. At China's National People's Congress the following year, Zhou went further in spelling out this new approach. He pledged that 'as far as it was possible', the Chinese people would use peaceful means to liberate Taiwan, and expressed optimism that peaceful liberation was becoming more likely. He called for Taiwan representatives to be sent to Peking, or elsewhere, to negotiate. He warned prophetically that the KMT was in constant danger of betrayal by the US, and promised that, regardless of their crimes, those who joined the 'patriotic ranks' and worked for peaceful reunification would be rewarded by the communist government, and given appropriate jobs. KMT personnel on Taiwan, including soldiers, would be allowed to visit friends and relations on the mainland, to help allay any anxieties they may have harboured about life there, or about their own future well-being. The KMT response was intransigent: 'What needs liberating now is . . . the mainland under the bloody communist reign.' Later that year, Zhou even went so far as to say that Chiang Kai-shek could 'make a contribution', and would be rewarded with a senior position. Still, Chiang condemned Zhou's blandishments as 'acts of deception', and reaffirmed that there was 'absolutely no possibility of any compromise' with Peking.

China's strategy was to sow doubt in Taiwan about the durability of US friendship, and about ultimate US ambitions in Taiwan. In July 1955 talks in Geneva between Peking and Washington, which had been going on for a year, were upgraded to ambassador level. The US was negotiating for the return of US citizens held prisoner in the People's Republic. The fear that Washington might trade off the prisoners' lives for a less clear-cut endorsement of the KMT claim to legitimacy was worrying to the KMT. With the prospect of a KMT return to the mainland now so remote, there was also a debate in the US over Taiwan's international position. Even official statements had described Taiwan's legal status as 'undetermined'. Hence the mainland's appeal was not directed at Taiwan nationalists, but at the KMT itself, and its mainlander power base, playing on the fear that the US might eventually support moves towards self-determination and even independence. The 'one China' rhetoric was designed to appeal to the mainlanders' overriding ambition to see Taiwan reunified as part of China, and the perception that this would be more easily achieved by negotiating with the communists than by continuing to rely on an untrustworthy US security umbrella.

This more conciliatory approach did not survive Mao Zedong's visionary frenzy of the 'Great Leap Forward', an attempt, launched in 1957, to galvanise China's masses into creating communism through sheer will-power and collective effort. With the Soviet Union's prestige at its height after the successful launching of the Sputnik satellite, Mao believed that the 'East wind was prevailing over the West wind'. Now was a good time to make a concerted assault on the decaying outposts of imperialism. In July 1958, Mao ordered a heavy bombardment of Quemoy and Matsu. The same debate about the strategic importance of the offshore islands resurfaced in

Washington. President Eisenhower was later to reveal that he believed the loss of Quemoy would be so catastrophic in its domino effect that it must be prevented even at the cost of using nuclear weapons against China. In September, US and Peking ambassadors to Poland held talks on the crisis in Warsaw. Later that month, the US said it would favour a reduction of KMT garrisons on the islands, in return for a communist acceptance of a ceasefire. Meanwhile Khruschchev had written to the White House rejecting the United States' 'atomic blackmail', and saying that the Soviet Union would support its Chinese allies. Chiang stood out against reducing his forces on the islands. The US navy did provide convoys to escort Nationalist troops to the island, but cooler heads prevailed, the islands were saved anyway, and the crisis defused.

The 1958 exchange of bombardments had several unexpected long-term effects. First, it created a fresh strain on already troubled Sino-Soviet relations, as Khrushchev took fright at the possible consequences of Mao's adventurism, and the Chinese felt themselves once again let down by the only lukewarm support from the Soviet Union in their struggle with the forces of imperialism. Second, the KMT was forced to acknowledge that the military conquest of the mainland was now improbable. In a joint statement with US Defence Secretary John Foster Dulles in October 1958, Chiang Kai-shek repeated that return to the mainland was still a sacred mission. But the two men asserted that the 'principal means' of accomplishing that mission was political – not through the use of force. The quid pro quo for Chiang was a firmer commitment from the US to help in defending the offshore islands, now it was made clear that the islands were seen not as a beach-head for invasion of the mainland, but as Taiwan's first line of defence. Third, China changed its stance. The focus of attention on the offshore islands had given rise to suggestions of some kind of a deal, whereby Quemoy and Matsu would be returned to China, while Taiwan would be placed under UN trusteeship. In November 1958, the communist Foreign Minister Chen Yi rejected such a proposal, saying that UN trusteeship would be 'nothing but US occupation', and rejecting also any calls for demilitarisation, or reference to the International Court of Justice. But this type of argument seemed to help persuade Peking that its interests did not really lie in the military conquest of the offshore islands. Not only did this run the risk of uncontrollable military escalation with the US, it might also serve to perpetrate the de facto division of China, by separating Taiwan from that part of its government's territorial control which most clearly impinged on mainland China.

In 1962, when the calamitous disruption of the Great Leap Forward and three years of natural disasters had brought China to mass famine and the brink of economic collapse, Chiang Kai-shek did again flirt briefly with the idea of a military victory. But the US quickly dissuaded him from the notion that he might be able to capitalise on perceived popular discontent in China to stage a Nationalist restoration. Ever since, Taiwan, armed to the teeth, and to technologically very high standards, has taken a defensive posture. For much of the next two decades, Quemoy and Matsu were the target and origin of ritual shelling. Often the shells were just a noisy way of disseminating propaganda literature, but they had symbolic value as evidence of the potential for armed hostility between the two Chinas, and of the belief on both sides of the straits that the civil war is still unresolved. Taiwan has kept 400 000–500 000 men under arms, and has stationed a third of its army on the offshore islands. The Taiwan Strait has been for the most part dominated by the ROC air force and navy. In 1970, the US naval patrol of the straits was discontinued. By then a tacit agreement on the limits of each Chinese navy's operation had been established, with the ROC fleet staying away from coastal waters plied by PRC ships. Occasionally through the 1960s, the KMT would mount nuisance raids on the mainland, sending in small numbers of marines to attack communist targets, and reconnaissance planes would overfly the mainland to garner intelligence. But the last raid was in 1969. In military terms, the two sides settled down to an uneasy truce, and a war of diplomatic attrition.

After the short-lived hysteria of the offshore islands campaign, the mainland reverted to the Zhou Enlai conciliatory approach. Even during the bombardment of the offshore islands, China's Defence Minister, the soon to be ousted Marshal Peng Dehuai, broadcast an appeal to 'compatriots in Taiwan' in October 1958. In an emotional plea, he returned to the idea that the US wanted to isolate Taiwan, and turn it into a US-controlled United Nations trustee. 'Chinese problems can only be settled by us Chinese. . . . There is only one China, not two, in the world,' he said, 'We only hope that you will not yield to American pressure, submit to their every whim and will, lose your sovereign rights, and so finally be deprived of shelter in the world and thrown into the sea.'

STALEMATE IN THE 1960s AND 1970s

After the second Taiwan Strait crisis, Taiwan–mainland relations were frozen into a war largely fought with words. American backing for the KMT effectively ensured that communist China could not take military action to break the log-jam; and KMT suppression of the Taiwanese nationalist movement at home meant that any aspirations of the Taiwanese towards self-determination were not allowed to rock the boat. However, the context in which this apparently immutable deadlock was located changed radically. In 1960, China's rift with the Soviet Union became public, and seemed irrevocable; as the 1960s wore on, China began taking the first steps towards normalising relations with the United States. Meanwhile, China itself had been torn apart by Mao's Great Proletarian Cultural Revolution, bringing isolationism abroad, and near civil war at home.

At one level, the Cultural Revolution was a power struggle at the top of China's leadership, whose protagonists were identified with two different approaches to China's development. On the one side were the Maoist fundamentalists, who had not been deterred by the catastrophe of the Great Leap Forward from believing that more rapid collectivisation, economic self-reliance and ideological rather than material incentives could propel China into a new age, closer to the communist stage of development. The targets of the zeal of the Maoists were 'capitalist roaders' who believed in more gradualist development, the retention of some material incentives, and the importation of technology where required for China's modernisation.

While the power struggle between these factions ebbed and flowed, policy towards Taiwan similarly oscillated between the two extremes already seen in the 1950s: the bellicosity of the Taiwan Strait crises, and the conciliatory approach adopted by Zhou Enlai. The ideological fundamentalists of Maoism took the aggressive line: Taiwan's domination by a 'renegade fascist Chiang clique', as 'puppets of US imperialism' was an affront to the rest of China and to 'liberate' Taiwan was a sacred mission from which China should not be deterred by fear of the international consequences. Official policy remained the same: that China was prepared to enter talks with a view to reaching agreement on peaceful reunification, but had not renounced the use of force should it deem it necessary. It was the emphasis between the stick and the carrot that shifted through the 1960s and 1970s. During the years of the Cultural Revolution's severest intensity, from 1966 to 1970, it was the hard line that dominated China's pronouncements, with official commentaries expressing scepticism about the prospects for a peaceful resolution. But with the internecine strife wrecking the unity of China's leadership, and an isolationist foreign policy alienating both the superpowers, China was not in a position to act on these warmongering cries. Rather, the Taiwan issue served as proof of the Maoist world vision, that it was still divided, though now into four groups: the socialist bloc, consisting of China, Albania, Romania, Vietnam and North Korea; the developing world; the imperialists led by the United States; and the 'revisionist', 'social hegemonists' of the Soviet bloc. The United States, Japan, and the Soviet Union were all accused of trying to split Taiwan from China, and foster some sort of 'two China' solution. For China's leaders, adjacent Taiwan and the excoriated Chiang Kai-shek were proof positive that the rest of the world was as bad as they said it was.

But as Zhou Enlai, more than anyone, tried to restore some rationality to Chinese foreign policy in the early 1970s, the softer line emerged again. In 1971, Zhou Enlai was asked whether Taiwan would not be impoverished by reunification with its larger, and already much poorer, neighbour. He replied that, on the contrary, Taiwan would be much better off, without income taxes, with all external debts cancelled, and with new central government subsidies. Later, in another interview, Zhou suggested that post-reunification Taiwan would be like Shanghai, China's most prosperous city. In

1972, Peking again started encouraging 'people-to-people' contact across the Taiwan Strait. It reined in its ritual imprecations against Chiang Kai-shek, and returned to the theme of peaceful reunification. In August, Zhou Enlai met a group of scholars from Taiwan. Again he stressed that living standards would be maintained, and raised the prospect of a 'long' period of transition, in which Taiwan's people would not have to accept the political and economic systems of communism. In further conciliatory gestures, in October, the senior leader, old Marshal Ye Jianying encouraged Taiwan compatriots to visit the mainland. Sun Yat-sen's image was favourably revived on the mainland, after a period of relative eclipse, partly in order to stress the common revolutionary heritage of Taiwan and China. Zhou Enlai even said Chiang Kai-shek could visit Peking, and pointed out that Foreign Minister Chen Yi had made this suggestion as early as 1965, but that it had been forgotten in the turmoil of the Cultural Revolution. In the wake of the Kissinger, Nixon and Tanaka visits to Peking, China played from a position of strength, as if it could afford to be magnanimous.

But China's new reunification rhetoric was subtly different from that of the late 1950s. It was now targeted as much at the native Taiwanese as at the KMT élite. China toned down its harangues against 'two Chinas' solutions. Then, on 28 February 1973, a meeting was held at Peking's Great Hall of the People to commemorate the February 28th Uprising. Politburo member Liao Chengzhi praised Taiwan's 'glorious revolutionary tradition', and called upon the Taiwanese to 'make contributions to the unification of the motherland'. However, this did not amount to backing Taiwan independence, other than as a weapon against the KMT. In one of his 1971 interviews, Zhou Enlai said that China would be pitiless toward the people of the Taiwan independence movement. They are no more, he said, than agents in the pay of Tokyo or Washington. China would never accept a plebiscite on the possible independence of Taiwan, because the issue does not exist. The Taiwanese are Han, that is, Chinese.

All of this was still largely in the realm of a propaganda war, in which defectors from the KMT played a major part. In 1965, the former KMT President Li Ts'ung-jen had gone over to Peking, and made speeches attacking the US and the

Chiang clique. In 1973, the former KMT General Fu Zuoyi, who had been a senior commander in north China, similarly encouraged his colleagues to follow his example and defect. He warned that, following the US President's visit to China, Taiwan could not rely on Washington, and made a plea for talks between Taiwan and the mainland: 'we are all Chinese. . . . Why shouldn't we talk for the sake of the sacred cause of unifying the motherland?' Sportsmen and women from Taiwan began to be invited to take part in tournaments on the mainland, and Liao Chengzhi spent a month in 1973 in Japan, visiting Taiwanese residents there.

The tide turned again in the mid-1970s, as the power struggle for the succession to Mao Zedong and Zhou Enlai gathered momentum. The campaigns first to 'criticise Lin Piao and Confucius' in 1974-5, and then the 'Deng Xiaoping Rightist Deviationist Wind' in 1976 heralded another phase of harder line rhetoric. Vilification of Chiang Kai-shek began again in 1974, and even Deng Xiaoping, briefly brought back from political oblivion as Zhou Enlai's help-mate and assumed successor, seemed to encourage a popular uprising against the US and the KMT. He stressed that 'at present prior consideration is given to the peaceful method', but warned that 'the future calls for the consideration of both the peaceful and non-peaceful method. . . . The development of patriotic forces [on Taiwan] can play a part in both peaceful liberation and in the non-peaceful method'. The 'Hearts and Minds' campaign continued alongside, with nearly 300 KMT prisoners of war held on the mainland released in 1975. But in January 1976, Zhou Enlai, the voice of moderation in foreign policy, died. Three months later Deng Xiaoping was again in disgrace, and the Maoist 'Gang of Four' staged their short-lived bid for absolute power when Mao himself died (which happened just a few months later, in September). Gang of Four member Zhang Zhunqiao, at the time seen as a future Prime Minister, advocated military invasion of Taiwan. He told a visiting US Senator that peaceful reunification was impossible. Sections of the army loyal to the Gang of Four staged manoeuvres along the Fujian coast and attempted to build military bases in Fujian for an independent invasion of Taiwan. After Mao's death, however, the Gang of Four were soon ousted by a more moderate leadership which was to pave the way for another return from the political grave by Deng Xiaoping, and a revival and intensification of the push for peaceful re-unification.

Throught the 1960s and 1970s, the KMT's response to China's tilts between belligerence and compromise was the same: no negotiation, no contact, and no compromise with the 'communist bandits'. Its policy was summed up in a few war-like slogans: 'Wipe out the Red Bandits and Recover the Mainland!', or 'Oppose Chinese Communists and Resist Soviet Russia!', and so on. Beneath this unchanging rhetoric, however, Taiwan's policy also underwent several shifts. Dur-ing the Cultural Revolution, Taiwan saw the opportunity to use China's internal divisions for its own ends. In his New Year's Day message of 1967, Chiang Kai-shek seemed to interpret the struggle on the mainland as one between Mao and himself, or less personally, between Maoism and the Three Principles of the People. In his National Day message in October that year, he suggested that the victims of the Maoists in the Cultural Revolution – like Liu Shaoqi, Peng Dehuai, Huang Kecheng and Deng Xiaoping – would be welcomed into the KMT's efforts to overthrow Mao. 'I propose an alliance of anti-Mao forces at home and abroad through the concentration of thought and action to destroy the handful of wandering ghosts led by Mao Zedong.' It was a remarkable call for 'forgetting all past feuds' in the joint struggle against Mao and his clique. It was also patently unrealistic. Chiang seemed almost to believe the Maoists' own propaganda, that the 'capitalist roaders' they were attacking were KMT spies and agents. In fact, if any one idea more than any other transcended the factional struggle of the CCP, it was detestation of Chiang and the commitment to reunifica-tion. More realistically, however, Chiang's pleas to the moder-ates in China were in Taiwan's self-interest. They were the sponsors of peaceful reunification, against the unpredictable adventurism of the Maoist leftists.

Chiang was also inspired by the possibilities opened up by the Vietnam War. Ever since the Korean conflict, it had seemed probable that the only way the KMT would ever stage a military comeback on the mainland would be as part of a broader conflict between the KMT and communism. Now, again, there seemed a chance that the US and China might find themselves at war, as the US bombed close to China's borders, and Chinese communists went to North Vietnam to help the war effort. The KMT again hoped to use the opportunity to attack China on a second front. The ROC even proposed sending its troops to invade Hainan island, as a bridgehead for advances on two fronts – against North Vietnam and China's Guangdong province. Again, Taiwan's offer was out of step with US ideas of containing the war, and certainly of keeping China out of it as a direct belligerent.

The world was changing around Taiwan. The repeated mainland warnings about the unreliability of the US alliance went hand in hand with a steady deterioriation of China's relations with the Soviet Union, to the extent that in 1969, after armed clashes on the Sino-Soviet border, war between the two communist giants seemed a real possibility. The prospect of US 'betrayal' and war in the communist camp made the KMT think the unthinkable, that maybe it should prepare the way for a shift in its global allegiances, to the Soviet Union.

6 Taiwan's Foreign Relations

INTRODUCTION

When Chiang Kai-shek sat down with a reluctant Winston Churchill and a supportive Franklin Roosevelt at Cairo in 1943, his government seemed to have achieved the peaks of international status. Chiang was only excluded from the summits of the Great Powers, with Stalin also in attendance, because it was not until the dying days of the Second World War that the Soviet Union declared war on Japan. In June 1945, the Republic of China became one of the founder members of the United Nations. As the government recognised as legitimate ruler of the world's most populous nation, it was only natural that the ROC should be given a permanent seat on the UN Security Council, along with the US, the Soviet Union, Britain and France. The ROC thus had a veto power over many of the most important decisions of this new world body for which such hopes were held.

The history of the ROC's foreign policy ever since then has been of the erosion of this international role. As the years solidified the division of the 'two Chinas', it seemed ever more anomalous that 'global' organisations should accord recognition to the government that rules less than two per cent of China's population and controls 0.38 per cent of its land area. In the Cold War of the 1950s, China, like Korea, Germany and Vietnam, was split into two halves, each recognised and backed by one of the two superpowers and its allies. But as the others moved towards reunification in the case of Vietnam, towards coexistence in the case of the two Germanies, and to armed truce in the case of the two Koreas, both 'Chinas' steadfastly resisted any moves towards the official perpetuation of 'two Chinas'. Diplomatic recognition was played by each side as a 'zero-sum game'. Dual recognition was not considered: countries must choose. It is a game that the ROC steadily lost, as, one by one, the countries of the

129

world, whatever their political colouring, took the pragmatic course and chose Peking, self-evidently a more realistic claimant to the title of 'Government of China'. The ROC's diplomatic recognition dwindled remorselessly. In the late 1940s, it lost the Soviet bloc, in the 1950s and 1960s, more and more of the newly emerging countries of the developing world, and in the 1970s, its biggest international friends, Japan and the United States.

The ROC's foreign policy has thus been, on the one hand, a losing battle to stem the tide of diplomatic defections, and on the other, a successful effort to mitigate the effects of diplomatic isolation by expanded non-political, and especially commercial, relations. By the end of the 1980s, Taiwan had only 26 countries which accorded it full diplomatic recognition, mostly small right-wing regimes in Latin America and the Caribbean. Yet Taiwan traded with virtually every country in the world, and with those with whom it still did not have economic relations, the barriers were by and large erected by the KMT itself. The dislocation between Taiwan's economic capacity and its political status had become acute, and Taiwan was forced to adapt to new realites by adopting a less ideologically rigid foreign policy. That meant some swallowing of diplomatic pride, but also a limited re-emergence on the international political stage as a player in its own right, rather than as a bargaining chip at the tables of the Great Powers.

RELATIONS WITH THE UNITED STATES

Relations between Taiwan and the United States have never been easy, for all Taiwan's dependence on Washington. In the 1950s, the ROC relied on the US for its very survival as an independent entity. How successful a communist invasion of Taiwan in 1950 would have been is unknowable. But it is improbable that, without US military backing, Taiwan could have survived the sporadic outbursts of patriotic fervour on the mainland over the next two decades. The economic triumphs of Taiwan also depended in large measure on US advice, financial assistance and subsequently, private investment. In the 1980s, as Taiwan experienced renewed surges of economic growth on the back of soaring exports, it was the

United States which, above all, supplied a market for its products, taking almost half of Taiwan's exports in the mid-1980s.

But this dependence on the US should not mask a deep sentiment of betrayal in Taiwan about the US attitude. Twice, the people of Taiwan feel they have been stabbed in the back by the power whose battles they thought they were fighting. First, in the late 1940s, the US backing for the savage imposition of KMT rule on the island was seen as a betrayal by those Taiwanese who, having suffered Japanese colonialism, thought that the United States, the strongest power in the world, might help them win the right to self-determination, or at least to freedom from arbitrary and despotic rule. Second, when Kissinger and Nixon went to Peking in 1971–2, and then President Carter switched diplomatic recognition from Taipei to Peking in December 1978, all sectors of society in Taiwan felt let down. The KMT felt betrayed by its old ally in the fight against global communism. Taiwanese nationalists had no desire to swap KMT mainland élite rule for CCP mainland élite rule, and saw the US concession in 1972 that there was 'only one China, and that Taiwan is part of China' as an abandonment of any hopes they still nurtured for independence or self-determination.

Hence, throughout the KMT's rule in Taiwan, there has been an ambivalent attitude to the US. At one level, Taiwan has become very ' Americanised': its cultural stereotypes have come from the US; American English is quite widely spoken; baseball is played, American pop music widely listened to; and clothing fashions ape American models. American political ideas have suffused even the younger ranks of the KMT. A large proportion of the educated élite have spent time at US colleges, and many businessmen and entrepreneurs have stayed on after a US education to make their first capital working for US companies, before returning to set up their own businesses at home. There are extensive personal and family links between Taiwan and the US. Many Taiwanese when they have made their first fortune choose to invest it in American real estate.

Yet, as in so many countries where a powerful foreign ally plays a dominant political and economic role, Taiwan already had a strong strain of nationalist anti-Americanism. In May

1957, the US embassy in Taipei was attacked, burnt and ransacked by a mob. The incident was sparked by the type of anti-foreign resentment more typical of the days of the 'treaty ports'. An American army sergeant shot a prowler he found in his garden. When he was tried and acquitted by an American military court, the widow of the dead man staged a protest outside the US Embassy, demanding 'consolation money'. It became a riot. There have been some suggestions of the official connivance or even involvement of Chiang Ching-kuo's security services in this outburst, which came at the time when the KMT had successfully stamped out almost all forms of protest. If it is true that the KMT were in some way behind the riot, their intention was perhaps to gain access to confidential US files in the embassy. What the incident certainly demonstrated, however, was the well-spring of anti-American resentment in Taiwan, waiting to be tapped. Sporadic outbreaks of this type of popular anti-American protest have continued to the present day, with several protests in 1988 against American negotiators by sections of society, like farmers, aggrieved at the danger to their livelihoods posed by the market-opening measures demanded by the US.

Since the debacle of US involvement in the Chinese civil war, American policy on China has been subject to a complex array of differing pressures. In the 1970s and 1980s, especially in the wake of the Soviet invasions of Czechoslovakia in 1968 and Afghanistan in 1979, geo-political considerations have been paramount. Nixon's and Carter's decision to play 'the China card' against perceived expansionism of a hostile Soviet empire was the clinching factor in the decision to open relations with China. In the late 1970s and 1980s, this was encouraged by the 'open door' policies of Deng Xiaoping. China seemed about to become a major commercial market, and one where the US stood to lose out by its anachronistic relationship with the Republic of China on Taiwan. But these forces for a fuller relationship with Peking had to contend with at least three countervailing pressures: the profound anti-communism of US foreign policy, which was slow to capitalise on the Sino-Soviet split to become a more explicitly anti-Soviet foreign policy; the importance of Taiwan to US Pacific strategy after the Second World War; and the residual feelings of loyalty for an old ally, Chiang Kai-shek.

To make sure these obligations of loyalty were not forgotten, the ROC has enjoyed the activities of a 'China lobby' in Washington. This was most prominent in the 1950s, but the remnants of a Taiwan lobby were influential in mitigating the worst potential side-effects of US recognition of China on 1 January 1979, and are still active on Taiwan's behalf today. The China lobby is no more than an informal coalition of individuals and groups who have used their influence with the administration and Congress to try to manoeuvre the passage of policy favourable to the KMT. It emerged in the 1930s and 1940s, when the KMT's T.V. Soong, Chiang Kai-shek himself, and Chiang's wife (and T.V.'s sister), Soong May-ling, cultivated their high-level US contacts assiduously to garner US help in propping up their faltering economy and abortive war effort. At the heart of the China lobby were a group of Chinese and Americans who were in effect on the KMT's payroll, their job to win friends and influence people. But they were able to draw on the backing from time to time of a wide range of people with no financial interest in the outcome of US policy – soldiers, Christians, right-wing politicians, and simply those who hoped to score political points off the Democrat Party and its administration under President Truman. This campaign was at its strongest in the frenzied months of the McCarthy witch-hunt in the early 1950s. In this sense the 'lobby' included Senator Joseph McCarthy himself, who based some of his allegations about communist infiltration of the US policy-making apparatus on the 'loss' of China, and General MacArthur, dismissed for refusing to heed administration strictures against broadening the Korean War into a continental crusade against communism. Around the efforts of these prominent men, a number of pro-KMT organisations sprang up, such as the 'Committee to Defend China by Aiding Anti-Communist China', which became active as early as 1949 in urging support for the KMT and railing against appeasement of the communists.

In the 1950s, American policy towards Taiwan satisfied neither the calls of the right wing for full-blooded commitment to the KMT drive to recover the mainland, nor those arguing for recognition of the Peking government. Yet it was firmly based on a perception of China and the Soviet Union as firm allies, forming a massive anti-American force at the centre of the Soviet bloc. In the early 1960s, the Sino-Soviet split shattered this world view. Still, the Kennedy and Johnson administrations in the US respected the basis for China policy laid in the days of the Korean War and its aftermath. Occasionally, they would delicately raise the hope of better relations with Peking. In 1962, Kennedy said 'We desire peace and we desire to live in amity with the Chinese people [on the mainland]'[1]. Similarly, Johnson was quoted as saying that 'Eventual reconciliation with [communist] China is necessary and possible'[2]. But these pious hopes were not reflected in policy. Kennedy's administration argued for 'keeping the door open' to China, but not for taking the initiative.

Through the 1960s, and the steady build-up of US involvement in the Vietnam War, American policy began to be transformed. The Sino-Soviet split seemed irreparable and, in 1969, verged close on full-scale warfare; US voting power in the UN was weakened by the advent of newly emerging independent countries generally sympathetic to Peking's claim to legitimacy; Taiwan seemed economically on the point of self-sufficiency and able to dispense with US aid; the cost and outcome of the Vietnam War led to a reassessment of US military commitments in Asia, made explicit in President Nixon's 1969 'Guam Doctrine' of gradual disengagement from the region; Peking acquired an atomic bomb, announcing its first explosion in October 1964 so joining the four other UN Security Council permanent members as the only nations to have an independent nuclear deterrent. All of these factors led the US to want to shun the prospect of war with communist China. From February 1965, that prospect once again seemed near as American planes bombed close to Chinese territory in North Vietnam.

One of the first glimpses of an evolving US policy came as Secretary of State Dean Rusk visited Taiwan in April 1964. He stressed the United States' obligations to the Nationalist government, and opposed handing over its seat to the communists. But he did not reaffirm US commitment to the Nationalists as the only legitimate government. It was one in a series of signals to Peking that the US was prepared to consider a 'two-China' option, backing Peking's accession to the United Nations, provided it did not entail KMT withdrawal. In 1965–6, the US partially lifted its ban on travel to mainland China, in place since the 1950s. In March 1966, Secretary of State Rusk spelled out a ten-point policy. He renounced the use of force against Peking, and stated that, should the communists be prepared to do the same, the US would welcome the establishment of friendly relations between the two countries.

The bait was not swallowed by Peking, embroiled in the Cultural Revolution at that time. A breakthrough had to wait for the Nixon administration, of 1969–74. His 'Guam Doctrine' of 1969 already implied diminished military support for Taiwan, and conciliation with Peking. Then on 25 February 1971, for the first time in an official public utterance by the US administration, he used the term 'People's Republic of China', saying he hoped it would 'play a constructive part in the family of nations'. The formal switch of government policy was marked in April by a State Department 'Statement on the Status of Taiwan'. It said that it regarded the status of Taiwan as undetermined, but that the Republic of China 'exercised legitimate authority' over Taiwan by virtue of its having accepted the Japanese surrender. The US, to the consternation of both Chinas, was formally pursuing a 'two-China policy. As for Taiwan, Nixon dropped plans for weapons sales that could have been interpreted as increasing the ROC's offensive strength, made a large-scale cut-back in US military assistance, stopped the Seventh Fleet from patrolling the Taiwan Strait, and blocked any more KMT commando raids on the mainland. Peking was well satisfied, and gave Nixon the reward he had hoped for. In July 1971, Nixon announced his proposed visit to mainland China. The next month Secretary of State William Rogers announced that the US was dropping its opposition to People's Republic of China membership of the United Nations. The US would make efforts to prevent the ROC being expelled from the UN, but would abide by the majority decision on which China would have the permanent seat in the Security Council. The US efforts to have two Chinese governments at the UN were doomed to failure in light of both governments' adamant objections to such a solution. In October, the ROC delegation walked out of the UN.

At the end of Richard Nixon's historic visit – a 'week that changed the world', as he put it – a joint communiqué was issued on 28 February 1972. This 'Shanghai Communiqué', although it did not entail the switch of diplomatic recognition, was a nail in the KMT's diplomatic coffin. It contained the following passage:

> The US acknowledges that all Chinese on either side of the Taiwan Strait maintain there is but one China and that Taiwan is part of China. The United States Government does not challenge that position. It reaffirms its interests in a peaceful settlement of the Taiwan question by the Chinese themselves. With this prospect in mind, the United States reaffirms the ultimate objective of the withdrawal of all US forces and military installations from Taiwan. In the meantime, it will progressively reduce its forces and military installations on Taiwan as the tension in the area diminishes.[3]

By accepting that there is 'but one China', the US waved goodbye to any halfway house of UN trusteeship or self-determination. By undertaking to reduce its military presence, the US abandoned the KMT to an uncertain future. The communiqué, following the ROC's withdrawal from the UN, undermined whatever credibility the KMT still had as the legitimate government of China. It created an untenable position where the US still officially recognised the ROC as the one government of all China, but deprived it of the wherewithal to give the claim any substance. The trickle of countries switching diplomatic recognition became a flood, so that, by the time the US formally switched its own diplomatic representation eight years later, only 21 countries still recognised Taipei as the legitimate government. Almost the only sop to KMT worries was the US expression of interest in a 'peaceful settlement'. This was as close to a guarantee of US backing in the event of a communist military adventure as the KMT was going to get.

Nevertheless, the 1954 Defence Pact was not abrogated, and although the US established a liaison office in Peking (under future President George Bush), its embassy remained in Taipei. After the path-breaking carried out by a right-wing Republican President, the full normalisation of relations was to await a liberal Democrat, Jimmy Carter, as President. Even then, it was a tortuous process. Seeking a diplomatic breakthrough in Asia, the Carter administration pursued the normalisation of relations with both Vietnam and China. In 1978, as relations between Vietnam and two of its neighbours – the Khmer Rouge in Cambodia and their sponsors in China – steadily worsened, it became apparent that the two goals were mutually exclusive. China's interest in fuller ties with the US was in part motivated by a growing fear of Soviet expansionism, and its strategic encirclement of China. From the 4500 miles of Sino-Soviet and Sino-Mongolian border, through the ethnically troubled regions of Turkestan, the tiny border with Afghanistan, the three long sections of Sino-Indian border, to Laos and Vietnam, China saw a map peopled by Soviet armed forces their clients or their friends. Vietnam was on the point of launching its December 1978 invasion of Cambodia, in what China saw as a bid for regional hegemony by a traditional rival. In November 1978 Vietnam had signed a 25 year treaty of friendship with the Soviet Union and had become, in Chinese eyes, the Soviet Union's 'Cuba in Asia'. China began seeking partners in a global coalition against 'Soviet social hegemonism'. The United States was the most important partner, but the partnership effectively precluded Washington – Hanoi normalisation.

On 15 December 1978, the United States and China announced the full normalisation of diplomatic relations. The US would terminate its diplomatic relations with what the announcement called not the 'Republic of China', but 'Taiwan', on 1 January 1979. The 1954 Defence Pact was abrogated, and all US military personnel would be withdrawn within four months. Clearly, the United States' extensive ties with Taiwan could not be dismantled overnight, nor was that the intention. The announcement of Sino-US normalisation stated that the US would 'maintain commercial, cultural, and other relations' without official government representation, and without diplomatic relations. In March 1979, the 'Taiwan Relations Act' provided a legal framework for these continued relations. The functions of the embassy would be taken over by a notionally non-governmental 'American Institute in Taiwan', with branches in Taipei and Kaohsiung. More vexing, however, was the question of US military links. The 'Taiwan Relations Act' commits the United States to

consider efforts to determine the future of Taiwan by other than peaceful means, including by boycotts or embargoes, a threat to the peace and security of the Western Pacific area, and of grave concern to the United States ... to provide Taiwan with arms of a defensive character ... and to maintain the capacity of the United States to resist any resort to force or other forms of coercion that would jeopardize the security, or the social and economic system, of the people of Taiwan.[4]

These provisions were in part designed to placate the resurgent 'China Lobby' of outraged right-wing opinion, and clearly went further than the announcement on normalising relations in committing the United States to the defence of Taiwan. Carter's 'appeasement' of the communists became an election issue. In a speech in May 1980, Presidential candidate Ronald Reagan openly declared he would favour a 'two-China' policy, with an official liaison office in Taipei as well as an embassy in Peking. Later, in June, he said he intended to re-open diplomatic relations with the ROC if elected. The realities of office were to temper this zeal, and the Reagan Presidency was in fact to mark a further improvement in relations with Peking at the expense of Taipei. At first, however, there was considerable suspicion of Reagan's intentions over Taiwan, and no slackening of China's sensitivity to alleged US meddling.

In Sino-US relations, the question of arms supplies has been contentious ever since the Taiwan Relations Act, which China regarded as reneging on US commitments. This issue continued to rankle until, in August 1982, China and the US issued a 'Second Shanghai Communiqué', in which the US agreed that its arms sales to Taiwan would not exceed 'either in qualitative or quantitative terms, the level of those supplied in recent years since the establishment of diplomatic relations ... and that they will be gradually reduced, leading to a final resolution of this issue over a period of time'[5].

Just as US congressional resistance to the implications of normalisation with Peking had led to the Taiwan Relations Act, so, in 1983, the Senate Foreign Relations Committee passed a resolution concerning the 'Future of the People of Taiwan'. It resolved that Taiwan's future should be settled peacefully, and in a 'manner acceptable to the people of Taiwan'. The resolution did not pass the Senate floor. Even after the Shanghai Communiqué, China carped about arms sales. In a 1986 interview, then Communist Party leader Hu Yaobang claimed that at the present rate, it would be 34 years before US arms sales to Taiwan finally petered out. And there were Chinese suggestions that the US was cheating, by transferring high technology and know-how that was not quantifiable but breached the 'qualitative' limit.[6]

Later in 1986, Deng Xiaoping was to say there was only one obstacle in Sino-US relations, that of Taiwan, but it was 'immense'. Taiwan will not evaporate as a problem for US policy-makers. But, meanwhile, relations with Taiwan have naturally been dented by the normalisation of relations with Peking. Taiwan's first official reaction, 'Five Principles', enunciated by President Chiang Ching-kuo in December 1978, was restrained, a plea more in sorrow that in anger for continued US security support, and for the continuation of ties between the two governments. Since then, relations, under the new guise of 'unofficial contacts', have remained close. The US has, as we have seen, continued to provide military technology and hardware, and economic relations have prospered, to Taiwan's advantage. By 1986, the size of the US global trade deficit began to dominate its bilateral relations with trade surplus countries, Taiwan among them. In 1986, the United States accounted for more than 80 per cent of Taiwan's massive trade surplus of US$16 billion, and again in 1987, when the surplus climbed further, to US$19 billion. The US put on pressure to dismantle tariff barriers and import quotas, and to revalue the local currency. Taiwan acceded, albeit more slowly than the US would have liked. It tried to argue that the issue ought not to be balanced trade, but fair trade, and pointed out that in 1986, Americans each spent US$78 on Taiwan's goods, whereas Taiwan residents spent US$284 a head on US imports. This argument did not cut much ice, and as protectionist tendencies gained ground in the US, especially in the run-up to the 1988 elections, the related issues of trade and currency began to sour bilateral relations quite severely.

But this is still an argument between friends. Taiwan knows that it needs the US, and that, in the present climate, an accommodation has been found in how Washington can deal with it while pursuing its goal of good relations with Peking. Taipei no longer feels under threat of imminent further sanctions forced on it by Peking by proxy through its Western allies. After the Peking massacre of June 1989, Taiwan was quick to make political capital out of the international opprobrium poured on the Peking regime. Yet it knew that there was no hope of going back, that there is no chance that Washington will de-recognise Peking. Instead, Taipei must do the best it can in the margins of global arrangements over which it has no control.

TAIWAN AND THE UNITED NATIONS

The Republic of China's permanent seat on the United Nations Security Council was its greatest asset in presenting itself internationally as a credible national government, rather than simply as a US surrogate. It was under threat from the outset. Almost every year between 1949 and 1971, a vote was taken in the UN General Assembly on whether or not to unseat the ROC and welcome the PRC into the UN.

At first, the battlelines were relatively well defined. The United States and its allies backed the KMT; the Soviet bloc supported the PRC, and indeed the Soviet Union boycotted the Security Council over the issue of Chinese representation for a crucial period on the run-up to the Korean War in 1950. In that year, the Soviet Union twice proposed resolutions to give the UN seat to Peking. So, too, did India, which as a newly independent country sided with the Soviet bloc against what was seen as Western imperialism in Asia. Both resolutions were easily defeated. Of the then 59 members of the UN, only 16 voted for Peking. Thereafter, throughout the 1950s, a US-sponsored resolution calling for a moratorium on discussion of the issue of Chinese representation was passed.

But the United States' in-built majority in the UN was gradually being whittled away by the accession of new members, especially the newly independent countries of Africa. By 1960, the votes against the ROC had climbed to 34 out of a total membership of 98, with 22 abstentions. The US resorted to a procedural defence of the ROC's position, replacing the 'moratorium' resolution with an 'Important Question' vote. That made the issue of Chinese representation an 'important question', which required a two-thirds majority in the General

Assembly. This eased the US lobbying task. If it could muster a simple majority for the 'Important Question' resolution, it need only ensure one-third of the votes against any proposal to oust the ROC.

However, as the 1950s wore on, it became apparent to Taipei that it could not rely indefinitely on US protection in the UN. It needed to try to garner support among some of the new members, whose natural, anti-colonial bias tended to be to vote for the PRC. A programme of aid and technical assistance for Africa was launched in 1961, and was to cover a total of 31 countries. Although the aid operation was dressed up as an enlightened push to disseminate the KMT's valuable development experience in the Third World, it was also designed to secure some African votes at the UN.

Nevertheless, the trend of voting patterns at the UN was shifting remorselessly against the ROC, with only a hiccup in the mid 1960s, as China slackened its own lobbying activities amid the internal preoccupations of the Cultural Revolution. In 1970, of 127 members, 52 voted against the 'Important Question' resolution, and 51 voted for the PRC in a subsequent resolution on ousting the ROC. For the first time, this gave the anti-ROC vote a majority when abstentions were taken into account. It did not achieve, however, the two-thirds majority needed. By the next year, after the Kissinger visit and the announcement that the US was going to support PRC membership, though not the unseating of the ROC, the 'Important Question' resolution was defeated, and in what had become an annual vote on an Albanian-sponsored resolution, the UN General Assembly voted overwhelmingly in favour of seating the PRC and of removing immediately 'all representatives of the Chiang Kai-shek clique who are unlawfully occupying the place of China in the United Nations'.[7]

By this time, it was by no means just the Soviet bloc and a few post-colonial governments that recognised the Peking government. Britain, anxious to keep lines open to secure the future of its colony in Hong Kong, also swayed by wanting to keep unity in the Commonwealth in the light of India's decision to recognise Peking, had severed its ties with the ROC as early as 1950. In 1964, France, another permanent Security Council member, had followed suit, as it sought to establish itself as a 'non-aligned' European power, not tied to Washington's bootlaces. In 1970, Canada, after 18 months of negotiation, also recognised the Peking government, using the formula over Taiwan that was to become a model first for Italy, in the same year, and then for the United States. With the loss of the UN seat, the tide of countries deserting the ROC became unstoppable. Between January 1971 and January 1979, and the normalisation of Sino-US relations, 46 countries ended their diplomatic relations with the ROC. In 1972 alone, Japan, Australia, New Zealand, Argentina and a number of small African and Carribean countries switched.

The loss of the UN seat also brought the end of the ROC's representation in a host of international organisations, like the World Bank and the International Monetary Fund, as well as the UN's own organisations. Taiwan entered a phase of acute diplomatic and political isolation.

TAIWAN AND JAPAN

After the United States, Taiwan's most important foreign relationship is with Japan. This is founded on a solid economic basis. In 1988, Japan provided nearly 30 per cent of Taiwan's imports, and just under 40 per cent of approved foreign investment in Taiwan. Meanwhile, Japan was also the mainland's most important trade partner outside Hong Kong. Japan's ability to outdo its competitors in dealing extensively with both Chinas dates back almost to the division of China, and has caused frequent strains in Tokyo's relations with both Peking and Taipei.

As Japan rebuilt under American occupation at the end of the Second World War, there was considerable sympathy across the political spectrum for maintaining as normal a relationship with the Peking government as possible. Despite the umbrella of US security protection, it seemed foolhardy to adopt a wholly hostile stance towards Japan's large continental neighbour. Policy formation was complicated by the close links that colonialism had built up between Japan and the mainland and Taiwan, and the presence of some 50 000 ethnic Chinese in Japan, many from the former colony of Taiwan. Ever since, there have been influential lobbies at both extremes of Japanese politics. Opposition parties, especially the Japan Communist Party and the larger Japanese Socialist Party, have consistently advocated closer ties with the mainland. They have been backed in this by large sections of liberal opinion, and much of the media. But the Japanese right wing has also been active in lobbying for the maintenance of ties with Taiwan.

However, in the early 1950s, foreign policy was not in Japan's control. Under American influence, Japan normalised relations with the ROC, and signed a peace treaty with the Taipei government in 1952, to coincide with the coming into effect of the San Francisco peace treaties. When, in 1952, Prime Minister Shigeru Yoshida told the Japanese parliament that he was willing to establish official Japanese representation in both Taipei and Shanghai, there was uproar in Washington. In the 'Yoshida letter', the Prime Minister was forced to confirm in writing to Secretary of State Dulles that Japan had no intention of concluding a bilateral agreement with the People's Republic of China. Japan became active on the ROC's behalf in the United Nations, and remained, as it had been in colonial days, an important market for Taiwan's exports. In Taiwan, Japan was not loathed as an ex-colonial power. On the contrary, for some of the Taiwanese population, with fresh memories of the KMT repression of the late 1940s, Japanese rule seemed almost like halcyon days in Taiwan's history. The KMT itself gained popular sympathy in Japan by the early repatriation of Japanese prisoners of war, and was grateful for Japan's diplomatic support. However, the KMT, like the Chinese communists, was to remain suspicious of Japan. The popular nostalgia in Taiwan for some aspects of Japanese rule, and the presence of Taiwanese pro-independence activists in Japan, led both the KMT and CCP to feel with some justification that Japan's ultimate ambition was to see a permanent division of Taiwan from China, enabling Japan to deal equally with both.

The KMT, moreover, was sensitive to the undeniable evidence that, behind the diplomatic facade, Japan was pursuing a 'two-China' policy. As early as 1952, Japan entered into an unofficial trade agreement with mainland China. By the early 1960s, as the Sino-Soviet split forced China to look elsewhere for economic partners, Japan–mainland trade showed rapid growth. This exploded into a diplomatic row in 1963–4, when it was revealed that Japan, through its Export–Import Bank, was providing official financial support for exports to the mainland. The KMT withdrew its ambassador from Tokyo, and former Prime Minister Yoshida wrote 'privately' but with official sanction to the ROC to promise that it would not happen again. When in 1965, the Japanese Prime Minister Eisaku Sato indicated that he would honour this commitment, the PRC cancelled a number of deals in the course of negotiation with Japan.

It was the issue of the largely small and uninhabited Senkaku or Diaoyutai Islands which was to inflame Taipei's relations with Tokyo. After the 1969 announcement of the Nixon 'Guam Doctrine', of disengagement from Asia, the US prepared to hand back to Japan both Okinawa and the Senkakus, which had been under US administration since the end of the war. In April 1971, the US announced that the islets would be handed over to Japan in 1972. Peking was nervous that this might foreshadow a Japanese role as the United States' security policeman in the western Pacific, re-arming and resurging as a regional military power, an eventuality Peking continues to regard with dismay. For the KMT, however, the possibility was not so alarming. In fact, with the US security blanket already looking threadbare, the KMT took some comfort in a November 1969 joint communiqué signed by Eisaku Sato and President Nixon, declaring that Korea and Taiwan were vital to Japan's security. The implicit acceptance by Japan of some responsibility for regional security, and of the idea that Taiwan was within its 'defence zone', seemed to offer some options in the event of the abrogation of the 1954 Defence Pact with the US. The 1951 US–Japan Defence Treaty had contained provisions implicitly envisaging co-operation in the defence of Taiwan. However, public opinion in Taiwan was outraged by its government's apparently conciliatory stance on acceding to the transfer of its perceived territory to the former colonial power. Japan was seen as an aggressor backed by a treacherous United States, which was just three months later to make its surprise announcement of President Nixon's impending China visit.

That announcement was a surprise to Japan as well. It undercut the position of the pro-Taiwan right wing, and made

Sino-Japanese normalisation inevitable. Prime Minister Tanaka visited China in September 1972, and concluded the normalisation of relations, announcing that Japan 'fully understood and respected' the PRC's view the 'Taiwan is an inalienable part of China'. The joint communiqué announcing this contained no reference to the 1952 Japan–ROC Peace Treaty. It was assumed to have lapsed.

Now, the boot was on the other foot. Japan continued to follow a 'two-Chinas' policy, but now it was Peking which protested when this became too blatant, and Taipei which took umbrage at continuing diplomatic slights. Since normalisation, Japan's relations with China have rarely been smooth, and a consistent irritant has been Japan's attitude to Taiwan. Peking does not object to Tokyo's 'unofficial' relations with Taiwan as such. Indeed, during the 1970s, while it was trying to coax the US into full normalisation, it was against China's interests to disrupt Tokyo's ties with Taipei too much, lest it deter Washington. However, China has been resentful of the scale of Japanese involvement in Taiwan, and wary of what it perceives as a dangerous right wing in Japanese politics, whose long-term aims are to see a revival of Japanese militarism, and whose policies also favour an upgrading of ties with Taiwan.

This fear has provided the background to Peking's extreme touchiness over anything which smacks of 'official' relations between Taipei and Tokyo. Thus, in 1974, flights between Japan and Taiwan had to be suspended following the negotiation of an air service agreement between the Japanese and Chinese governments. Peking categorically refused to allow the Taiwan flag carrier, China Airlines, to land at the same airport as its own national airline. A bitter row with Taipei ensued, and after a year a complex arrangement was instituted whereby planes from the two Chinas both flew to Tokyo airport, but with a six-hour interval between flights, to ensure that the rival airlines were not on the ground at the same time. In the end, when Tokyo opened its new Narita airport in 1978, the problem was resolved. China Airlines had to make do with facilities at Tokyo's less prestigous, but more convenient, Haneda airport. Similarly, in 1977, there was an incident at a Syrian port when two ships flying the different Chinese flags berthed at the same time, and China insisted that the ROC-flagged vessel take down its standard before being allowed to unload its cargo.

In the late 1980s, this sensitivity about Japanese double-dealing intensified in Peking. China viewed some aspects of the Nakasone administration from 1982 to 1987 with unease. It seemed to mark a reawakening of Japanese national pride accompanied by a resurgence of militarism. So the period was marked by bitter Chinese polemics against Japanese attempts to play down in its school textbooks the atrocities inflicted on China by Japanese invaders, and against Nakasone's 1985 visit to the Yasukuni shrine to honour Japan's war dead. The issue of Japan's defence spending also provoked concern in Peking. Inevitably, the fear of a right-wing revival also led to sensitivity about Japan's relations with Taiwan. In 1987, Japan angered Peking by engaging in official contact with the ROC over the transportation of 11 North Korean defectors from Japan to Taiwan.

This worry about 'official' links with the ROC surfaced most bitterly in a complicated wrangle over the so-called 'Kokaryo' dormitory. This provided accommodation for Chinese students in Kyoto, and in 1952 had been bought from a private owner by the government of the ROC. In 1977, a court had ruled that, as of the date of the Sino-Japanese normalisation in 1972, the ownership of the dormitory had passed to Peking automatically. The ROC continued to appeal against this judgement, and in 1987 won a case which upheld its right to the dormitory. Peking was outraged, both by the verdict, but also, more crucially, by the fact that the courts had accepted a suit filed on behalf of the ROC. For Peking, the issued became a clear-cut case of whether or not Japan would abide by its commitment to recognise a sole legitimate government of China, including Taiwan. A conspiracy was suspected, with the court ruling corruptly influenced by the pro-Taiwan lobby. For Japan, the issue impinged on the constitutional separation of powers. As in its dealings with the US congress, Peking wilfully or by design seemed to overlook the executive branch of government's theoretical inability to intervene in decisions by the legislative or judicial branches.

Taiwan, aggrieved as it may have felt at the desertion of Japan to the PRC had no option but to accept it, and to accomodate itself to maintaining relations at as full a level as possible. In this it has had considerable success. Indeed, although private commercial dealings are not subject to any official discouragement from Peking, the mainland government has clearly been peeved that Japanese investors have preferred to deal with Taiwan. Sino-Japanese trade had flourished, especially since the signing in 1978 of a Treaty of Friendship, but Peking has repeatedly grumbled about the Japanese reluctance to supply the two elements of foreign assistance it values above all others in its modernisation drive: the transfer of high technology and private investment. While Japan has been generous in providing development finance on favourable terms, and while Japanese consumer goods have helped meet the demand for better living standards on the mainland, Japanese investors have actually been slower to risk their capital in China than they have in Taiwan. On the trade issue, Taipei and Peking are at one in complaining about the Japanese resistance to imports. As Taiwan faces unrelenting pressure from the US to slash its bilateral trade surplus, it in turn has put pressure on Japan to balance its trade with Taiwan. Geographic proximity, historical ties and the steady expansion of Japan's already massive economy all make Japan the obvious first target for Taiwan's export diversification drive. But in 1987 and 1988, exports to Japan increased by only 11.4 per cent and 26.2 per cent respectively, while imports from Japan grew 34.3 per cent in 1987 and 17.9 per cent in 1988, leaving Japan in 1988 with a bilateral trade surplus with Taiwan still in excess of US$5 billion.

TAIWAN AND THE SOVIET BLOC

It has been mentioned in passing that, as China sank into the chaos of the Cultural Revolution, and the Sino-Soviet rift widened beyond repair, Chiang Kai-shek began to toy with the idea of a shift in the ROC's global alliances. This is one of the most curious episodes in the ROC's diplomatic history. In his speeches around 1965, Chiang began to stress that it was the Chinese communists, not the Soviet Union, that posed the biggest threat to world peace. In 1967, the then Prime Minister Yen Chia-kan reversed the government's usual formulation that 'those who are not our friends are our enemies', saying instead that 'those who are not our enemies are our friends'. This clearly held out the offer of some kind of *rapprochement* with the Soviet Union, in an effort further to isolate mainland China.

The Soviet Union showed signs of interest in the approach. Soviet publications began carrying occasional references to Taiwan as a 'country', and a Soviet representative at the UN hinted that the Soviet Union might back the accession of the PRC to the UN, only provided the ROC kept its seat. These delicate hints were given more substance when Soviet journalist, Victor Louis, went to Taiwan in October 1968. Although Louis went as a 'private individual', there was little doubt that he was acting as a broker for the Moscow government. He was widely reported as having held long talks with Defence Minister Chiang Ching-kuo, and as making several secret return trips to Taiwan. In May the following year, a Taiwan Professor, Ku Yu-hsin, who was a member of the National Assembly and former Education Minister, visited Moscow.

The contacts were never officially acknowledged, and, in public, the ROC stuck to its anti-Soviet line, that the communist regime in Peking had been installed as a result of Soviet conspiracy. Whatever quiet attempts at *rapprochement* were made in the late 1960s came to nought, and relations with the Soviet bloc reverted to the frosty distance that had characterised them since 1949. The reported overtures, however, were enough to alarm Peking, which has said that one of the eventualities which might make it take up arms against Taiwan would be a military alliance with China's enemies. In the 1960s and 1970s, the principal enemy was the Soviet Union.

The rigid ban on contacts with socialist countries began to relax in the 1980s, under the influence of more pragmatic foreign policies in all of Peking, Taipei and Moscow. The main thrust of Soviet leader Mikhail Gorbachev's July 1986 'Vladivostok Initiative' had been to add impetus to normalising Sino-Soviet relations. But it also contained a commitment to the Soviet Union's role as an Asian power, and to peaceful co-existence. To that end, the Soviet Union has since then pursued better relations in Asia not just with the major countries that had been hostile to it, China and Japan, but also with countries where politics had precluded it from any relations – South Korea and Taiwan. There was interest in commercial ties with these two as well as Japan, to help in the development of the vast expanses of Soviet Asia. Just as with China it was the Soviet Union's East European allies who set the pace in normalising relations, so it was with South Korea and Taiwan.

In 1980, Taiwan lifted its trade embargo on most of the communist world (but not the Soviet Union or China), though it still barred direct trade, forcing its exporters to deal thorough intermediaries, among which Japanese trading houses played a prominent role. The trade was trivial in comparison to Taiwan's global role, but as protectionist pressures in the US mounted, and the diversification drive gathered momentum, its potential was taken more seriously. With the Soviet Union in particular, there appeared to be an economic complementarity, between the vast untapped resources of Soviet Asia, and Taiwan's surpluses of capital and shortage of resources. The same is true to a lesser extent of some of the more beleaguered socialist economies, notably Vietnam, but also Poland.

In September 1987, two Polish scholars were given permission to attend a medical conference in Taipei the following spring. They are believed to be the first such 'official' visitors from a communist country. In January 1988, the ban on direct trade was lifted for most of the socialist world, with Vietnam, Laos, Kampuchea and Cuba added to the list the following year. By April 1990, the only countries still subject to the ban on direct trade were the Soviet Union, North Korea and mainland China itself. In October 1988, a 60-strong Taiwanese trade delegation went to Moscow. In March 1989, two Soviet beauty queens were allowed to compete in Taiwan, and in May, as Mikhail Gorbachev completed his historic *rapprochement* with Deng Xiaoping in Peking, two Soviet officials arrived in Taipei for the annual meeting of the Pacific Basin Economic Council, the first 'official' visit.

Taiwan's most important socialist partner was Hungary, which by the late 1980s had one of the most market-oriented economies in Eastern Europe. But in 1989, Taiwan failed to win Hungarian approval for a trade mission in Budapest. Hungary had outraged North Korea in February 1989 by establishing full diplomatic relations with South Korea but it seemed to be more cautious in its dealings with Taiwan, apparently less worried about North Korean fury than about antagonising Peking.

RELATIONS WITH THE OVERSEAS CHINESE

It will be recalled that the Chinese Revolution of 1911, which Taiwan regards as the foundation of its present system of government, was conducted in large measure by Chinese living overseas. The KMT has never forgotten the importance of the overseas Chinese to its diplomacy, and has competed with Peking for influence, and later investment, among these communities. An Overseas Chinese Affairs Commission was set up in 1952, to interest itself in the welfare of overseas Chinese, particularly those living in regimes which had recognised the communist government. Even in the 1989 elections, about 20 seats in the parliament, the Legislative Yuan, were still reserved for presidential appointees representing overseas Chinese in Hong Kong, the United States and elsewhere. Ostensibly, overseas Chinese were also to be encouraged to return home and take up public office, but, in practice, population pressures on Taiwan made this a very muted policy.

There are as many as 24 million people of Chinese ethnic origin living outside China, Taiwan, Hong Kong and Macao. The largest such communities are in non-communist South-East Asia, especially Indonesia and Malaysia, but also in the United States and Europe. In some countries, they have divided into explicitly pro-Taipei or pro-Peking lobbies, and, for example, in Indonesia in the mid-1960s, have been regarded as a dangerous fifth column encouraging revolution. More usually, they have followed the policies of their domestic governments, and have refrained from overt interference in China policy. Their prime interest to Taiwan has been commercial, both as significant sources of investment, and as a network of commercial contact and intelligence. After the economic reforms in China in the late 1970s, Taiwan found itself in competition with the mainland for overseas Chinese capital. Many had emotional ties with their ancestral home, and favoured China for that reason rather than commercial choice.

However, as a haven for Taiwan's own overseas investment in the late 1980s, South-East Asia was an obvious choice. Taiwan invested heavily in Indonesia, Malaysia, Thailand and the Philippines. In 1988, it overtook Japan to become the largest single new investor in the Philippines. The motives were commercial. In face of rising costs at home, the South-East Asian countries offered cheap labour, abundant natural resources and, by and large, political stability. But Taiwan was quick to try to use its economic muscle to win political kudos, much to the chagrin of Peking. In 1988, Malaysian Prime Minister Dr Mahathir Mohamad visited Taipei. Of most concern to Peking, however, were calls in the Philippines for a formalisation of ties with Taipei. In 1989, an attempt was made to pass a 'Taiwan Relations Act' in the Philippines Congress. President Aquino, herself of overseas Chinese origin, said that when she visited Peking in 1988, Chinese leaders told her they had no objections to Philippines–Taiwan economic links. Mrs Aquino may have been disingenuous. The suggestion that Manila might somehow up-grade its ties with Taipei, and occasional references in government statements to the 'Republic of China', caused fury in Peking, and stiff warnings of the possible consequences.

In 1989, after the Peking massacre, the ideological campaign for the hearts and minds of overseas Chinese stepped up. The Taiwan lobby in the US, founded in the immigrant community, again became active. As mainland Chinese students and intellectuals went into exile and set up anti-Peking 'pro-democracy' fronts, Taiwan offered money to help them study. It also offered money to other mainland students already studying abroad, but loath to return to the mainland. The memory of Sun Yat-sen and his band of exiled patriots came back to haunt the blood-stained chambers of the Peking leadership.

TAIWAN'S CURRENT FOREIGN POLICY

As part of the process of wholesale reform affecting Taiwan's political life from 1986 onward, foreign policy, too, underwent a major transformation. Taiwan's leaders called the new approach 'pragmatic', the mainland berated it as 'flexible' or 'elastic'. What it meant was a softening of diplomatic pride and a concerted effort to use Taiwan's commercial strength as a substitute for formal diplomatic links.

By April 1990, only 26 countries had full diplomatic relations with the Republic of China. The number had remained more or less constant throughout the 1980s, although the list of countries had changed somewhat. There was still a trickle of countries switching to Peking, like Colombia, Lesotho and the Ivory Coast in the early 1980s, Nicaragua in 1984 and Uruguay in 1988. Generally, Taiwan would take the initiative and terminate diplomatic relations once the other country had recognised Peking. But, largely by dint of its ability to offer substantial economic assistance, Taiwan was able to claim some new diplomatic partners, mostly small Caribbean or Pacific States, like Dominica, Saint Lucia and Tuvalu. As late as November 1988, the Bahamas, which hitherto had had ties with neither China, recognised the ROC.

In July 1989, Grenada for a short while made history by establishing what is regarded as 'dual recognition'. It established full relations with Taiwan, without breaking relations with Peking, which it had recognised in 1985. It took a month for Peking to take the initiative and break relations with Grenada itself. Although short-lived, it was an important interlude. The ROC Foreign Minister said that although Grenada may have looked on this arrangement as 'dual recognition', the ROC did not. The implication, however, was that if other countries wanted to try and adopt a 'two-China' diplomacy, the ROC would not stand in their way. Later in 1989, Grenada's example was followed by Liberia and Belize, and Taiwan's Foreign Ministry claimed more countries were in the pipeline. The switch to Taipei was accompanied by generous financial assistance from Taiwan. China fulminated about 'silver bullet diplomacy', and the KMT's 'one China, one Taiwan' policy.

Of the 26 states recognising the Republic of China by April 1990, four stand out in importance: Saudi Arabia, South Korea, the Vatican and South Africa. Of these, only the relationship with South Africa seemed totally secure. Staunchly anti-communist, royalist Saudi Arabia has been one

of Taiwan's best international friends. Its supplies of oil have
helped Taiwan to weather the two oil shocks, and Taiwan in
return has been lavish in providing technical assistance in
areas like petrochemicals, electric power and the food and
high-tech industries. But in the late 1980s, Peking has been
assiduously courting the Riyadh government. Anxious to find
a role in the Middle East, Peking's position on the UN
Security Council gives it some leverage in trying to prise
diplomatic recognition out of the Saudis. The courtship took a
turn which alarmed both Israel and the US in 1987, with the
supply of Chinese-built surface-to-surface missiles to Saudi
Arabia. The missiles had the capacity to carry nuclear war-
heads, and Israel was within their range. The irony for Israel
was that large-scale clandestine military co-operation had
been in progress for a number of years between its own armed
forces and China. In March 1988, the highest-level Saudi
visitor so far, a deputy foreign minister, visited Peking. In
November, Taipei was provoked into a public expression of
concern by the news that Saudi Arabia was going to open a
trade mission in Peking. That may also explain the rapid
welcome Taipei gave that month to the establishment of a
Palestinian state, despite its own close Israeli links. By March
the following year, agreement had been reached on a recipro-
cal mainland Chinese trade mission in Riyadh. The next
month, Bahrain announced it was to open full diplomatic
relations with Peking. This left Saudi Arabia isolated as the
only member of the Gulf Co-operation Council not to recognise Peking.

With South Korea, the dangers of a switch of recognition
seem less imminent, although in January 1988, the newly
elected President Roh Tae-woo set as his prime foreign policy
a 'northward policy' of pursuing better relations with the
Soviet Union and mainland China. As the fiercely anti-
communist half of a divided country, the Korean example is
important in more than just diplomatic terms. South Korea
has for a number of years taken a less transigent 'one country'
policy than Taiwan. Both Koreas have observer status at the
UN, and South Korea could accept, and welcome, dual
membership. Its leaders have proposed summit meetings with
North Korea's Kim Il-sung, and it is the North's refusal to
deal with the South Korean government which is the obstacle

to official contacts. Similarly, the South would accept a 'cross-recognition' solution, whereby Japan and the United States would recognise North Korea, in exchange for Soviet and Chinese recognition of the South. In the climate of the late 1980s, both the Soviet Union and China, keen to improve their economic ties with South Korea, and to see military tension on the peninsula ease, might have been expected to favour some such breaking of the by then 35-year diplomatic log-jam. Moreover, both communist giants had lost patience with the economic bankruptcy of the North Korean regime, with Kim Il-sung's imperviousness to the reforms sweeping the communist world, and with the North Korean state's occasional and destabilising sponsoring of international terrorism. Yet, while Kim Il-sung lives, it is still, on balance, unlikely that either Peking or Moscow will carry out what he would regard as gross betrayal – the recognition of the Seoul government. Peking has another reason for deferring cross-recognition – the fear that it might be taken as a model for the future status of Taiwan. But with the Sino-Soviet *rapprochement* of the late 1980s, North Korea had lost its strongest card – its adroit manoeuvring between its two neighbours, playing on the fear that abandonment by one would lead Kim Il-sung to move entirely into the other's camp.

But within these constraints, China has been moving fast to improve its ties with Seoul. In 1987 at the Asian Games, and at the Olympics a year later, it sent large teams of athletes. In June 1988, the South Korean government had started to refer to the People's Republic of China as 'China', and the ROC as 'Taiwan'. Direct trade and investment links between South Korea and China gathered pace. The now openly acknowledged direct dealing gave South Korean exporters a competitive edge over their rivals from Taiwan, who still had to deal indirectly with the mainland, and pay middlemen's fees. In August 1988, an export-processing zone was set up on the Shandong Peninsula of north-east China, specifically to attract South Korean investment. Provincial level trade offices in Seoul gave Peking inchoate diplomatic relations.

Naturally, these developments caused strains in Seoul–Taipei relations. In August 1988, President Lee Teng-hui spoke of 'worrying differences' with the South Koreans over attitudes to communist regimes. Bilateral tensions also appeared. In early 1989, there was a furore in Taiwan over the navy's decision to buy South Korean built frigates, at a time when Taiwan's own shipping industry faced troubled times. Another row ensued in February 1989, when South Korea seized a Taiwanese fishing boat for allegedly sinking a South Korean vessel, which had, in fact, been rammed by mistake because of a navigational error.

The Vatican, too, has been trying to improve its relations with Peking, and has down-graded its representation in Taipei in readiness. Pope John Paul was known to want to visit China, to set the seal on a healing of the rift between the Catholic Church and China. There is a 'patriotic' Catholic Church in China which is schismatic, appointing its own bishops. In the ideologically confused climate of mainland China in the 1980s this Church flourished, as did the Protestant faith and the underground 'Roman' Catholic religion, which remained loyal to the Vatican. In November 1988, a visit to China by Cardinal Jaime Sin, the Archbishop of Manila, led to a thaw in China's relations with the Vatican. A Roman Catholic priest was released from prison, and there was speculation that the Holy See, too, might sacrifice its relations with Taiwan, to bring the world's most populous nation back into official contact with the Vatican. Such a switch by the Vatican must inevitably have been delayed by the Peking massacre of June 1989, but in the long run, the Church's unity may outweigh human rights considerations.

No such fears colour Taiwan's relations with South Africa, although the stability of the apartheid regime itself must be open to question. Unlike South Korea, which competes in Africa for diplomatic influence with North Korea, Taiwan has no important black African connections. As partial economic sanctions limit Pretoria's freedom of manoeuvre, it has found Taiwan a willing partner. In 1987, two-way trade reached more than US$1 billion, over 1 per cent of Taiwan's total trade, and nearly 3 per cent of South Africa's. This volume was expected to triple by 1990. South Africa was important as a source of coal and as a market for Taiwan's consumer goods. The black homelands of South Africa offered an attractive source of cheap labour in the internationalisation of Taiwanese industry and by 1988, it was estimated that Taiwan businesses had invested over US$100 million in more than 120 factories in South Africa. In 1988, as Taiwan became the world's largest buyer of gold in an effort to massage its trade figures, it also provided large indirect support to South Africa's economy. The gold was largely bought from the US, but mined in South Africa. The two countries also are believed to share military intelligence, and to conduct joint nuclear research. The pariah status of the Taipei regime gave it few qualms about pursuing its links with one of its few remaining reliably anti-communist partners.

There are three kinds of country in the world as viewed from the Taipei Ministry of Foreign Affairs: there are those with whom it has diplomatic relations; there is the most important group, which recognise the Peking government and have no official ties with Taipei; and there is the dwindling band of largely insignificant countries which recognise neither. This group of about 20 includes Israel, Bahrain until April 1989, and most importantly Indonesia and Singapore. Israel, like South Korea, however, has made plain its desire for diplomatic relations with China. The price of a Chinese involvement in the Middle East peace process may well be recognition of Israel. In a sense, there is a game of diplomatic brinkmanship on this issue between Peking and Moscow, each anxious not to antagonise their Palestinian and other Arab connections, but wary of isolating themselves from negotiations on the region's future.

Indonesia 'froze' its relations with Peking in 1967, as a result of China's alleged complicity in the communist uprising of 1965, the suppression of which brought President Suharto to power. In February 1989, in the fringes of the gathering of international dignitaries in Tokyo for the funeral of Japanese Emperor Hirohito, Suharto met Chinese Foreign Minister Qian Qichen, and the two countries made a surprise announcement that they would start 'unfreezing' talks. Indonesia was still nervous at China's strategic influence in South-East Asia, and at the potential volatility of its own ethnic Chinese population. But its efforts to play what it saw as its natural role, given its size, as a leader of non-communist South-East Asia, and in particular to mediate in the Cambodian conflict, were hampered by its lack of official ties with Peking.

Indonesia is an important destination for Taiwan's investment and exports, but diplomatically, its resumption of ties with the PRC is not a disaster for Taipei. The knock-on effect, however, is likely to be damaging. Singapore has always said it will follow Jakarta in establishing relations with Peking, and confirmed as much after the February 1989 announcement. Singapore's Prime Minister Lee Kuan-yew has profited from the absence of official ties with either China to put himself in the unique position of being the one world leader warmly welcomed in both Taipei and Peking. He enjoyed a close friendship with Chiang Ching-kuo, and was quick to establish a similar rapport with his successor Lee Teng-hui, whose first overseas trip as President – and indeed the first official foreign visit by a Taiwan Head of State for 12 years – was to Singapore in March 1998. The pall cast by the Tokyo announcement did not prevent the Taiwan official media from reporting the trip in up-beat terms. Taipei and Singapore have close trade, investment and military links. The Singapore army exercises frequently in Taiwan, and the navy has bought Taiwan-built vessels. But Singaporean Chinese also invest in the mainland, and in foreign policy, especially in maintaining South-east Asia's resolutely anti-Vietnamese stance, Singapore and Peking have found a lot of common ground. With Hong Kong reverting to Peking sovereignty in 1997, Singapore seemed well-placed to take over the former colony's role as an entrepôt for indirect trade, and as an intermediary in the event that government-to-government talks between Peking and Taipei take off. In 1988, there were rumours that 'parliamentary' talks between Legislative Yuan members and members of the National People's Congress might take place in Singapore. Once official relations with Peking are established, however, it will be hard for Singapore to fulfil such a role. But Taiwan has steeled itself to such diplomatic set-backs. The emphasis of its foreign policy now is on the breadth and continuity of unofficial ties. The battle for diplomatic recognition as the sole legitimate government of China is tacitly acknowledged as lost.

7 China Changes Tack: Peking's 1980s Taiwan Policy

INTRODUCTION

Following the death of Mao Zedong in 1976, China shook off the isolationism and ideological fanaticism of the Cultural Revolution. In December 1978, at the third plenum of the Central Committee of the 11th Congress of the CCP, Deng Xiaoping emerged in control as China's paramount leader. He started debunking many of the sacred cows of Maoism, and pursuing a course of radical economic reform. Over the decade he was to rewrite the ground rules of Chinese politics. No longer, as under Mao was 'politics in command'. Rather 'economic development' was the 'key link', the ultimate arbiter of both domestic and foreign policy. It was, to a certain extent, a revival of the ideals of Zhou Enlai. Even before Deng took over, Mao's chosen successor, Hua Guofeng, had trumpeted a policy formulation first put forward by Zhou in 1964, the 'four modernisations'. In foreign policy, too, there was a revival of Zhou Enlai's ideals of 'peaceful co-existence', that is of pragmatic co-operation even with ideological foes.

China's foreign policy in the 1980s began to enter a fourth phase. After the 'leaning to one side' phase of Soviet alliance in the 1950s, the isolationism and identification with the third world of the 1960s, there had been in the 1970s a period of seeking friendships in what amounted to a global coalition against perceived Soviet expansionism. By the end of the 1980s, this had been superseded by the normalisation of relations with the Soviet Union, and a more genuinely 'independent' stance between the two superpowers, with foreign policy often dictated by economic advantage.

In Taiwan policy, too, Zhou Enlai's conciliatory approach, first enunciated in 1955, was revived, elaborated and formalised. Again 'peaceful reunification' was stressed. A year before Mao, in 1975, Chiang Kai-shek had died. The death of the two bitterest antagonists among the old civil warriors seemed to mark a transition to a new generation of leaders for whom the six decades of intermittent KMT–CCP civil war were not a vivid memory. Post-Mao China was changing fast, opening to the West economically and politically. Its image in the West became benign, even friendly. With the old guard in Taiwan also dying off, a younger generation was taking its place, well-indoctrinated in the ideal of Chinese reunification, but perhaps without the same emotional antipathy to the Chinese communists. China began negotiating about once intractable territorial issues – Hong Kong, Macao and the Soviet, Mongolian and Indian borders. It did not seem wholly inconceivable that the KMT, too, might be enticed into a dialogue with Peking. Not that the CCP for a moment dropped its insistence on its sovereignty over Taiwan. Nor did it ever renounce its right to use force to bring about reunification if peaceful means failed, or took too long.

CHINA'S NEW APPROACH – THE NINE PRINCIPLES

On 1 January 1979, diplomatic relations were formally opened between the People's Republic of China and the United States. The previous October Deng Xiaoping had visited Japan, to coincide with the ratification of the China–Japan Treaty of Peace and Friendship. In December, at the eleventh plenum, Deng Xiaoping's line had won out in the Party's own policy battle. 'Class struggle' was jettisoned as a slogan, to be replaced by 'socialist modernisation' under a guiding principle of pragmatism ('seeking truth from facts'). 'Peaceful *reunification* of the motherland' was made a strategic policy, and the rhetoric of both armed and peaceful *liberation* was cast aside. 1 January 1979 was also marked by a message from the Standing Committee of the National People's Congress (NPC) to Compatriots in Taiwan, setting the basis for Taiwan policy to this day.

Many of China's formal approaches to Taiwan have come from organs or spokespeople of either the NPC, or the Chinese People's Political Consultative Committee (CPPCC). The NPC is China's legislature, which also gives it constitutional law-making powers for the 'separated territories' of Taiwan, Hong Kong and Macao. Until the late 1980s it tended to act purely as a rubber stamp for turning Communist Party policy into law. The CPPCC has had even less power. It was a relic of the 'united front' policy of the civil war, and hence included members not just of the Communist Party, but of other political parties of the 1940s, including a section of the Kuomintang which had become loyal to the communists. It was natural that these two 'popular' bodies should be the channel for 'official' communication with Taiwan, rather than arms of the government, whose top organ is the State Council. Governmental pronouncements would have implied dealing on equal terms with the government in Taipei. As the decade wore on, the Communist Party was itself to make direct appeals to Taiwan, but not to the government there. Rather, it addressed itself to the KMT, and revived the rhetoric of party co-operation, calling for a 'third United Front' with the KMT.

China's policy on Taiwan in the 1980s was, like so many policies both on the mainland and in Taiwan, subject to numerical encapsulation. In this case, it was summed up as the 'three links', the 'four exchanges' and the 'nine principles concerning the return of Taiwan to the motherland for the peaceful reunification of China.' The first two of these slogans originated in the New Year's Day message in 1979. It made no mention of military threats. Indeed, it included the announcement that, as of that day, the government had ordered the People's Liberation Army to stop the bombardment of Quemoy. The 'three links' the message proposed were in trade, transport and mail. It urged the development of economic links, and of air, shipping and postal services to facilitate them, and to allow relatives and friends to visit each other. The 'four exchanges' were academic, cultural, sports and technological exchanges – in other words the full panoply of bilateral relations shorn of any overtly 'political' content.

The message marked a stepping up of China's efforts to bring reunification closer. It stressed the urgency of the task: 'It is an issue no one can evade or try to.' This point was emphasised again the same afternoon, by Deng Xiaoping himself, when, at a meeting of the National Committee of the CPPCC, he said that the question of returning Taiwan to the motherland had now been placed on the day-to-day agenda. Later that month, in a speech to the US Congress, Deng Xiaoping formally announced that China would no longer use the term 'liberation' in relation to Taiwan.

Although the 1979 New Year message proposed these various means of expanding contacts with Taiwan, and promoted national reunification to an immediate policy goal, it had nothing to say on the future status of Taiwan, or its relationship with the Peking government. It was not even clear whether Taiwan would be, as most Chinese rhetoric implied, simply a 'province of China', or whether it would be, as Zhou Enlai had hinted in the early 1970s, 'like Shanghai', a municipality directly under the State Council, or whether it would be like Tibet and other 'minority nationality' areas, an 'autonomous region' of China. The experience of Tibet and other autonomous regions was little advertisement for even this, the most 'hands-off' arrangement that seemed to be on offer at the time under China's constitution. This lack of clarity about what was actually being proposed bolstered the KMT's intransigence. Fond of the numbers game itself, it responded with 'three noes': no contact, no compromise and no negotiation with the communist bandits.

A concrete proposal had to await the 'nine principles'. They were elaborated by the late Marshal Ye Jianying in an interview with the official news agency in September 1981, when he was Chairman of the Standing Committee of the NPC. The nine principles, which were still upheld almost a decade later, were:

(1) A proposal that the KMT and the CCP hold talks for an 'exhaustive exchange of views'.
(2) A call for family reunion visits, and for the so-called 'three links', and 'four exchanges'.
(3) A guarantee of a 'high degree of autonomy as a special administrative region' for Taiwan after reunification. No time limit was set on this, unlike in the subsequent agreement reached in 1984 with Britain over the future of Hong Kong, or in 1987 with Portugal over the future of Macao. Also unlike Hong Kong, Taiwan is allowed to keep its own armed forces. Marshal Ye also offered a pledge of non-interference from Peking in 'local affairs'.
(4) Taiwan's current socio-economic system to be preserved, as will be its way of life, economic and cultural relations

with other countries. No encroachment of private property rights, on the right of inheritance, or on foreign investment. As for principle 3, no time limit was set on this.

(5) 'People in authority' and others on Taiwan may take up leadership posts in national political bodies, and participate in running the state.

(6) The central government's coffers will be available to bail the Taiwan economy out of financial difficulties, should they arise (Marshal Ye did not cover the more likely eventuality of the central government needing financial assistance from the bulging bank balances of the 'Taiwan authorities').

(7) Taiwan residents will be able to settle on the mainland without fear of discrimination.

(8) Taiwan industrialists and businessmen will be encouraged to invest in the mainland, and their rights and profits will be guaranteed.

(9) A call for proposals from all nationalities, public figures and mass organisations in Taiwan on reunification. Proposals on affairs of state should be made 'through various channels'.[2]

The ideas embodied in the 'nine principles' were later to be encapsulated in the slogan 'one-country – two systems'. That formulation did not gain currency until the negotiations with Britain over Hong Kong. But Deng Xiaoping was to tell British Prime Minister Margaret Thatcher in December 1984 that 'the one country two systems proposal did not begin with Hong Kong, but with the issue of Taiwan. Although the nine-point statement ... was not called "One country – two systems", in fact, that was what is was.'[3] Hong Kong was both a dry run for the reintegration of Taiwan, and China's best chance of demonstrating to the sceptical Taiwan public that it was feasible. On 16 July 1982, Peng Zhen, a vice-chairman of the CCP, and its leading constitutional expert, spoke to the NPC's Standing Committee. Taiwan, Hong Kong and Macao, he said, would become 'Special Administrative Regions' of the People's Republic of China. He said that the three regions would be allowed to retain their capitalist economic systems, their way of life and their cultural freedom, provided they accepted the ultimate political sovereignty of the Peking government. Later in 1982, the NPC adopted a new Constitution for the People's Republic, which incorporated (in Article 31) provision for the existence of such 'special' regions with different socio-economic systems.

Meanwhile, the Peking government was continuing efforts to prove its new open, liberal, trustworthy and unvengeful stance towards Taiwan. In March 1982, more than 4000 former KMT party, military and intelligence personnel were freed from jail. Later, China was to promise 'understanding' to those who had KMT tattoos indelibly inscribed on their bodies. In July, NPC Vice-chairman Liao Chengzhi wrote to Chiang Ching-kuo, as a 'childhood friend'. Couched in placatory, even affectionate tones, his letter recalled a youthful friendship, acquaintance in Moscow in the 1930s, and a last 'brief rendezvous' in Nanking in 1946. But it told Chiang he had 'unshirkable responsibility' to enter into peace talks with former 'school-mates and close friends'.⁴ It said Chiang's father's remains should, after reunification, be brought back to his native soil, exploiting Confucian notions of filial piety in the cause of reunification. Liao offered to go to Taipei to meet Chiang. The next year, in June 1983, Zhou Enlai's widow, Deng Yingchao, Chair of the United Front talking shop, the CPPCC, made the additional clarification that 'after reunification the CCP and the KMT will supervise, co-operate and co-exist with one another for a long time to come.'⁵

Taiwan was being offered much more genuine autonomy than Hong Kong. Not only was there no time limit placed on the period of guaranteed continued capitalism, but Taiwan was also to be allowed to keep its own troops, provided they did not constitute a threat to the mainland. In July 1983, Deng Xiaoping confirmed further that 'the mainland will station neither troops nor administrative personnel in Taiwan', a right Peking has staunchly refused to yield in negotiations over Hong Kong. Deng also proposed that the talks take place between the CCP and the KMT 'on an equal basis, rather than negotiations between the central and local authorities'. The same year, Prime Minister Zhao Ziyang added that 'the mainland will not collect any tax from or impose any levies of money on Taiwan.... Taiwan may also develop its trade relations, exchanges and co-operation with foreign countries in economics, technology and culture.'⁶

As negotiations with Britain over Hong Kong proceeded through 1984, China's commentators were at pains to point out the parallels for Taiwan. The economic troubles of Taiwan in the mid-1980s were blamed by mainland analysts on its diplomatic isolation and uncertain future, leading to a brain-drain of the professional élite. Naïvely, it was implied that Hong Kong would be spared such loss of confidence. However, the crucial difference was also underlined: Hong Kong was a question of resuming sovereignty, and hence involved negotiation with the colonial power; Taiwan was a matter of peaceful reunification, and fell within the ambit of 'China's internal affairs'.

Nevertheless, the Hong Kong negotiations, and developments there since the 1984 'Joint Declaration' with Britain became Peking's most important propaganda tool in the battle for public opinion in Taiwan. It is perhaps worth pausing to reflect on quite how extraordinary it was for the Chinese Communist Party to propose a 'one-country – two systems' formula for Hong Kong, Macao and Taiwan. Ever since its foundation in 1921, the CCP had held to the view that capitalism was a dying form of social organisation. Even under Deng, the party still insisted on the 'superiority of socialism' that was to be demonstrated by its ability to achieve more equitable and efficient mobilisation of economic resources than capitalism. China's Constitution, even as revised in 1982, still maintained that the People's Republic was a socialist country. Yet here was China's government promising both to wicked imperialist powers, and to its old civil war adversary the KMT, that the territories they controlled could keep their capitalist systems. What is more, Peking was pledging autonomy and limited non-interference in two of its wealthiest regions at a time of hectic modernisation in the rest of the country. Indeed, some of the official justifications of the policy seemed aimed as much at soothing outraged socialist sensibilities at home as at reassuring 'compatriots' in Hong Kong and Taiwan. In 1984, Deng Xiaoping felt it necessary to clarify that 'the main system in China must be socialism.... The socialist system practised by one billion people on the mainland will not be changed.'[7]

It is thus not surprising that many outside China were sceptical about the one country – two systems approach. What value did the constitutional provisions for 'special administrative regions' have, it was asked? The very preamble to the constitution seemed to make it all conditional on adherence to the 'Four Cardinal Principles', which boil down to Communist Party rule and the maintenance of a Marxist–Leninist ideology. The same revision of the constitution that legitimised 'special regions', also deleted the constitutional guarantees of the 'four great freedoms', of speaking out freely, airing views fully, holding great debates, and posting big character wall-posters. What guarantee was there that the radical turn-around in party policy over Hong Kong and Taiwan was durable – did it not all hinge on Deng's own position as the linchpin of a reformist government? In 1984, Deng also addressed this concern, pointing out that the policy 'is not my personal idea ... but a principle and law adopted by the National People's Congress.... If it is correct, nobody can change it.'[8] But what if the policy turned out not to be 'correct'? Hong Kong was to be the testing ground.

THE HONG KONG EXAMPLE

The tiny, barren island of Hong Kong had been ceded to Britain as a result of the first Opium War of 1840–42. Britain's sovereignty was confirmed by the 1842 Treaty of Nanking. Some twenty years later, in 1860, the Kowloon Peninsula, on the mainland of China just over the water from the island, was also ceded to Britain in perpetuity. In 1898, Britain's colony was further enlarged, in the 'scramble for concessions', by the addition of the so-called 'New Territories' on the mainland, and of the 'Outlying Islands'. These, however, were only leased to Britain, for 99 years. They were thus due to revert to China in 1997. Since the establishment of the People's Republic of China, the Peking government has never recognised the treaties giving Britain control of the colony. Along with other agreements reached during the Ch'ing's decline, they were regarded as 'unequal', imposed by force of arms on a weakened Chinese state, and invalid. This ruled out the possibility of negotiating with Britain over the future of Hong Kong. Since the British government insisted on the legality of its position by dint of these treaties, to have opened talks would have implied that China accepted the basis of the treaties.

This fundamental difference of opinion did not stop Hong Kong enjoying miraculous economic growth. It became the port of refuge for many of the capitalists fleeing communist China. Its fine natural harbour made it a flourishing entrepôt port. Like Taiwan, it became an exporting giant in its own right, specialising in labour-intensive manufacturing. It became an important regional financial and communications centre. It was of positive benefit to Peking, as the intermediary between its socialist economy and the capitalist world. By some estimates, in the 1970s, as much as 40 per cent of China's foreign exchange earnings derived from Hong Kong. Equally, however, Hong Kong was wholly dependent on the mainland for supplies of water and food. Nor was there much prospect that Britain would go to war with China to protect its colony. By choosing to overlook the uncertainties of Hong Kong's status, China's leaders had contributed to a symbiotic relationship with the colony that seemed in everybody's interests. China showed no great urgency about recovering sovereignty over all colonial possessions. Indeed, in 1975, when Portugal, shedding itself of its colonial possessions in the wake of its revolution, offered Macao back to China, Peking declined the offer.

It was Britain that rocked the boat over Hong Kong, by its perverse insistence on the legality of its occupation. The expiry of the lease on the New Territories and Outlying Islands gave a sense of looming crisis. Even if China could be persuaded to recognise the 'unequal' treaties, Hong Kong, bereft of its other accretions, would have been an unviable island. Meanwhile, investment, and in particular land tenure and construction in the areas due to revert to China in 1997, was bound to be constrained by the fact that, legally, there could be no title to ownership beyond 30 June 1997. The obdurate logicality of a Western-style legal system had made the status quo unfeasible.

Faced with this, China had to find a path between on one hand, killing the Hong Kong golden goose by immediately reasserting its claim to sovereignty, and on the other hand, disavowing its past policy and setting a dangerous precedent by granting Britain an extension on the lease. China realised that if it threatened to take back Hong Kong at once, the effect on economic confidence would be disastrous. But then so too would a decision to carry on ignoring the problem and failure to make its position clear. The 'one country – two systems' formula found China a way out of this impasse. It could maintain its insistence that the treaties were invalid, but condescend to negotiate because it recognised that 'problems left over from history' created specific difficulties for Hong Kong. Similarly, Peking could argue that its claim to sovereignty remained unimpaired and yet leave Hong Kong to prosper to the benefit of its own inhabitants and China itself just as it had before. It was a remarkably imaginitive and ambitious attempt to square the circle.

The result was the Sino-British 'Joint Declaration' on the future of Hong Kong, initialled on 1 September 1984.[9] It restored Hong Kong to Chinese sovereignty as of 1 July 1997, but outlined a series of measures designed to ensure that Hong Kong's socio-economic system stayed fundamentally unchanged for 50 years after that. The 'Hong Kong Special Administrative Region' would enjoy a 'high degree of autonomy', including executive, legislative and judicial power, as well as that of final adjudication, except in foreign and defence affairs; laws would remain basically unchanged; its government would be composed of local inhabitants; the legislature would be 'constituted by elections'; Hong Kong would remain a free port, a separate customs territory and an international finance centre. These policies would be embodied in a 'Basic Law', a kind of subconstitution for the Special Administrative Region, drawn up in consultation with local people, and passed by the NPC in Peking.

The Joint Declaration was accompanied by much self-congratulation in London and Peking. For the Chinese government, its importance was greatly enhanced by its status as a precursor for similar negotiations one day with the KMT. Taiwan's official statements on the agreement were scathing. Communists could not be trusted. Hong Kong's prosperity was doomed. For the agreement with Britain to succeed as propaganda in Taiwan, at least three conditions needed to be met: confidence in the Hong Kong economy had to survive; Chinese leaders had to abide by the joint declaration, especially, in respecting the 'high degree of autonomy'; and those leaders had to appear capable of continuing to respect the Joint Declaration after 1997. By the time of the Peking massacre in June 1989, the Joint Declaration had failed on all three counts.

At first, however, after the Joint Declaration was signed, Hong Kong's economy continued to boom. Even capital investment held up remarkably well. But this was illusory. The business cycle in Hong Kong is notoriously short, and before the 1990s there still seemed ample time for entrepreneurs to make their pile and decamp to Australia, Canada, the United States or elsewhere. In the meantime, there was no shortage of evidence of an alarming exodus of the professional and capitalist classes. Of those who stayed, many had already prepared themselves a bolt-hole by acquiring another passport. Britain had mean-spiritedly refused right of abode even to those born in its colony, about 3.28 million out of a population of nearly 6 million in 1989. The economy became vulnerable to political swings on the mainland. In the winter of 1986–7, the Hong Kong Stock Exchange, an effective barometer of economic health in the colony, plunged after student demonstrations in cities across China led to the dismissal of Communist party leader Hu Yaobang, and a backlash against political freedoms of expression on the mainland.

In addition to these 'accidental' by-products of political association with the mainland, China patently was interfering quite extensively in the pre-1997 arrangements. The chief of the bureau of its official news agency became, in effect, China's ambassador to Hong Kong. 'Joint Liaison Group' meetings between Britain and China on arrangements for the handover became a channel for Chinese views on policy to be known. Britain talked about the importance of 'convergence' between its colonial administration's actions up to 1997, and China's intentions thereafter. While the strength of this argument was irrefutable, it too often seemed to surface as Chinese pressure to tone down some of the more unpalatable implications of the Joint Declaration. In particular, China seemed reluctant to let Britain go too far in meeting the stipulation that the legislature should be 'constituted by elections'. A 'democracy' lobby grew in Hong Kong, arguing that the only meaningful safeguard against Peking's interference would be the presence of a strong local parliament, directly elected by universal suffrage, and thus with a popular mandate to speak for the people of Hong Kong. But, until the 1989 Peking massacre changed it views, Britain preferred to go slowly on the introduction of direct elections for the legislature, the Legislative Council, which until 1991 was to be entirely composed of appointed and indirectly elected members. Peking's apparent aversion to political participation by the people of Hong Kong also showed itself in insensitivity to the demands of the environmental lobby. In 1986, the increasingly politicised Hong Kong population, demanding the right to an environmentally safe future, organised a million-strong petition calling for the scrapping or relocation of a nuclear plant being built nearby in Guangdong province.

These fears about rule from Peking exploded in the aftermath of the Peking massacre in June 1989. The shock and outrage felt in Hong Kong were founded in the genuine sense of cross-border kinship that Chinese communities everywhere experienced. But also, the massacre seemed to undermine the very foundations of the Joint Declaration and the Basic Law. How could a government which would send soldiers with automatic rifles to suppress peaceful demonstrations in its own capital be trusted to implement its promises in a capitalist enclave? The Peking government tried to calm fears that anything in its attitude to Hong Kong had changed. But it proceeded to worsen the impact on local feelings by warning Hong Kong residents against meddling in Peking politics, by accusing some of them of helping instigate what it regarded as a counter-revolution, and by re-confirming that it would not give up its right to station the People's Liberation Army in Hong Kong if it felt it necessary. Taiwan felt vindicated, not just in its traditional view of the Peking regime as 'barbaric', but in the scorn it poured on the 'Hong Kong model'.

CHINA'S PRAGMATIC FOREIGN POLICY IN THE LATE 1980s

The 'Joint Declaration' on Hong Kong was the most striking example of the new pragmatism with which China under Deng Xiaoping conducted its foreign policy. It was followed in 1987 by a similar agreement with Portugal over Macao, arranging for a reversion to Chinese sovereignty in 1999. As

China's Prime Minister Li Peng was to point out in 1988, this made 'the question of the early reunification of Taiwan with the mainland ... stand out very prominently before the Chinese people'. Of the separated territories, only Taiwan was left. What is more, Peking had meanwhile been engaged in a similarly pragmatic process of negotiation over its other territorial 'problems left over from history' – its extensive land borders.

The most important of these borders is that with the Soviet Union, which is about 4500 miles in length. There are two sections, divided by the Mongolian People's Republic. The eastern section of the border, between Manchuria and Soviet Asia, is largely demarcated by the Amur and Ussuri rivers. China and the Soviet Union long disputed sovereignty over the hundreds of mainly tiny and uninhabited riverine islands. It was on one of the larger of these islands that the worst clashes of the 1969 Sino-Soviet border fighting erupted. On the western sector of the border, between Chinese- and Soviet-controlled Turkestan, as much as 8000 square miles of land in the Pamir mountain range is in contention.

The dispute is on two levels. There is actual disagreement about who should control what piece of land and there is the more philosophical dimension. China has rejected the original nineteenth-century border treaties as 'unequal'. It has wanted the Soviet Union to repudiate them, and renegotiate the borders afresh. The Soviet Union, a patchwork of increasingly restive national republics, has been adamant that the old issues of its territorial integrity could not be reopened.

In the 1980s, this deadlock was broken by flexibility on both sides. China no longer made so much of its demand for a formal renunciation of the tsarist treaties. The Soviet Union, keen to mend fences with Peking, made significant territorial concessions. These were contained in Mikhail Gorbachev's July 1986 'Vladivostok Initiative'. He conceded that the river border in the eastern sector could follow the main navigational channel, rather than, as the Soviet Union had previously insisted, extend to the Chinese bank of the river. This is the 'Thalweg' principle generally accepted in international law. The Chinese discretion on the issue of the treaties and Gorbachev's climbdown on this point enabled border talks to resume in 1987, after stalling repeatedly since the 1950s, most recently in the late 1970s, after a resumption following the fighting of 1969. By October 1988, the two sides were able to announce that they had reached agreement on the demarcation of a long section of the eastern border. This demonstrated flexibility on both sides, since the precise path of the 'main navigational channel' was in many places open to question.

In the 1980s, China also entered negotiations on almost all its other land borders – with Nepal in 1979, India in 1981, Mongolia in 1982, Bhutan in 1984 and Burma in 1985. In many cases, China was in fact resuming talks and refining agreements reached in an earlier phase of international pragmatism, the early 1960s, but the businesslike approach to its borders, many of which had been subject to a high degree of armed tension, was convincing evidence of Peking's new international image.

The administration of the border with the Mongolian People's Republic was agreed in November 1988, as part of the *rapprochement* with the Soviet bloc in general. The Soviet satellite had been established in 1921, and formally recognised as a *de facto* independent nation since shortly after the founding of the PRC. The Kuomintang still claims Outer Mongolia as as province of the Republic of China, despite Chiang Kai-shek's agreement to recognise its independence in 1946, at the time of Stalin's dealings with him as China's internationally recognised leader. In the late 1970s and early 1980s, Soviet troop deployments in Mongolia, and along the Sino-Soviet border, had become one of the 'three obstacles' in Chinese eyes to full normalisation of Sino-Soviet relations. But announcements in 1986 and 1988 of big reductions in the numbers of Soviet troops there had effectively removed the Mongolian issue as a stumbling-block between Peking and Moscow.

The Sino-Indian border was even more problematic. Of the three sections of the border, two are disputed. In the 1950s, China built a strategically important highway linking Xinjiang and Tibet through an area in its remote west, known as Aksai Chin, some 14 500 square miles in extent. India asserted its sovereignty over the region, as part of Jammu and Kashmir. China in 1962 then tried to demonstrate its claim at the other end of the border, the eastern sector. Here, China repudiates the British-imposed 'McMahon Line', which puts some 38 000

square miles of what China regards as the Tibetan Autonomous Region, inside India. India has now granted full
statehood to what used to be called the 'North East Frontier
Area', as Arunachal Pradesh. In 1962 China launched a
punitive invasion into this area to establish its claim, and then
withdrew to the 'line of actual control' having 'taught India a
lesson', a particularly bloody one, leaving an estimated 40 000
Indian dead. On the Indian border, China's unstated position
has always been pragmatic. It has wanted to do a 'package
deal', rather than adopt the sector by sector approach advocated by India. In other words, China would be prepared to
formalise the status quo, dropping its claim to Arunachal
Pradesh, which it does not control, in return for Indian
acceptance of the legitimacy of its actual control of the Aksai
Chin. In India, however, the humiliation of the 1962 war left
a lingering antipathy to any such horse-trading, and a parliamentary resolution calling on its leaders never to cede a
'single inch' of Indian territory. With the difficulty, not faced
by the leaders in Peking, of having to seek approval from an
electorate, India's leaders were unable to proceed to a full
normalisation of relations with China. They were buttressed in
this intransigence by an informal pattern of superpower allegiances on the subcontinent. While the United States and
China backed Pakistan, India's friendship with the Soviet
Union blossomed.

However, this web untangled in the 1980s. The Soviet
Union agreed to withdraw its troops from Afghanistan in
1988, easing tension with the United States, Pakistan and
China at a stroke. India's intransigence towards China seemed
out of keeping with the fluid new pattern of regional relationships. In December 1988, Rajiv Gandhi went to Peking to set
a symbolic seal on a new era of co-operation with China. In
doing so, he acceded to the Chinese suggestion that the border
dispute should not be allowed to stand in the way of good
relations in other areas. It was another major victory for
China's pragmatic approach to its territorial wrangles.

CHINA'S TAIWAN POLICY IN THE LATE 1980s

China's responsible new attitude to its land neighbours and its
willingness to negotiate with the heirs of the old imperialists

both served to underline its conciliatory line on Taiwan. The big difference, of course, was that it did not acknowledge that Taiwan had ever left Chinese control. It was not a question of negotiating with a foreign power over the return of territory unjustly wrested from Peking's sovereignty. Rather, it was a matter of persuading a local Chinese authority to drop its absurd claim to legitimacy over all of China, and admitting, as almost all of the rest of the world had, that Peking was the seat of the true Chinese government.

In this sense, a more reliable indicator of Chinese policy towards Taiwan was its handling of nationalist unrest in Tibet. Under Chinese suzerainty on and off since the Mongols, Tibet had been re-incorporated into China in 1951. A nationalist uprising in 1959 was put down with great brutality, and Tibet's god-king, the Dalai Lama, fled to India with tens of thousands of his followers. The distinctive age-old traditions of Tibetan Buddhism were ravaged by the excesses of young Maoists during the Cultural Revolution. In the 1980s, a more liberal climate prevailed. Communist Party leader Hu Yaobang even went so far as to apologise to Tibetans for past Chinese mistakes, and the area was opened up for tourism. But in the new, somewhat more relaxed climate, loyalty to the Dalai Lama and a nationalist movement for the independence of Tibet moved into the open. This led to a series of violent anti-Chinese demonstrations in the Tibetan capital Lhasa, starting in October 1987, and leading to bloody Chinese reprisals, most notably a mass protest in March 1989, followed by the declaration of martial law in Lhasa. The extent of Chinese 'flexibility' on Tibet was to agree to hold talks with the Dalai Lama, provided he drop his claim to independence. In June 1988, to the dismay of many of his followers, the Dalai Lama did just that. He offered a Hong Kong- or Taiwan-style solution: China could retain its control over Tibetan defence and foreign policy, in return for more genuine autonomy for the Tibetans. Even that was not enough to allow talks to go ahead. The Dalai Lama proposed sending a team of negotiators from the Tibetan parliament in exile, the Kashag. Since China could not recognise the legitimacy of this body, and since the Dalai Lama further antagonised Peking by proposing that a foreign legal adviser join his negotiating team, talks were slow to materialise.

The KMT found itself in a awkward position over Tibet. On the one hand, the widespread international sympathy for the Tibetan cause seemed to offer a good opportunity to score propaganda points off Peking. On the other hand, the KMT, too, claims sovereignty over Tibet, and to back an independence movement would be heretical. What is more, as with pro-democracy protests in China proper, KMT backing would only serve to fuel Peking's claims that anti-government protests were an international conspiracy fanned by Taipei. So, in October 1987, the 'Mongolian and Tibetan Affairs Commission' in Taipei, reacting to the first of the big protests, said that it would back anti-communist activity in Tibet provided it stopped short of calls for independence. It also claimed to have close contacts with the Dalai Lama, and to have reached a 'political understanding' with him on a number of unspecified points.

The Peking government's uncompromising and brutal handling of the unrest in Tibet, however, helped destroy the image so painstakingly built up of a reformed, reasonable regime. Tibet, after all, was an 'Autonomous Region'. Would it not act just as savagely if it saw developments in the 'Taiwan Special Administrative Region' moving in a way it disapproved of? Certainly, Peking's attitude to the new stirrings in the late 1980s of the Taiwan independence movement were just as uncompromising. As the opposition in Taiwan had regrouped through the 1980s, Peking had been extremely wary of any sign that it might adopt a pro-independence stance. This was exacerbated by China's deepening suspicions of US and Japanese intentions. With a right-wing American president deemed susceptible to the arguments of the Taiwan lobby, and an apparent resurgence of the Japanese right under Nakasone, Peking repeatedly warned that some elements in the West were plotting for a 'two Chinas' solution.

In a 1986 interview, then Communist Party leader Hu Yaobang spelled out China's concerns. He analysed the US leadership as split over Taiwan, with some of its members wanting to see some form of independence for Taiwan. Some, he said, still saw Taiwan as MacArthur's 'unsinkable aircraft carrier' and, he implied, would hence do all they could to undermine the ultimate goal of Chinese reunification. But he also raised a more subtle fear:

I have the impression that some people in the United States government want to use Taiwan as a pawn to bring about an absolute change in China's foreign and domestic policies, so that we would become a faithful ally of the United States. If these groups gain the upper hand, it would be very dangerous. We have repeatedly stated that China will not become an ally. We want to be friendly but not an ally.[10]

What Hu seemed to be worried about was the US exploitation of the powerful pull of the reunification issue, to persuade China to make major shifts in both its foreign policy and its own socio-economic system – that is, offering to use the considerable US influence in Taiwan in favour of reunification if China was 'good', and tilted further to the West. If there really were such a current of opinion in Washington, it was far-fetched and naïve. But Hu's voicing of such a fear was revealing of China's insecurities over Taiwan, and of the background to its staunch opposition to the Taiwan independence movement. Ironically, when Hu Yaobang was forced to resign his post in January 1987, one of the criticisms thrown at him was directed at remarks he had made the previous November, in which he implied that the people of Taiwan might be allowed some say in their future.

This hostility to any idea of self-determination for the people of Taiwan placed Peking in something of a quandary as to how to treat the emergent opposition there. Taiwan's Democratic Progressive Party in 1987 was ahead of the KMT in pushing for contact with the mainland. It represented a strand of middle class opinion which saw the KMT's 'three noes' policy as anachronistic and self-defeating. In this sense, it was a welcome development for Peking. In June, 1986, Deng Xiaoping was reported as speaking to a foreign visitor of his frustration with the KMT. It had 'turned a deaf ear' to Peking's proposals for contact and peaceful reunification. The opposition in Taiwan were at least willing to countenance contact, but the DPP also wanted self-determination. It did not go so far as to advocate sedition – independence for Taiwan. However, self-determination, to the extent that it required Taiwan's own people to decide on the future of the island without reference to Peking, was only a hair-split away from a full-blown call for independence. So the DPP's motives in supporting greater contact with China were the exact converse of Peking's – greater contact would formalise the de facto separation of Taiwan. Instead of bringing reunification closer, it would help postpone it indefinitely.

Peking never relented in its tirades against any manifestation of Taiwanese 'splitism'. Despite the predominantly soothing tone of its overtures to Taiwan, Peking would occasionally remind the island that it had never renounced the use of force if peaceful reunification were deemed to have been thwarted. One event that would clearly be seen as provocative of armed intervention would be a Taiwanese declaration of independence. Even less dramatic developments might lead to the use of force. Deng also told his June 1986 visitor, 'When patience runs out, and peaceful compromise is refused, there is no other way but force.' Similarly, the deputy Prime Minister Yao Yilin used a press conference in the aftermath of the accord with Portugal over Macao in March 1987 to remind Taiwan that Peking's patience with the peaceful approach was not inexhaustible.

The brief flirtation with the idea of harnessing anti-KMT resentment as a means of advancing China's cause proved short-lived in the mid-1980s, as it had a decade earlier, and Peking again found itself making common cause with the KMT. We have seen how Liao Chengzhi as early as 1982 had written in chummy tones to Chiang Chiang-kuo playing on respect for his dead father. In 1985, on the fortieth anniversary of the Japanese surrender, China mounted a full-scale rehabilitation of Chiang Kai-shek and his role in the anti-Japanese war. CCP official history had long taken the line that Chiang had not fought the Japanese, leaving the CCP to win the war. Now, however, his 'patriotic spirit and personal sacrifices' were lauded. Television and cinema dramatised the newly-perceived heroism of Chiang *père et fils*.

This reflected a growing awareness in Peking that the best chance of a negotiated settlement lay with the KMT old guard. There was a greater likelihood of an acceptable compromise while the reins of power were still in the hands of men with a life-long commitment to Chinese reunification, than when a new generation of Taiwanese leaders without the ties of blood and history on the mainland were in control. Chiang Ching-kuo himself seemed to be the only man of the ancestry and stature who could effect any dramatic shift in KMT mainland policy. But by 1986 he was already 76, and in poor health, suffering from diabetes and a weak heart that needed a pacemaker. His constitutional successor was a native Taiwanese, Lee Teng-hui. The opposition in Taiwan was gaining ground. A concerted bid for Chiang Ching-kuo's backing seemed a sensible option.

Indeed, Chiang Ching-kuo was to sponsor a dramatic revision of the KMT's mainland policy before his death, but not in the direction the CCP had hoped. It mourned his death, however, with no hint of criticism. China's then Communist Party leader Zhao Ziyang addressed the first public message from the Party to the KMT since 1949, expressing the CCP's 'deep condolences', and hailing Chiang for upholding a one-China policy, opposing the independence of Taiwan, and standing for the reunification of the country.

The elegiac tone of Zhao Ziyang's message of condolence masked a real worry in Peking. This surfaced most clearly later, in November 1988, in an article in the official magazine *Outlook*, that was subsequently, and highly unusually, withdrawn. The article made detailed allegations about US interference in the process of securing the succession to Chiang Ching-kuo for Lee Teng-hui. The thrust of the argument was that the US was taking sides in factional struggles within the KMT and the armed forces to back those who would be 'content to retain sovereignty over part of the country and refuse peace talks'. To this end, the US was continuing to violate the spirit of the Second Shanghai Communiqué on arms sales, and was striving to build up its economic links with Taiwan so that it would be even more dependent on Washington, and reluctant to rejoin China. Although the inflammatory article was retracted – perhaps in order not to ruffle relations with Washington just as a date for the long-awaited Sino-Soviet summit meeting was being set – the views expressed did accord with the new CCP orthodoxy over the government in Taiwan. The CCP simply no longer believed that the KMT was serious about reunification. Whereas the KMT under Chiang Ching-kuo was regarded as pursuing a misguided policy of 'reunification under Sun Yat-sen's three principles', now, no credence was given to the KMT's official and constitutional commitment to reunification. China's rhetoric would constantly remind the KMT of this commitment. But looking at Taiwan's 'flexible' diplomacy, they would conclude that 'some people in the KMT' have 'retreated from the previous stand of "one China"'.

This became a main theme of early 1989 articles, speeches and events on the mainland to commemorate the tenth anniversary of the 1979 'message to compatriots'. Developments in Taiwan itself seemed to be making Peking more impatient. At the March 1988 National People's Congress, the President Yang Shang-kun had stressed the 'urgency' of reunification. Later that year, in August, a Chinese American scholar, James Hsiung, arrived in Taipei claiming to have had talks on the future of Taiwan at the highest level, and to be conveying new Chinese thinking. Peking would formally eschew reunification by force; it would rewrite its constitution to down-grade the role of the Communist Party; and it would offer the KMT a place in a 'coalition government'. All Taiwan would have to do would be to accept Peking sovereignty and foreswear independence. The KMT shrugged off the message dismissively and its authenticity was never confirmed. But it came at a time when Peking's strategy seemed at a dead end. China now had much of what it wanted in terms of the 'three communications' and the 'four exchanges'. And all this had achieved was sharper definition of Taiwan as a separate country. Now the KMT old guard had lost out once and for all in the power struggle within the Taiwan party, and the old guard in Peking seemed also to be on the way out. It is not inconceivable that Deng Xiaoping and his peer group might have sponsored some such leak, in an effort to go down in history as the unifiers of China's sacred territory.

They might even fear that their successors, the second and third echelons of Chinese leaders, whose performance has so often failed to meet the stringent requirements of the old guard, might 'go soft' on Taiwan. This is unrealistic, however. Even though they might lack the emotional fervour about reunification of their elders, younger Chinese leaders are not going to give Taiwan up. The January 1979 'message to compatriots' explained this neatly; 'Who among the descendants of the Yellow Emperor wishes to go down in history as a traitor?'

After the Peking massacre and, in particular, when Taiwan's independence became the major issue at the December 1989 elections, hints of further compromise were forgotten. The divided, weak and unstable Peking leadership reverted to basics, among which reunification with Taiwan on its terms figured large.

8 Political Reform in Taiwan 1986–89

THE PRESSURES ON CHIANG CHING-KUO

By 1984–6, the authoritarian one-party rule of the KMT on Taiwan was unsustainable. International and domestic factors were contributing to a build-up of pressure for reform both within and outside the party. The KMT was faced with the choice of harsher repression or some sort of liberalisation. To the surprise of many, in view of his parentage and background, Chiang Ching-kuo chose the path of reform.

Internationally, the picture had been transformed by Washington's recognition of Peking. Deng Xiaoping had been to Washington and was fêted as *Time* magazine's 'man of the year'. China's image had improved beyond recognition, so that its coaxing words to compatriots on Taiwan seemed winningly reasonable to many. The KMT, meanwhile, was locked into its 40-year-old, and now clearly quite forlorn, claim to sovereignty over China. What is more, with the 'reformers' on the mainland now in the ascendancy, its own autocratic practices effectively prevented it from advertising itself as a 'beacon of democracy' in a grimly totalitarian China. Just as importantly, for all the formalities of the diplomatic position, Taiwan still relied on tacit US support for its continued survival. US-backed dictatorships around the world seemed to be crumbling: the Shah of Iran and Nicaragua's Somosa in 1979; Marcos in the Philippines in 1986; Chun Doo-hwan in South Korea a year later. The lesson of Iran and the Philippines, in particular, seemed to be that US backing would not be unstinting if the regime failed to meet popular demands for political participation.

At home, the KMT was rocked by a series of scandals. Not only did the financial quagmire of the Cathay scandal in 1985 threaten to besmirch the reputation of many of the Party's most senior figures, but there had been an even worse revelation regarding the country's intelligence services. In

October 1984, Henry Liu, a Chinese American who had written a critical biography of Chiang Kai-shek, was murdered in California. It transpired that a top intelligence official had conspired with Taiwanese gangsters 'to teach him a lesson'. The KMT's arrogation to itself of powers beyond not just its own laws, but those of its most important friend, made reform seem a necessity.

Meanwhile, the 'dangwai' opposition in parliament were gaining in maturity and organisation as the result of several years of open activity in the Legislative Yuan. If the KMT were to keep the electoral majority it needed to mitigate the manifest unfairness of its huge numerical preponderance in the Legislature, it would have to clean up its act. The rising living standards on the island, and the exposure to, in particular, American democratic values, made a younger generation less willing to put up with the restrictions of martial law. Nor did the muzzling of the opposition by occasional arrests, tight media controls and law-suits help the KMT's image as a party of the people.

So Chiang Ching-kuo put his weight behind a radical series of reforms of the political system and of policy to the mainland. His own prestige seemed crucial to the success of this effort, in the face of the presumed resistance of much of the KMT old guard and of the military. Still unswayed from their abhorrence of communism and suspicion of mainland intentions, conservatives feared that the liberalisation would entail instability, and hence strategic vulnerability. Chiang had around him a balanced force of conservatives and reformers. His Prime Minister, Yu Kuo-hwa, the former central bank governor, was among the staunchest of conservatives. But in 1984, President Chiang had chosen a reformist vice-president, Lee Teng-hui. Lee, a Taiwan native, was not seen at the time as a serious candidate for the succession. He was a popular academic and technocrat, but it was thought that the successor would have to be a mainlander, and perhaps even a Chiang. Ching-kuo's son, Hsaio-wu, and half-brother Wego were both mooted until, in 1986, Chiang Ching-kuo ruled out any such 'dynastic' solution.

But Chiang Ching-kuo further bolstered the forces of reform by rehabilitating one of Taiwan's most popular politicians, Lee Huan, first as education minister in 1984, and then, in

1987, in the key post of KMT Secretary General. Lee Huan, a mainlander, had been an old comrade of Chiang's from the China Youth Corps, and long identified with the liberal wing of the KMT. But he had been held responsible by party elders for the 1977 Chungli Incident, because he had advocated a policy of moderation and co-operation with the emergent opposition, and had in that year been banished to a university post.

Nevertheless, when Chiang Ching-kuo died in January 1988, and Lee Teng-hui took over, in accordance with the Constitution, he was still seen by many as a stopgap, and as an improbable candidate for Chiang's other post, the Chairmanship of the KMT. Conservative forces were rumoured to be rallying around the frail figure of Chiang Kai-shek's widow, the nonagenarian Soong May-ling, who had returned from the US for the centenary celebrations for her husband in 1986. However, with the backing of the reformists now in the majority in the KMT hierarchy, as well as the key tacit support of the military Chief-of-Staff, General Hau Pei-ts'un, Lee was soon made acting Chairman of the KMT, and confirmed in the post at its 13th National Congress in July 1988. Despite the alleged weakness of his own position, Lee Teng-hui was soon to show himself intent on pursuing reform with even greater gusto than his predecessor. The 13th Congress stacked the Party leadership with his supporters, and paved the way for the resignation the following year of the conservative Premier Yu. He was replaced by Lee Huan. The young technocrat James Soong got Lee Huan's top Party job as Secretary General, and the KMT leadership seemed united behind a policy of gradual but fundamental reform.

THE LIFTING OF MARTIAL LAW

In March 1986, President Chiang set the reform ball rolling. He formed a 12-member committee to discuss four important questions: the lifting of martial law, the formation of new political parties, rejuvenation of the legislature, and strengthening local government. In May, Chiang, in his capacity as chairman of the KMT, instructed the Party to open talks with the opposition about political reforms. The 'dangwai', who already had the organisation of an embryonic political party, were encouraged. In May, they staged in Taipei the largest opposition rally since the Kaohsiung riot, calling for political reforms. A 'dangwai' organisation, 'the Research Association for Public Policy' was given permission to set up a network of branch offices around Taiwan, bringing the 'dangwai' one step closer to the status of a fully-fledged opposition party.

In October that year President Chiang said that martial law would soon be terminated, and that new political parties would be allowed to form. The oppositionists had already jumped the gun. In September, the Democratic Progressive Party had been founded, and stated its intention of campaigning as a party. The party was illegal, but it was not banned. It was allowed to contest the election campaign, in the most dramatic gesture yet made to political liberalisation and pluralism, even though official pronouncements referred to its name in inverted commas, a tactic used for years to facilitate discussion of organisations' and individuals' titles on the mainland. Other opposition parties followed suit. In the next year, a dozen political parties sprang up, although none was to match the DPP in organisation or mass appeal. In early 1989, the law governing new political parties finally was passed, and the 'DPP' became the DPP.

Through the first half of 1987, the Legislative Yuan ploughed its way through drafts of a new National Security Law, designed to replace martial law. On 23 June 1987, the new law was passed. This was followed by the lifting of martial law on 14 July, except on Quemoy and Matsu. As the world was transfixed by the spectacle of people power in South Korea for the second time in just over two years forcing democratic reform on an Asian dictatorship, Taiwan moved less flamboyantly to its own rendezvous with the forces of political liberalisation.

The lifting of the 'emergency decree' (martial law) restored constitutional rights of freedom of assembly and association. The Taiwan Garrison Command lost its control of vetting of exit and entry permits into Taiwan. The military also lost their power to screen or confiscate publications without a trial. Only military personnel would be subjected to military trial. The DPP boycotted the vote on the National Security Law, claiming it was 'old wine in new bottles', an attempt to foist an unreconstructed authoritarianism on Taiwan's people by a change of legal nomenclature. It was still seditious to violate the constitution – in other words, to call for independence – or to advocate communism. The military retained effective control of certain 'strategic' areas of Taiwan, primarily along the western coast. The provisions to cover the new freedoms of association and assembly were not defined, but postponed until the enactment of further legislation.

Limited as the reform was in itself, however, it did serve both as a powerful symbol of the KMT's commitment to political change, and, as part of a package of other measures, contributed to a major liberalisation. Throughout the next two years, day-to-day political life was dominated by the passage of legislation to cater for the new situation. Political parties, trades unions, a freer media and street protest all had to be accommodated. The Legislative Yuan itself became a forum for heated debate – and occasional fisticuffs – as the DPP tried to make up in bluster what it lacked in numerical representation.

In September 1987, a draft of a March and Assembly Law was approved by the Executive Yuan. Outdoor marches and meetings required government approval. At least three days' advance notice had to be given, and anyone 'hurling insults or slander' could face up to two years' jail or forced labour. The law was widely flouted and street protests became an almost daily occurrence. Three DPP leaders were charged under the new law for involvement in scuffles that had broken out at protests against the National Security Law.

On 1 January 1988, press restrictions were eased. Since 1951, the number of newspapers granted publication licences had been frozen at 31, and the number of pages had also been restricted. In 1955, pages were limited to six per newspaper, and only increased to twelve in 1974. Under the new arrangement pages were to be between four and twenty-four. As soon as the restrictions were eased, eight applications for new licences were filed, including one for a new news agency, to break the monopoly of the government-owned Central News Agency. Licences were slow to be granted, and it was November 1988 before the first explicitly pro-opposition paper was licensed. It was sponsored by Kang Ning-hsiang, and held up because of its proposed title – *Capital*. As everyone knows,

China's 'capital' is not Taipei, where it was based, or even Peking, but Nanking, seat of the KMT's pre-war government. But in the meantime, even the existing press was becoming more outspoken and heterodox.

The liberalisation also encompassed a series of amnesties on political prisoners. In May 1987, six of the eight 'Formosa' magazine defendants, jailed for their alleged part in the 1979 Kaohsiung riot, were freed. Most returned to active politics in the DPP although a seventh, Shih Ming-teh, remained in jail and an eighth, Hsu Hsin-liang, was in exile in the US. In December 1986, he had tried to return to Taiwan just before the elections, challenging the government to try him on sedition charges. He was turned away at the airport, where a large crowd had gathered to welcome him home. The pretext for refusing him entry was his lack of proper travel documents. But the government wanted to avoid an embarrassing political trial, and the presence of a potential rallying-point for the protest vote. Three years later, on the eve of the next elections, Hsu Hsin-liang did succeed in slipping unnoticed, by boat, back to Taiwan. He was apprehended, jailed and prosecuted on charges of sedition. After a July 1987 'clemency programme' releasing 23 political prisoners to coincide with the lifting of martial law, the government claimed that 144 people had been released in recent years. It said that only 70 people were still in jail on sedition charges, and that they had had their sentences shortened. The next year, President Lee Teng-hui sponsored another amnesty to mark his 100 days in office, covering 31 political prisoners. Again, however, this liberalisation had strict limits. As late as January 1988, two prominent churchmen, accused of advocating Taiwan independence, were given lengthy prison sentences.

REFORM OF THE LEGISLATURE

With the lifting of martial law, the KMT at a stroke robbed the opposition of its major platform. As in other authoritarian societies, like South Korea under Chun Doo-hwan and the Philippines under Marcos, the opposition had been united largely by its hostility to the government. When, suddenly, the focus of that unity is removed – Marcos himself in the

Philippines in 1986, or the demand for direct presidential elections in South Korea the next year – fissures start appearing almost immediately in opposition ranks. The same was true in Taiwan. The fundamental split had already been apparent. It was between those who wanted to concentrate on democratic reform on Taiwan itself, and those who wanted to air the issue of Taiwan's international status directly. The two issues were, however, inseparable, because of the peculiar structure of Taiwan's elected organs of government. Despite these fundamental tactical differences, all sections of the opposition could rally round the demand that parliament had to be made more representative of Taiwan itself, or else democratic reform, the legalisation of political parties and greater freedoms of expression would have no institutional outlet. Hence, even those DPP members who saw the issue of electoral reform as only one part of a self-determining process which would ultimately lead to Taiwanese independence, could unite behind a platform of demanding the end of the domination of parliament by geriatric mainlanders. The issue took the place of martial law as the nexus of anti-government protest.

A visit to Taipei's Legislative Yuan in mid-1989 was a rather bizarre experience. Debates often seemed dominated by histrionic performances by DPP members. One fiery orator, Ju Gao-jeng, although a moderate in DPP terms, had acquired a reputation as a firebrand, and the nickname 'Rambo' because of his at times quite literally pugnacious approach to political debate. Meanwhile, the KMT was able to field equally passionate debaters from among its 'young Turks'. But the seats in the Legislative Yuan would often be almost deserted. A sprinkling of ancient-looking gentlemen, some of them in traditional Chinese dress, could be seen on the benches, sometimes snoozing. Many of their peers, however, were unable or unwilling to turn up. As a KMT spokesman put it in 1988 with a most un-Chinese candour, 'Some are robust, but many are senile'. As the KMT tried to sharpen its image as a reformist, forward-looking party, its insistence on the presence in the legislature of many who were by now senile and decrepit was a serious embarrassment.

However, the KMT was, of course, constrained by its constitutional commitment to the mainland. Reform of the legislature weakened its claim to form the government of all China and it also might send the wrong signals to Peking about its intentions as to its 'one China' policy. But if the KMT did not reform, death would do the job for it. Although dying mainland delegates could be replaced by nominees, that, too, would be a feebler proof of mainland legitimacy. There was little option but to grasp the nettle as President Chiang had in March 1986, and address the question of parliamentary reform.

The KMT had two choices: to reform the Legislative Yuan and National Assembly, or to make them redundant. The only way to achieve the latter would be to up-grade the importance of the Taiwan Provincial Assembly, so that it became a genuine local government, and supplanted the 'national' bodies, the Legislative Yuan and the National Assembly, as the focus for political activism on Taiwan. The 'national' elected organs would then wither away into less and less importance, existing purely as symbolic vestiges of the dream of reunification. The KMT rejected this route. The 'General Rules for Provincial, City and County Self-Government' instituted in 1947 as the constitutional basis for local government in National China were suspended in 1949. Since then, local government on Taiwan has functioned under special administrative decrees issued by the Executive Yuan. In other words, the organs of local government have been unconstitutional. There have been a number of calls for the 'legalisation' of local government, but the KMT has shied away from the implications. For instance, as provided under the 1946 Constitution, the provincial governor would have to be elected by popular vote, rather than, as at present, be appointed by the President subject to the approval of the Taiwan Provincial Assembly. Since the President of the Republic is only elected indirectly, by the National Assembly, a popularly elected local governor would be a rival source of ultimate authority. Although it is conceivable that, in time, Taiwan might be ready to countenance a provincial governor with a popular mandate as a de facto President, that was certainly not the case in the late 1980s. Other suggestions have tried to tinker with the administrative divisions of Taiwan. In 1988, 40 of the 77 members of the provincial assembly signed a petition demanding that Taiwan be split into five provinces and two municipalities. This, they argued, would make the popular election of governors feasible without raising worries that any one governor would be more popular than the President. But the same year, the KMT rejected demands for a beefing up of the provincial government. One of the main planks in the opposition's platform became the demand for the institution of direct elections for the Taiwan Provincial Governorship, and their reinstatement for the mayoralties of Kaohsiung and Taipei.

Already, however, efforts to enhance the status of the Provincial Assembly were at odds with the decision to allow an opposition party to contest the 'national level' elections. Once seated in the Legislative Yuan and National Assembly, it was inevitable that first the 'dangwai', and then the DPP would focus on reforms of those bodies. In 1988, the KMT adopted the second road to electoral reform, that of the constitutionally formed legislature for all of China.

In the December 1986 elections for the National Assembly and Legislative Yuan, the DPP fared rather well. It won nearly 24 per cent of the popular vote. This, however, left it with 12 seats out of 323 in the Legislative Yuan, and 11 out of nearly 1000 in the National Assembly. Seventy-three 'supplementary' seats had been at stake in the Legislative Yuan, of which the KMT won 59, and an independent one. In addition, there were 27 Presidential appointees representing overseas Chinese interests and professional and aboriginal groups. In the National Assembly, there were 84 elected seats, of which the KMT won 68, and independents five. It was not surprising that parliamentary reform became the key opposition demand.

The KMT went through various complex sums before arriving at the version of reform that would cover the next elections (in 1989 and 1992 for the Legislative Yuan, and 1992 for the National Assembly). In January 1989, an agreed formula was finally approved as a new 'Election and Recall Law' approved by the Legislative Yuan. The number of seats in the Legislative Yuan open to Taiwan candidates would be increased from 100 to 130, of whom 79 would be directly elected. The National Assembly would have 230 local members in 1992, and 375 in 1998. The Control Yuan, which by 1989 had about 60 surviving members, would have the seats open to indirect election (by the Taiwan Provincial Assembly, and City Councils of Taipei and Kaohsiung) increased from 32 to 54.

Meanwhile, elderly delegates who died would not be replaced. Until 1987, as old legislators passed away, they were replaced by people the KMT claimed were runners-up in the 1947–8 elections. Many have wondered whether these men really were runners-up, or whether their seats in the legislature were a bizarre fraud perpetrated on Taiwan's people. Now, since the average age of the mainland deputies was over 80, it could be expected that their numbers would dwindle rapidly. To accelerate the pace of transition further, elderly delegates would be encouraged to retire. They would be enticed with severance pay of NT$3.7 billion (about US$130 000), to the fury of the opposition, who regarded them as 'old thieves', scrounging off the government, rarely turning up to debates, and clinging to an outmoded conservatism. Nevertheless, many of the 'old thieves' were apparently reluctant to retire. It was anticipated that after the 1989 elections, the Legislative Yuan would still have a 50 per cent mainland representation, and that while a wholly locally elected parliament would come, it would be a ten-year process.

The KMT dismissed the notion that parliamentary reform weakened the claim to mainland legitimacy. It argued that the claim rested on the 1946 constitution, and the fact that it was adopted, unlike the West German or South Korean constitutions before the country was divided. The government formed under that Constitution could institute whatever parliamentary reforms it liked, because it was still the only government representing the wishes of the Chinese people.

REFORM OF THE KMT

Reform fitted ill with the KMT's structure. It was a mass party, with some 2.4 million members by the time of its 13th Congress in July 1988, but it was also still the party that had been remoulded by Sun Yat-sen in the 1920s on Soviet, Marxist–Leninist principles. Hence it was run by a small centralised clique, dominated by the old mainland élite. This was out of step not just with the population of Taiwan as a whole, but with the KMT itself. By now, 65–70 per cent of its members were Taiwanese, still less than the percentage of Taiwan natives in the population at large, but nevertheless significant enough an infusion of new blood to make the KMT seem unduly unrepresentative. Its candidates for the popularly elected assemblies were nominated by the Party, and imposed, usually unopposed, on local constituencies. But these individuals became the focus of a reformist tendency within the KMT itself. Almost all Taiwan-born second-generation mainlanders, they were the one section of the KMT which could lay claim to a genuine popular mandate from Taiwan itself. They became known, collectively, as 'young Turks', criticising the old guard with almost as much vehemence as the DPP and pressing for faster reform, both of the political system and of mainland policy. Yet, at the top of the party itself, in the Standing Committee of the Central Committee, this group was completely unrepresented.

At its 13th Congress, the Party pledged to reform itself. The Central Committee was, for the first time, elected. It was expanded from 150 to 180 members. In the past, these members had been nominated by the Party Chairman, and rubber-stamped by Congress. This time, there were 360 candidates and only half of these were Chairman's nominees, 33 of whom failed to win seats. The Central Standing Committee had 31 members, and for the first time, a majority of these (16) were native Taiwanese.

But, perhaps to reassure the party's elders that reform was not out of hand, the Congress was dominated as much by an emphasis on continuity as on reform. All three key-note speeches, from Lee Teng-hui, Yu Kuo-hwa and Lee Huan stressed the importance of stability. Lee Teng-hui's opening address was made from a podium where he was dwarfed by massive portraits of the three guiding lights of the KMT's past – Sun Yat-sen, Chiang Kai-shek (both of whom are written into the KMT Constitution as holders for all eternity of their KMT titles) and Chiang Ching-kuo. In an even more potent symbol of Lee Teng-hui's unwillingness to rock the historical boat, the curtain-raiser to the first session of the Congress proper was an appearance by the enfeebled Soong May-ling. Her imprimatur seemed to set the seal on Lee

Teng-hui's accession, and put paid to rumours of entrenched conservative resistance to the party coming under the control of a man who had never set foot on the mainland.

In fact, the token opposition at the Congress to Lee Teng-hui's promotion from acting to permanent KMT Chairman came from the other wing of the party, the radical 'young Turks'. The charismatic leader of this faction, Jaw Shao-kong, led a small group of abstainers who remained seated while the other 1209 Congress delegates stood up to signify their approval of Lee's appointment. But even Jaw's protest was not directed at Lee himself. He had argued for a secret ballot, rather than the public and docile acceptance of the Party's decision. Jaw and his followers had been disgruntled from the start of the Congress. Like the CCP, the KMT is reluctant to hold a meeting if it cannot predict the outcome. Hence the most important issue in Taiwan's politics, the reform of parliament, did not even figure on the Congress agenda. Not only did the 'young Turks' want the issue discussed, but also they were dismayed at what they saw as the foot-dragging on electoral reform displayed by Lee Teng-hui, in whom they had vested great hopes. Like the DPP, many of the 'young Turks' wanted to see a legislature composed entirely of delegates elected on Taiwan, sooner rather than later. Their key point of difference was that they were not proposing the disbandment of parliament and totally fresh elections, casting doubt as that would on the 1946 Constitution's enduring vitality. Rather, the 'young Turks' wanted to see a more rapid programme for adding supplementary seats, and firmer action taken to oust the 'old thieves'.

Despite these set-backs, the 13th KMT Congress did represent a major victory for the reformist trend in the party. The Congress failed to live up to the billing the KMT had given it in advance, as a turning-point towards pluralism, openness and reform. To that end, the KMT had invited more international media attention than for many years, seeing the Congress as a good opportunity to advertise its new look. The Congress also failed to provide major new policy initiatives. But that was never really the point for KMT leaders. In this, as in many other respects, there were great similarities with another 13th Party Congress – that of the Chinese Communist Party in Peking in October 1987. Both put in place a new leadership, and consolidated the positions of their acting, reformist Chairmen – Lee Teng-hui and Zhao Ziyang – by confirming them in office and giving them the opportunity to slot some of their supporters into key positions. Both were heavy on the rhetoric of reform. Even many of the slogans were the same – democratisation, reform, openness, separation of party and government. But both in terms of actual policy did little more than legitimise changes that were already in train. Both parties were in a process of ideological catching up with the real world, and of handing the reins of power over from an ageing revolutionary generation to a younger leadership. The similarities betray the Leninist origins the parties share. The Peking massacre a year later was to suggest that, despite its arcane constitutional posture, the KMT had in fact gone a great deal further in institutionalising the rule of a revolutionary party, and catering for reform and the succession without turmoil.

After the Congress, the KMT emerged as a coalition of at least three main strands of opinion. On the right were the old guard, whose most prominent representative was still at the time Yu Kuo-hwa. The Congress had seen some attempt by the old guard to marshal their forces. Conservative veteran Wang Sheng returned from his exile as ambassador to Paraguay, having been consigned there in 1983, in belated disgrace for his conduct as chief of the military's political warfare division at the time of the Chungli and Kaohsiung incidents. This old guard probably still looked to the 'Chiang Dynasty'. Chiang Wego, Ching-kuo's half-brother and the influential head of the National Security Council had been moved upstairs to the KMT's advisory committee, but three of Chiang Ching-kuo's sons, legitimate and otherwise, did well in the Central Committee elections, all figuring among the top 15 vote-winners. The conservative position had moderated over the years, but its fundamental precepts were the same: mainland preoccupations should come first. That implied caution in liberalising both the political structure and the economy, lest it lead to destabilisation, or a weakening of the commitment to eventual reunification, which, in Taiwan as on the mainland, had replaced 'liberation' or 'recovery' in even the most conservative sloganeering.

At the Party's other extreme were the 'young Turks', Taiwan-born politicians with, in many cases, a genuine popular following. When the new law on political parties came into force in 1989, and obliged parties to select election candidates through primary elections, the power base of such young deputies could be expected to grow. Not only would they be able to demonstrate a following in the population at large, but also they would have been chosen in a democratic process within the Party itself. The 'young Turks' took a radical position not just on electoral reform, but on relations with the mainland as well, arguing for a greater and faster loosening of the bars on contact. In terms of economic policy, they constituted the extreme wing of the Party's 'liberalising' tendency, arguing for the state's disengagement from its still dominant role in many sectors of the economy – especially finance and banking. They were also able to capitalise on the growing popular discontent with the levels of environmental pollution. Because they were KMT members and delegates, but not in the government, they were able to criticise with freedom. They began to seem the most effective opposition force to the KMT in their own right.

Between these two extremes, the KMT was steered by a group of young, mainland-born technocrats. Like the 'young Turks', many of these men were educated in the United States. Urbane and cosmopolitan, they were able to present the KMT's anachronistic structure in apparently reasonable terms, practising politics as the art of the possible, rather than fired by great ideological myths. Prominent among this group were James Soong, who, at 46, became the Party's Secretary General in 1989, Ma Ying-cheou, who, aged 38, was to head its Mainland Affairs Committee, and so pilot through the dramatic reforms of the late 1980s, and Frederick Chien, who was brought back from his posting as de facto ambassador to Washington, to head the important Council for Economic Planning and Development.

At this time many in the KMT would talk of Japan's Liberal Democratic Party as a model. The Japanese system appealed for its stability. The LDP was attractive because it had managed to cling on to power apparently without major challenge, despite operating in a system where the electorate had real choice. By accommodating different factional interests within one party, it was felt, the KMT could ride out the political reforms and still emerge as the perpetual party of government. As the LDP lurched from crisis to crisis in 1988–9, the analogy was less frequently drawn. The KMT, too, was often hit by financial scandals, and did little in public to address the question of whether or not this type of arrogance of power is inevitable when there is no effective opposition outside the party.

THE DEMOCRATIC PROGRESSIVE PARTY

The DPP, too, was a coalition more than a solid party. It represented an alliance between various forces who had long been opposed to the KMT: moderate 'dangwai' politicians, the Taiwan independence movement, and labour and social welfare activists. Its main appeal was as a 'Taiwanese' party, capitalising on the KMT's history as a mainland-imposed élite, and on the traditional desire of the native Taiwanese simply to be left alone by the external powers who have repeatedly tried to govern them.

But in eschewing a class-based approach in favour of one based on nationalism, the DPP faced two hurdles. First, the KMT robbed it of its major platform by lifting martial law, and then undermined its next major policy goal by agreeing to significant electoral reform. The DPP was thus pushed inexorably towards the open espousal of independence as its major goal, and was vulnerable to charges, especially after the Peking massacre in 1989, that it was a group of immature and dangerous hotheads.

The KMT also stacked the decks against the DPP in a number of ways in the run-up to the 1989 elections. The DPP by then had a mere 12 000 members, and so was chronically under-funded. This was a crucial constraint in the 1989 elections, which were marked by an unprecedented level of vote-buying, reflecting past practice, rising affluence, increased electoral competition and widespread voter apathy. Fund-raising activities under the new law were banned until eight days before the elections. So too, were advertisements on radio or television by individual candidates. Unlimited advertising by parties was permitted, however, giving the KMT, with its extensive business interests, a chance to accentuate further the pro-government bias of the media. The DPP also alleged widespread gerrymandering of electoral boundaries. After the 1986 elections, the DPP boycotted the subsequent Control Yuan elections, in protest at what it said was KMT-inspired malpractice in the Legislative Yuan and National Assembly polls. The DPP also suffered from the fact that several of its leading members were former political prisoners disbarred from standing for parliament. In addition, the pro-independence politics of some of the DPP's most prominent leaders were still seditious. In 1988–9, the government took little action to enforce the National Security Act provision barring associations from 'violating the Constitution'. If a vigorous DPP seemed to be gaining ground as an avowedly separatist party, however, this tolerance might soon be stretched beyond its unstated boundaries.

Perhaps the DPP's biggest problem in trying to present itself as a credible opposition party was its factionalism. It had been split virtually since its founding in September 1986 into at least three warring factions. One of the party's stars was still the veteran 'dangwai' politician, Kang Ning-hsiang. As the one opposition politician with whom Chiang Ching-kuo would enter into a dialogue, Kang was long the moderate face of opposition to the KMT. The 1986 elections were a personal triumph for him; he won more votes than anyone apart from the popular Jaw Shao-kong in Taipei district. But he tended to seem increasingly isolated between the DPP's two major factions, and was humiliated at its 1988 Congress, which was marked by a bitter power struggle. This 'moderate' wing of the DPP was further damaged by the resignation in December 1988 of one of its founder members, Fei Hsi-ping, who called the party leaders 'fascists'. He was a rarity in the DPP, the one elderly, mainland-elected Legislative Yuan member in the party. As such, he had been urged by his party colleagues to resign his Legislative Yuan seat *pour encourager les autres*. Mr Fei agreed to do so only on condition that the Party took a less extreme position on the retirement question. When the Party refused to accept, for example, the retention of some seats for mainland delegates in a restructured parliament, Fei Hsi-ping made his vitriolic exit from the DPP.

The differences between the other two factions in the DPP centre on two questions: should the DPP play the part of a 'loyal opposition' and foreswear its tactics of street protest and other extra-parliamentary activity? And should it concentrate on internal democratic reform, or on Taiwan's international status? From 1987 to 1988, the party was led by a Chairman from the more extreme of these factions, the 'New Movement', Yao Chia-wen. At the time, the DPP was still cautiously talking of 'self-determination' rather than 'independence'. The thrust of its campaign was that Taiwanese nationalist and democratic aspirations could only be realised by an act of self-determination on the question of mainland rule. Furthermore, while parliament was so structurally unrepresentative, the Party had no option but to take its message to the streets. It had to counteract four decades of 'false consciousness' inculcated in Taiwanese by a society and educational system which taught them *ad nauseam* that 'Taiwan was part of China'. To bring this message across, it was not enough to rely on the limited forum of orthodox political debate.

This faction lost out, narrowly, at the October 1988 DPP Congress. Huang Hsin-chieh, a former cell-mate of Yao Chia-wen after they were both jailed following the Kaohsiung incident, defeated him in the contest for the chairmanship. Huang led the so-called 'Formosa' faction, arguing that the issue of independence should be shelved pending democratic reforms on Taiwan itself. He also advocated a more orderly approach to political campaigning, to prove that the DPP had become a responsible political party and could attract broad electoral support. The other main point at issue was the question of contracts with mainland China. Whereas the independence advocates, like Yao Chia-wen, thought the sudden unleashing of Taiwan–mainland links in 1987 and 1988 was 'rash', and posed a security threat, the 'Formosa' faction, like the KMT 'young Turks', saw greater contact as the surest way of solidifying the status quo and deferring the question of reunification.

Crossing all these tendencies in the DPP was another debate, about whether the party should adopt a more class-based approach. Taiwan's seven million strong industrial workforce represented the largest single sectional interest, if 'Taiwanese consciousness' is discounted. The KMT, with its eyes on Japan, hoped that party politics could evolve without the growth of a strong workers' party. The DPP, meanwhile, was a middle-class party, with its roots in the intelligentsia frustrated by years of stifling political repression. In 1987, one of the DPP's elected Legislative Yuan members, Wang Yi-hsiung, resigned to form a Labour Party, which was slow to develop into more than a pressure group, and, in the manner of fringe parties the world over, split almost as soon as it was founded. By February 1989, it had only 1000 members, of whom 200 defected under a charismatic textile worker, Lou Mei-wen, to form a more radical 'Workers' Party'. The radicals championed a more activist labour movement, reject-ing Wang as too moderate, and as an opportunist. The radicals' platform stressed extra-legal action to agitate for workers' rights, as opposed to the gradualist approach dedi-cated to legal improvements and parliamentary campaigns favoured by Wang Yi-hsiung.

In the December 1989 elections, the first since martial law, and hence the first it contested as a legal party, the DPP made a major advance. It achieved its initial target of 35 per cent of the popular vote. This won the party a number of important local government positions, notably the county magistracy in Taipei County, which, as the more extreme DPP members liked to point out, 'surrounded the capital' and gave them a stranglehold on central government. The DPP also gained 21 seats in the Legislative Yuan, passing the twenty-seat threshold which would allow them to intiate legislation, and cross the dividing line between a fringe party engaged in legislative guerrilla warfare, and a true opposition formulating positive policies.

However, the election results highlighted structural prob-lems for both major parties, and for the process of political development itself. For the DPP, the election was likely to intensify the rift between its two major factions. The domi-nant, moderate tendency could point to the success at even chronically unfair elections as a vindication of their gradualist approach. However, in advance of the elections 32 DPP candidates had formed a 'New Nation Alliance', and cam-paigned openly on the platform of independence for Taiwan. Twenty of these candidates were elected, and achieved the biggest rallies and strongest show of popular backing of any candidates. They, too, were able to claim that the elections proved the viability of their approach.

For the KMT, the elections posed a dilemma. The opposi-tion vote was admitted to signal a need for change. The creeping progress towards representative democracy was clearly not satisfying enough people. However, the campaign had shown once again how democratisation is inseparable in Taiwan from an upsurge in pro-independence activity. If the KMT enforced the law and prosecuted the 'New Nation Alliance', it would be faced with a wave of protest. If, on the other hand, it took no action against them, the independence movement would in any event gather strength. The KMT's attitude was further swayed by the presidential elections of March 1989 in the National Assembly. Lee Teng-hui's re-election still depended on support in this body, still overwhelmingly dominated by ageing mainlanders.

The structural problem was that the elections seemed to institutionalise a two-party system. Of those parties, one, the KMT, had its historical roots on the mainland, the other, the DPP, in anti-mainlander Taiwanese nationalism. Some DPP candidates, for example, refused to make campaign speeches in Mandarin, insisting on Taiwanese. However, this polarisation around the issue of the Taiwan–mainland divide and independence now seemed at odds with the concerns of the electorate. Public opinion polls (of dubious reliability, but nonetheless indicative of an undoubted social phenomenon) suggested that only 15 per cent of the electorate positively supported independence. Voters were more concerned with candidates' personalities and attributes, and with 'pocketbook' issues like pollution, traffic congestion, the stock market, corruption and street crime. On many of these issues, it was hard to distinguish the two parties. Even as it moved towards representative democracy. Taiwan's political system was evolving in a way that still left it adrift from the needs of its society.

THE GROWTH OF PROTEST

The more liberal political climate of Taiwan in the late 1980s spawned more than just new political parties. There was also an upsurge in other forms of anti-government activity – street marches, rallies and demonstrations, some of which turned violent, and strikes and boycott campaigns. In July 1988, it was reported that there had been more than 1400 such protests in Taiwan in the previous 12 months. There were several reasons for this phenomenon. The first was the sheer novelty of relative liberalism. For the first time many people who would normally have steered clear of political protest felt able to express their grievances without fear of intolerable retribution. Second, as the two main political parties were organised around constitutional issues more than class or interest groups, sectional interests found them an inadequate channel for the expression of their demands. Finally, the still unrepresentative nature of government made mainstream politics a cumbersome and ineffectual mechanism for dealing with particular demands.

Many of the protests were specifically political. The DPP, under the influence of the more radical 'New Movement', followed a deliberate strategy in 1987–8 of taking to the streets. They drew attention to their demands, and focused on instances of political repression, like the continuing detention and occasional hunger strikes of Shih Ming-teh, or the arrest and trial of the returned dissident Hsu Hsin-liang. Others focused on narrowly sectional economic interests, or on environmental concerns.

Of the 'economic' protests, two groups felt with some justification that they had been comparatively disadvantaged in Taiwan's economic boom: industrial workers and farmers. As noted in Chapter 4, in the package of reforms that followed martial law, reform of labour legislation was less sweeping than in some other areas. Strikes were still illegal in almost all cases. A revised Arbitration Dispute Law, passed in June 1988, still banned strikes when a dispute was in the course of arbitration. Taiwan's first 'legal' strike, by some bus drivers that August, was in fact legal for only three hours. Trades unions were still largely KMT-dominated 'house' unions. The protections guaranteed by the new Labour Standards Law were frequently flouted by managements which faced little organised resistance from the workforce. In early 1989, the government's sensitivity on this issue was highlighted when it expelled an Irish priest, Neil Magill, who had been active in a church-sponsored educational effort to teach workers their rights.

The workers' fundamental grievance, however, was an almost insoluble one. They wanted a greater share in the prosperity of Taiwan which had in large measure been bought, despite the relatively equal distribution of wealth, at the expense of low labour costs. One confrontation occurred in November 1988, when Nestlé laid off 17 workers at its factory in the Hsinchu Science-based Industrial Park because it now found it cheaper to import instant coffee. The rest of the 100-strong workforce walked out in sympathy, and barricaded the plant's European management into the factory overnight. The Chinese New Year holidays in 1988 and 1989 both saw several labour disputes. The festival was traditionally marked by 'thirteenth month' bonus payments, which suffered as employers found their profits squeezed. Strikes began to afflict virtually every sector of the economy, but the public sector was especially badly hit. Not only did public enterprises tend to be large, unlike the small-scale, family-run businesses in the private sector, whose structure discouraged labour militancy. It was also harder for the state-owned companies to withstand worker demands by turning to the estimated 100 000 illegal immigrants from the Philippines, Malaysia and elsewhere in low-paid jobs in Taiwan by 1989.

Farmers in Taiwan, too, became disenchanted with the KMT and its economic policies, seen as kowtowing to US pressure at the expense of the agricultural sector especially, which had after all laid the foundations for the 'economic miracle'. A farmers' protest was at the root of the most serious civil disturbance in Taiwan since the 1947 suppression of Taiwanese resistance – the 'May 20th' incident in 1988. It began as a peaceful demonstration by farmers, protesting at what they saw as government inaction in the face of alleged US dumping of fruit and poultry products, at the high price of government-monopolised fertiliser, and at the lack of proper health insurance arrangements for farm workers. However, the protests escalated into an 18-hour street battle with riot police, leaving 200 people injured and 122 under arrest. Why the spark of a routine economic protest should have ignited such a blazing riot remains a mystery. The government blamed the opposition for inciting the riot. Conspiracy theorists saw the hand of discomfited KMT hardliners behind the disturbance – by fomenting a riot their arguments about the dangers of political liberalisation would be vindicated. The incident generated its own cycle of protest, as the DPP organised marches, rallies and sit-ins to register anger at the behaviour of the riot police, and at the detention of what they claimed were large numbers of peaceable farmers. Whatever the background, the incident did serve to show the disaffection of the rural community, who see their livelihoods ever more under threat from the KMT's import liberalisation policies, and who have taken to the streets on many other occasions to vent their feelings of frustration and anxiety about this.

The other main motive for popular protest has been environmental concerns. In 1987, a KMT spokesman rather patronisingly suggested that the opposition should forget about chimera like independence, and should concentrate on issues that really matter, 'like pollution and parking'. The opposition did not pick up the gauntlet, but the environment became a major political issue. The environmental lobby threw into doubt not just the future of the planned fourth nuclear power plant; it also caused China Petroleum Corporation and Formosa Plastics to look overseas for sites for new naphtha crackers, a vital import-substituting facility in the petrochemicals industry. The new stringency with which environment controls were enforced had meant that Taiwan was no longer a cheap and welcoming home for 'dirty industries'. At the local level, however, anti-pollution protest was more often bought off with politically expedient but environmentally irrelevant compensation payments. The most serious of many environmental protests was the siege in October 1988 of 18 petrochemical plants in the southern district of Lin Yuan. An estimated 20 000 local residents were involved in protest at the pollution of fishponds and coastal waters. The protest brought the temporary shutdown of two of Taiwan's largest naphtha crackers, and was only ended by a compensation payment of more than NT$250 million.

This wave of protest was disconcerting to more than just the KMT old guard. Taiwan valued its image as a haven of stability, labour harmony and social order. The KMT was aware that its strongest asset was not its willingness to countenance reform; it was as the guardian of stability. Hence, in the 1989 election campaign, even its more reformist leaders stressed law and order. In February 1989, Lee Teng-hui made an unprecedented appearance before the Constitutional Research Committee of the National Assembly. He presented himself, unusually, not as a reformer, but as the hard man. Whatever measures are necessary, he said, would be taken to protect the public good. His reassurances were addressed not just at alarm about the proliferation of street protest, but at the concern over the number of scandals involving people in public office. Nevertheless, the KMT, for all the rhetoric of reform, had decided to play its strong suit, and run on a law-and-order ticket.

9 Taiwan's Opening to Mainland China

THE 1980s DEBATE IN TAIWAN ON MAINLAND POLICY

By the mid-1980s, Taiwan's intransigence in the face of Peking's blandishments was beginning to appear positively churlish. On one side of the straits, the government was coming up with startling new initiatives, was opening its economy and society to an extent undreamed of during the Cultural Revolution, and was adopting a pragmatic and flexible approach to many of the foreign policy issues which had seemed intractable since 1949. In Taipei, on the other hand, the government seemed set in the aspic of a previous era. It still mouthed the rhetoric of national reunification under its style of political tutelage, but all the world's major powers now recognised Peking as the legitimate government of 'one China' and that 'Taiwan is part of China'.

The Chinese courtship of Taiwan was a two-tier affair. There were immediate proposals – the 'three communications' and the 'four establishments' – for opening contact, and there was the ultimate aim of 'peaceful reunification', on the basis of 'one country – two systems'. The KMT strategy assumed that the former was the thin end of a wedge that would inevitably lead to the latter. Or, conversely, that to accept contact with China would lead to the strengthening of the 'two Chinas' mode of thought, and hence undermine both the status quo, and the basis of the KMT's own legitimacy. Any contacts with the communist mainland of China were unacceptable, it was argued, because communism is a holistic, totalitarian system. You cannot trade with, or invest in, China without dealing with some branch of government. You cannot even visit the mainland as a 'private tourist' without dealing with the state-controlled travel organisations. You cannot send letters there without going through the Chinese post office. All of this implies having truck with organs of the communist

203

state. Dealing with them acknowledges their existence, and implies some degree of recognition of their legitimacy. Better to shun all contact, until communism withers under the incompetence of its economic management and the repression of popular discontent. Then, one fine day, the KMT will be welcomed back to introduce the rationale of the market and its own, but differing, brand of one-party authoritarianism.

But the Straits are only 100 miles wide. With China, figuratively, standing beckoning on the other shore, it was inevitable that some in Taiwan would bow to curiosity, nostalgia or the profit motive and be lured into business or travel in China. This is exactly what happened in the 1980s. Indirect trade, via Hong Kong and Japan, began to flourish. Talked up by Peking, and denied by Taipei, it is hard to put an accurate figure on the extent of this clandestine trade. But some estimates put bilateral business for 1985 as high as US$1 billion. Uncertain as to the direction of its own policy, the KMT government seemed to turn a blind eye to much of this. Since the trade was indirect, the government claimed it was impossible to monitor or control it. Similarly, the number of Taiwan residents who slipped into mainland China during this period is unknowable. Some guesses went as high as 10 000 a year by the mid-1980s. Going via Hong Kong or Japan, the mainland authorities accepted their need for discretion, hoping that if they were given a good reception, and did good business, or enjoyed emotional reunions with long-lost kin or loved ones, then they would prove a positive force within Taiwan for Peking's policies.

So while the KMT staunchly defended its 'three noes' policy of refusing all contact, compromise and negotiation with the communists, it winked at a steady build-up of commercial, political and personal pressures for accepting contact. Meanwhile, it showed some signs of baulking at its international isolation. In 1984, Taiwan sent a team to the Los Angeles Olympics, as 'Taipei, China', in deference to Peking's sensitivities. In 1986, the nomenclature issue surfaced again, in a potentially more worrisome form. The People's Republic of China was admitted to the Asian Development Bank (ADB), of which the Republic of China was a founder member. By now, the ADB was the only important body among the ten international organisations to which the ROC still belonged. Debate over what Taipei should do was heated. Whereas, in the early 1970s, it had seemed straightforward that the ROC should withdraw once the PRC was admitted to a body of which it was a member, because 'there is only one China', now there was a strong current of opinion arguing that the ROC should not give up the status and privileges of ADB membership, simply because of the organisation's misguided decision to admit Peking. A compromise was reached. Taiwan decided to stay in the ADB, which would allow it to keep its membership under the name 'Taipei, China'. However, Taiwan would refuse formally to accept the name-change, and would boycott ADB meetings when the other 'China' attended.

The breakthrough in relations with the mainland occurred in a very different, and quite unexpected, way. In May 1986, a China Airlines Boeing 747 cargo aircraft from Taiwan was diverted to Canton when on a flight from Bangkok to Hong Kong. One of the three crew members on board, the captain, Wang Hsi-chuen, announced he wanted to defect and stay in China. There had been a number of defections both ways across the Taiwan Straits over the years. Normally, a defector would be received with open arms by the host country, rewarded and used as a propaganda tool in the war of words with the other China. This time it was a bit more complicated. China was sitting on not just an expensive piece of China Airlines' hardware, but two other crew members, both of whom wanted to go back to Taiwan. When Peking offered talks on the situation, President Chiang Ching-kuo had a difficult choice to make. On the one hand, there could be no gainsaying that to enter talks would be an 'official' contact. Since, at the time, even private, indirect trade was banned, to meet communist officials would seem to go against the most fundamental principles of established mainland policy. On the other hand, there was clearly a humanitarian issue involved here. Two Taiwan citizens were stranded in the communist wasteland through no fault of their own. What was worse, Peking was magnanimously offering talks to find a solution to the potentially tricky problem. To the horror of some of the KMT old guard, Chiang Ching-kuo accepted the olive branch. Three days of talks ensued in Hong Kong. They stalled at first on the Taiwan side's insistence that Wang Hsi-chuen be returned as well as the plane and the others, despite his repeated public statements that he wanted to stay in China with his long-lost father and brothers, and was fed up with the lack of political freedom of Taiwan. In the end, Taiwan caved in, and granted Wang his perverse wish to live under communism, resulting in the return of the aircraft and the two crew members.

The issue had been a double bind for Chiang Ching-kuo. Had he not agreed to the talks, Taiwan's reputation for stubborn intransigence would have been enhanced. But, as it was, Taipei came off much the worse in the talks. Chiang's hardline allies at home were in a state of shock at the sudden dropping of four decades of consistent policy, despite the government's harping on the non-official 'humanitarian' nature of the contact. And internationally, Peking had appeared reasonable, flexible and understanding. By agreeing to talks in Hong Kong as acceptable 'neutral' territory, it had achieved the additional propaganda bonus of reassuring the colony that it really did intend to respect the autonomy promised under the 1984 Joint Declaration. Meanwhile, Taipei, having at first truculently refused to accept Peking's statesmanlike handling of an international aviation mishap, still appeared grudging and inflexible.

For many in Taiwan, including much of the budding young technocratic élite in the KMT and in the government bureaucracy, however, the 'jumbo' talks were a beacon of hope. It seemed that at long last the government was about to recognise the reality staring at it every time it looked at a map: even if there were only one China, literally more than 99 per cent of it was beyond its control, just 100 miles away. It was foolish, unprofitable and ultimately perilous to pretend it did not exist.

THE CHANGE FINALLY COMES

The expectation of change generated by the 'jumbo' incident, however, was not to be fulfilled for more than a year. In April 1987, Taiwan again boycotted the Asian Development Bank meetings, and the following month vehemently denied that one of its shipping companies was holding compensation talks in China through its insurance agent, over a collision in which 17 mainland fishermen died. There were other, non-accidental maritime disasters, and Taiwan troops were reprimanded by their government for their 'excessive' action in sinking a mainland fishing boat in March. China still complained of Taiwan harassment of its fishing fleet in a series of subsequent clashes, but, perhaps in an attempt to lure Taipei into talks, was very slow to publicise the incidents. Taiwan took the opportunity of a major forest fire that summer on China's north-eastern borders to send, without Chinese permission, emergency relief by hot air balloon, in a continuation of the old-style propaganda war.

But beneath this unchanged surface, over this period, more and more influential voices joined the chorus calling for an easing of mainland policy. In June 1987, Tao Pai-chuan, an adviser to Chiang Ching-kuo, added what seemed to be a quasi-official endorsement to this line, in an article in the mass circulation *China Daily News*. The following month, the first step was taken in what was soon to accelerate into a major rush for contact with the mainland. The first reform was a relatively minor one. Direct tourist travel to Hong Kong was legalised. Before then, the requirement to demonstrate a business need to obtain a visa for travel to Hong Kong had been one means of at least slowing down the number of Taiwan residents making clandestine side-trips across the border. In August, the blanket ban on the publication of mainland-produced books was lifted, and the copyright of mainland Chinese authors was protected. The dissident astro-physicist Fang Lizhi had the dubious privilege of seeing his writings legally reprinted in Taiwan. Meanwhile, Taiwan's academics were routinely allowed to take part in conferences alongside their mainland counterparts, and August saw a rash of officially-inspired commentaries in the press arguing for legalising private exchanges with the mainland. In one in August, the Chinese–American scholar Chiu Hungda, whose thinking often reflected that of the KMT, argued that Taiwan nationals should be allowed to visit family in China, that academic exchanges across the straits should be permitted for research purposes, and that some mainlanders should be allowed to come and settle in Taiwan.

As the speculation of a formal shift in government policy mounted, two young journalists jumped the gun. The reporters

Hsu Lu and Li Yung-teh of the liberal *Independence Evening Post* arrived in Peking in September 1987, amid a blaze of publicity, to file stories from the mainland. They wrote pieces typical of the type of coverage the mainland was to get on Taiwan when its wish to see reporters come was fulfilled. Hsu and Lu stressed the drab poverty of Chinese everyday life. Their reports helped encourage the KMT that, far from needing to worry about the pernicious ideological influences to which visitors to the mainland would be exposed, there were actually significant propaganda benefits to Taipei to be derived from letting people see 'socialism with Chinese characteristics' in action.

Finally, on 15 October 1987, the long-awaited liberalisation was announced. In view of the intensive preparation of the ground, the announcement was considerably less far-reaching than expected. Taiwan residents with two or more 'close' relatives on the mainland would be allowed to visit them, via Hong Kong or Tokyo. Only family reunions, of up to three months in any one year, would be sanctioned. The Red Cross, through offices in Taipei and Kaohsiung, would be the channel for arranging the visits. The decision, said the government, was a response to humanitarian concern for Taiwan's elderly mainlanders, many of whom had arrived in Taiwan as enlisted men in the late 1940s, and had been told that they would soon return victorious to see once again the wives and families they had left behind.

Even this modest relaxation seems to have been wrung with great difficulty from the upper echelons of the KMT against the wishes of its old guard. As late as August, Prime Minister Yu Kuo-hwa said in an interview that no such move was being contemplated. The Party Secretary-General, Lee Huan, on the other hand, was now saying that it did not matter if people returned to the mainland and stayed there, and that Taiwan should be able to cope with family visits from the mainland. In October, the government spokesman Shaw Yu-ming said that visits from the mainland were impossible, because Taiwan could not hope to squeeze in the numbers of those who would want to stay. Already, a tone of smug self-confidence about Taiwan's relative attractions in the competition for Chinese loyalties was beginning to suffuse official remarks about mainland contact.

On 2 November 1987, the Red Cross offices duly opened to receive applications from people who wanted to visit the mainland. They were swamped. Family ties are, quite literally, the life-blood of Chinese culture. It was not just rhetorical posturing when the KMT said its motives in allowing the family reunions were humanitarian. After four decades of separation, families found each other again. The media were filled with the tear-stained faces of long-delayed meetings between mother and son, sister and brother, even husband and wife. As if to emphasise the continuity of family life, as well as the principle of eventual reunification, the Taiwan Supreme Court ruled that pre-1949 mainland marriages were still binding. Of the hundreds of thousands of soldiers who left their wives behind in the late 1940s, a hefty proportion were thus confirmed as bigamists.

But the visitors to the mainland were not just mainlanders seeking their immediate kin. Not only were the Red Cross slack in checking on the reality of claimed family ties; but the change also encouraged many more to make the trip without approval. By the end of the year, 26 000 people had lodged applications with the Red Cross, and tens of thousands of others had quietly visited the mainland without informing the authorities. Peking welcomed them with open arms. Visa requirements for 'Taiwan compatriots' were eased; they were charged domestic room-rates at hotels, rather than the much higher prices paid by other overseas Chinese, let alone foreigners. The Special Economic Zone in Shenzhen, near Hong Kong, announced preferential terms for Taiwan investors. Peking's flag-carrier airline, CAAC, laid on new flights on its Hong Kong routes to cater for the influx. It was not just familial affection that accounted for the warm welcome afforded Taiwan compatriots; China also eased its customs regulations to allow Taiwan residents to bring in five 'ordinary' consumer goods items, among which were listed typewriters, sewing machines and even electronic organs.

But the KMT continued to insist that, apart from the 'humanitarian' adjustment to travel regulations, its policy was unchanged. In the nervous period that followed the death of Chiang Ching-kuo in January 1988, and the accession of the Taiwanese Lee Teng-hui, government and Party spokesmen were at pains to stress that the 'three noes' policy was still in place. In February, Lee broke with the stiff and aloof traditions of his predecessors by giving a press conference. But his message was the same. There would be no official contact with China. The government would 'not encourage' commercial ties with the mainland. The family reunion policy was being studied, and would be reviewed.

The contacts across the Taiwan Strait, however, had now developed a momentum of their own, and there was still the feeling of some imminent breakthrough in the air. In January, a dissident Taiwanese publisher, Lei Yu-chi, travelled to Hong Kong for a meeting with China's de facto deputy ambassador there, the number two in the local branch of the New China News Agency. Both men described the meeting as the first contact between a Chinese official and a Taiwanese politician. Lei had made no secret of his intention to discuss reunification in Hong Kong, but was not barred from making the trip. It was fruitless, however. He failed to win the assurance he was seeking that China would never reunify by force. At this time, Peking was taking fright at the conclusion some in Taiwan were drawing from the smoothness with which contacts had been resumed with the mainland – that Taiwan's separate status could be preserved while fostering greater links. In March, China's Prime Minister Li Peng departed from his prepared text in his address to the National People's Congress in Peking to warn that China would not stand idly by if the Taiwan independence movement were to hamper efforts at peaceful reunification. Nevertheless, despite this chilling note, there seemed little doubt in Taiwan that having dipped its toe in mainland waters, there was not that much risk in paddling a bit in the shallows. The family reunion policy had been a roaring success. Not only was it enormously popular; it also scored notable propaganda points, as wealthy Taiwan residents impressed their relatives with their affluence, and came back appalled at the backwardness of the economic and social life endured by their mainland compatriots.

THE TRADE AND INVESTMENT DEBATE

To a certain extent, the 1987–8 reforms in mainland policy did little more than reflect changes that had already happened, especially in the commercial world. The KMT's China policy, like its economic direction, was becoming trade-led. By 1987, two-way trade across the Taiwan Strait was estimated at as much as US$1.6 billion, or 1.8 per cent of Taiwan's total trade. The government seemed to be formalising a policy its businessmen had already been putting into practice with considerable success.

There were several reasons for the boom in Taiwan–mainland trade in the 1980s. The most important was the economic direction pursued by the Peking government in 1980s. Deng Xiaoping's embrace of 'economic development' as the 'key link' required a reliance on foreign capital, development finance and technology. It also implied a divorce of foreign trade policy from the old ideological shibboleths. China was able to trade freely with its ideological enemies in the Soviet Union as well as with the West. It pursued commercial links with South Korea. China sold hundreds of millions of dollars worth of weaponry to both Iran and Iraq during the Gulf War. It sustained clandestine ties with both Israel and South Africa. Only Vietnam and its Indo-Chinese clients, with whom it was engaged in a long-running diplomatic and occasionally military confrontation across the Sino-Vietnamese shared border, remained, for most of the decade, beyond the commercial pale. By the late 1980s, however, trade with Laos was resumed, though partly to loosen Hanoi's domination over its satellite and in 1989 trade resumed across the Sino-Vietnamese border. With Taiwan, not only were there no political objections to pursuing trade; it was actively promoted, as one of the 'three communications' which the current orthodoxy held would hasten Chinese reunification.

Eyeing this burgeoning market, Taiwan's traders were naturally attracted. The global trading environment was becoming tougher. Taiwan's reliance on the US market in particular made it highly vulnerable to protectionist pressures there. While the Reagan and Bush administrations in Washington were both avowedly committed to free trade principles, the regional interests represented in Congress had an almost structural protectionist bias. Senators and representatives seeking local votes would always find the threat to their industries from foreign penetration of the US market a more popular platform than an argument based on the necessity of a free US market for the health of the global economy. Mainland Chinese theorists would at times paint the US dominance of Taiwan's export markets as a conspiracy, designed to perpetrate 'two Chinas'. Market diversification became both a commercial imperative for Taiwan, and an ideological goal for the mainland.

What is more, the two economies seemed remarkably complementary. Taiwan was awash with surplus capital, but facing serious pressures on two fronts: local production costs, especially wage rates, were rising, and the markets for its labour-intensive manufactures were under threat from cheaper competition. In some cases, notably textiles, the pressure in fact came from the mainland, which in the mid-1980s overtook Taiwan as the United States' major foreign textiles supplier. Mainland China, on the other hand, was chronically short of investment capital, was flooded with under-employed cheap labour, and was unable to meet the demand for consumer goods produced by the success of the agricultural reforms of the early 1980s. It was also, potentially, a supplier of some of the raw materials that Taiwan had to import from distant and perhaps unstable countries – oil from the Middle East and coal from South Africa.

The mainland therefore seemed an obvious target both for the diversification of Taiwan's export markets, and for the internationalisation of its industries into investment in lower cost production centres. Within Taiwan's business circles, a powerful lobby built up for the freeing of trade restrictions. After the 1984 agreement on the future of Hong Kong, and the 1987–8 drive in South Korea for economic links with China, this lobby acquired another argument. Its competitors were gaining a significant commercial advantage. They were able to sell directly into China, thereby avoiding the incremental costs – shipping, storage and brokerage fees – that Taiwan's businessmen were forced into by the insistence that only indirect trade with the mainland was permissible, and that only because it was unstoppable. Second, the access to mainland raw materials, even the indirect importing of which was still banned in Taiwan, might give Hong Kong's and South Korea's industries an edge over Taiwan's in third markets. Suppose, for example, that Peking, anxious to secure a better relationship with South Korea, were to start selling it

coal at 'friendship' prices, a tactic Peking had used in the past
in its commercial diplomacy. These commercial worries are
especially galling to Taiwan. It was ideally placed geograph-
ically to deal with the open economies of China's Special
Economic Zones (SEZ) on the southern seaboard, and with
the coastal provinces of Guangdong, Fujian, and from 1988,
when it became a province and SEZ in its own right, Hainan
island. This was not just Taiwan's backyard. It was, so the
government insisted, part of the same country. They spoke
almost the same language, and there were extensive cultural
and family links between these areas and Taiwan.

The business lobby was supported in its call for an economic opening to China by both the KMT 'young Turks' and
the moderate factions of the DPP. Through the first half of
1988, the debate became one of the central issues in Taiwan
politics. The 13th KMT National Congress, held in July, was
anticipated as the forum for the announcement of a policy
change. Meanwhile, however, KMT and government spokesmen rehearsed the old arguments against economic ties with
China. First, there was the old stand-by, that because China
was a communist country any commercial dealings implied
official contact and hence a degree of unacceptable recognition
of the regime. Second, it was argued that mainland politics
were fundamentally unstable, and that communists were simply unreliable, and bad business partners. The use of intermediaries for trade thus made sound commercial sense as an
insurance policy, and any degree of economic dependence on
the mainland as an export market was too great a risk. Third,
besides the dangers of a change in economic policy by the
volatile Peking government, there was also the risk of a
change in Taiwan policy. A less gradualist approach by the
communists to reunification would be greatly helped were
Taiwan to rely on the mainland for any of its strategic
imports. Fourth, what China wanted to buy were relatively
low-technology consumer goods. Despite its reforms and
potential, it was still not that important a market, and
certainly was not a substitute in this regard for the West and
the US in particular. The chimera of mainland purchasing
power might encourage Taiwan's industry to continue to push
the products which had been the basis of its success in the
previous decade, and so hamper the drive to invest, modern-

ise, automate and move up-market, which was seen as essential to the island's long-term continued prosperity. Fifth, as government spokesman Shaw Yu-ming put it in April 1988, 'premature and unhealthy development of direct trade with China may fuel the Taiwan independence movement'. One of the very few ways left in which Taiwan did *not* behave as an independent country was its arms-length handling of dealings with China.

Nevertheless, there were marked changes in the government's attitude to trade with the mainland. Indirect trade was now acknowledged, and tacitly encouraged. Government spokesmen would suggest that there was a ceiling on the trade – of 5 per cent of Taiwan's global import–export business. This would still make China Taiwan's third largest trading partner, behind only the US and Japan, if Hong Kong were excluded because so much of the Hong Kong trade is in any event entrepôt business for the mainland. But the view seemed to be that this was a tolerable upper level at which dependence on the mainland would still not be strategically risky. In October 1987, the first liberalisation of import policy covered herbal medicine from the mainland. It could now be bought direct from wholesalers in Hong Kong, without recourse to Taiwan's official importing agency. This was a more significant change than might appear – traditional Chinese medicines are a staple in many Taiwan homes.

Indirect Taiwan investment in the mainland was also booming. After the July 1987 easing of the control on the export of capital, this became as hard to prevent as indirect trade. Up to US$5 million could be taken out each year without specific approval. Since most of the mainland investment was in labour-intensive manufacturing and assembly operations, the amounts of capital required were, individually, not that large, and so did not need to be reported. Indeed, many of the arrangements were contractual rather than equity investments. As manufacturers in Hong Kong had been doing for some years, Taiwan entrepreneurs retained their market share by winning orders direct, and then sub-contracting to cheaper labour countries. Thus the estimates for the amount of money from Taiwan that was pouring into coastal China are unreliable. One plausible US study reckoned that US$114 million was invested by Taiwan residents in Fujian province alone in 1987. In July 1988, China capitalised on the debate on the eve of the KMT Congress to promulgate a package of preferential investment for Taiwan investors. In March 1990, China published figures claiming that Taiwan investment in the mainland now totalled US$1bn, or over 6 per cent of all foreign investment.

While it tacitly supported trade, however, official policy was to condemn indirect investment. So the expectation was that the 13th Party Congress of the KMT would ease trade policy but set its face against investment. After all, investment links, which implied a far greater faith in the communist legal system, seemed a much more obvious infringement of the still sacrosanct 'three noes' policy. In fact, the KMT Congress passed a resolution 'encouraging any economic activity which will help compatriots on the mainland build a free enterprise economy'. This elliptical clause did seem a fairly direct endorsement of investment. Yet only two days before it was passed, a deputy Minister for Economic Affairs had said that anyone caught engaging in direct investment would be punished, and KMT spokesmen seemed split as to the true meaning of the resolution. Indirect investment, however, unlike most of the KMT's recommendations, did not become law in the next year, by which time the Peking massacre in June 1989 had turned the clock back in that respect at least, and provided a sufficient disincentive in itself to investment in the mainland.

Nor did the Congress result in the KMT's backing for the opening of direct trade. Some import liberalisation was allowed, to extend the list of permissible raw materials imports to cover such vital supplies as coal and cotton. These two provide interesting case studies. In May 1988, the Chairman of Occidental Petroleum, Armand Hammer, who was involved in projects in both the USSR and China, had arrived in Taiwan and reported that Deng Xiaoping wanted to sell coal from an occidental joint venture in China to Taiwan as well as to South Korea. Armand Hammer was, of course, famous as one of Moscow's most important conduits to the capitalist world ever since Lenin's day. He was rebuffed, however, in Taipei, with the time-worn arguments about the risks of strategic dependence. Coal was especially tricky, because more than three-quarters of Taiwan's coal purchases were made by the public sector – Taiwan Power Corporation and China Steel – which would be even more loath to engage in contacts which could be construed as 'government to government'. Cotton, on the other hand, was a largely private sector import, for the large numbers of textiles and clothing factories. Many did take advantage of the relaxation, with the result that in March 1989, Guangdong province received an instruction from the central government not to sell cotton to Taiwan at a time of a shortfall in supplies on the mainland. KMT trade officials could afford a modicum of *schadenfreude* at this, the communist unreliability they had always warned of.

THE THIRTEENTH CONGRESS AND AFTER: MAINLAND FEVER

In most ways, therefore, the 13th KMT Congress was, on mainland policy, a catching-up process with changes that had already taken place. In some areas, like investment, its recommendations were not taken up by government, leaving official policy still lagging behind reality. But the Congress provided an added boost to the already hectic pace at which contacts with the mainland were proliferating, and blurred still further the already hazy dividing line between permissible 'people to people' contacts, and outlawed 'official' exchanges.

Already, in April, rules on private travel had been relaxed to allow the Red Cross to assist those claiming less close blood-ties on the mainland to go as well. Government employees, including soldiers and teachers, however, were still barred. So popular had the relaxation been, and so much of a propaganda bonus both on the mainland as the Taiwan visitors flaunted their affluence, and at home as people spoke in pitying terms of the poverty and repression of life on the mainland, that in the same month, the Red Cross was entrusted with establishing postal links. It was allowed to deliver mail to the mainland, via Hong Kong, embellished with an improving frank calling for the reunification of China under the three principles of the people.

The KMT Congress recommended a further relaxation, resolving that three of the 'four exchanges' be initiated – sporting, cultural and academic (but not technological) – and that some journalists be allowed to go on reporting trips, following the scathing indictments of the achievements of communism that most of those who had gone illegally had written. It also recommended that some family visits be allowed the other way. The proposal was extremely restricted. Indeed one of the hottest issues at the Congress was over a minor modification. The original suggestion was that main-landers should be allowed to come to Taiwan for the funeral of a close relative. The Congress expanded this to sanction also 'death-bed' visits to ailing relations. It was also proposed that mainland students in Europe, Japan or the US who 'renounce communism' be allowed to come to Taiwan.

These proposals were slow to be implemented by the government. But in October a mainland passport-holder, the mathematician Chang Ching-lung, who was the son of a KMT war hero, made history. He took three months' sabbati-cal from his lectureship at Cleveland State University to teach at the Chung-yuan Christian University in Taoyuan. Also in October, the Party recommended that small groups of main-land-based students be permitted to come to Taiwan. Other 'outstanding' mainlanders would also be allowed to come, and the KMT embarrassed the Peking government by approving a visit by the dissident Fang Lizhi, although, unsurprisingly, he was not able to make the trip. In November, in another 'humanitarian' gesture to its old warriors, the Taipei govern-ment announced that about 2000 KMT soldiers who had been stranded on the mainland in 1949 would be allowed to come to Taiwan to settle, accompanied by their spouses and chil-dren under the age of majority. In a parallel move, to defuse tension, the government announced that it was abandoning its practice of rewarding mainland pilots who defected with handsome payments of gold and money.

Meanwhile, indirect trade boomed. Estimates for the total two-way trade in 1988 vary from US$2.3 to US$2.7 billion, making China Taiwan's fourth largest trading partner, if Hong Kong is excluded. In September, a ferry service opened between Shanghai and Taiwan, with Naha in Okinawa acting as a stopping-off point, where passengers and cargo could shift from mainland-flagged to ROC-flagged vessels or vice versa. The next month, a mainland Chinese news agency reported that the port of Shipu in Zhejiang province would be expanded to cater for the Taiwan trade. It claimed that over 2000 Taiwan fishing and cargo boats had taken shelter in Shipu's harbour from stormy weather in 1988.

This proliferation of commercial contacts inevitably raised the tricky question of how the communists' laws should be treated. In August, Taiwan denied a mainland report that a commercial arbitration panel was already meeting in Hong Kong. But it did allow mainlanders to instruct contacts in Taiwan to claim the labour insurance benefits earned by dead relatives. In December, in a landmark decision, the Taiwan Supreme Court ruled that it was not seditious to engage in direct dealings with the communist mainland. The next month, the Justice Ministry produced a draft law which provided for a maximum three-year prison sentence for those caught conducting direct business with the mainland. At the same time, work started on legislation to recognise mainland law which covered 'private' transactions, like inheritance and marriage. In April 1989, the mainland official press reported on the establishment of a joint law office in the south-eastern coastal town of Fuzhou to handle commercial disputes and contracts. The next month, a Taiwan government spokesman said that the cabinet was considering draft regulations on indirect investment by Taiwan entrepreneurs in the mainland. This was flourishing, despite still being illegal. In another significant move towards legal co-operation, an alleged murderer was extradited to Taiwan from China via Singapore in April.

The flow of visitors from Taiwan to the mainland gathered pace. In 1988, Taiwan figures put the number who had gone under Red Cross auspices at about 200 000. Peking figures put the total number of Taiwan visitors at 330 000. The position of delegations pursuing the 'four exchanges' was at first confused. In August, seven traditional Chinese doctors from Taiwan took part in a seminar in Fujian province. The next month, however, a delegation from Taiwan's official Academia Sinica was banned from participating in the plenary session of the International Council of Scientific Unions in Peking. In a compromise typical of the state of flux of mainland policy at this time, however, they were allowed to go, but only as 'private individuals'. In November, the Executive Yuan decided to follow the KMT Congress recommendation and lift the ban on attendance at all international sporting, academic and cultural activities on the mainland. Now people could go to civilian meetings sponsored by international bodies of which Taiwan was a member.

The most important area affected by this was sport. But before athletes from Taiwan were able to compete on the mainland, the perennial bugbear of nomenclature reared its head again. The 'Asian Development Bank' solution had been for Taiwan to acquiesce, under protest, to remaining a member under the name 'Taipei, China' (*Taibei, Zhonghua*). This includes a shortened version of the official title for China used in both the names 'People's Republic of China' and 'Republic of China'. Now, Peking decided to turn the screw a little tighter, and to demand that Taiwan's sports teams call themselves the less symbolic 'Chinese, Taipei' (*Taibei, Zhongguo*). This was a sticking point for Taipei, an example of the line beyond which it would not go. Earlier, in another example of these limits on the new openness, a KMT 'young Turk' legislator Hu Chiu-yuan had been dismissed from the Party after a trip to Peking. He was said to have met Li Xiannian, China's former President, and now chairman of the Chinese People's Political Consultative Committee, and had reportedly discussed the terms for China's reunification. Similarly, the DPP Chairman Huang Hsin-chieh had lost his travel rights for an illicit trip to the mainland made in July.

These wrangles aside, the momentum of contact with the mainland seemed unstoppable. In April 1989, it received the most dramatic boost of all, when the government announced its decision to send a delegation to the Asian Development Bank meeting in May. It was to be held in Peking. In typical fashion, the Taipei government insisted that their policy had not shifted from the hallowed 'three noes'; it was only because the ADB, not the Peking government, was the host and had extended the invitation that it was possible for Taiwan to attend. Nevertheless, the decision caused a furore in Taiwan. Its delegation was at the highest of levels, led by the Finance Minister, Mrs Shirley Kuo. What really rankled with hardline sensibilities at home was that they actually stood for the communist Chinese National Anthem, claiming feebly afterwards that they had no choice.

The decision to attend the ADB meeting resulted from a conjunction of two parallel trends in policy. One was the gradual easing on contacts with the mainland. In April, the nomenclature issue settled in favour of 'Taipei, China', the first Taiwan sports team – a group of gymnasts – had competed in Peking. The other was Taiwan's decision that it wanted to rejoin as many of the international bodies from which it had been expelled as possible. This was another aspect of the 'flexible' or 'pragmatic' diplomacy discussed in the context of bilateral relations in Chapter 6. The KMT had decided that international diplomatic flexibility was less a threat to its international status than it was a partial guarantee of its future security. To this end, it wanted to regain access to the full panoply of multinational forums, culminating in the United Nations. In the more immediate future, it wanted to join the General Agreement on Tariffs and Trade (GATT), the Organisation for Economic Co-operation and Development (OECD) and the World Bank and International Monetary Fund (IMF).

The auguries for the GATT looked quite hopeful. Taiwan had significantly freed its own markets, and in 1987, China had agreed that post-1997 Hong Kong could retain separate GATT membership. These hopes suffered a set-back in 1989, however. The degree of centralisation, import control and price subsidy still imposed by the Peking government meant that the GATT deferred approving the PRC's own application to 'rejoin' the GATT, even before the Peking massacre changed the world's perceptions of the communist regime. Peking used intense diplomatic pressure to try to prevent Taiwan being granted separate membership on its own. Membership of the OECD, the 'club' of the developed, industrial Western countries and Japan, would be a remarkable badge of merit for Taiwan's economic performance, and would provide a forum for meeting with the leaders of the 'free world' on equal terms. Similarly, the IMF and the World Bank were the world's most powerful multilateral financial bodies, and if membership could be achieved, Taiwan might be able to turn its towering external financial position to political as well as economic advantage.

But all of this was still a pipe-dream. The only important multilateral body to which Taiwan still belonged was the ADB. If Taiwan were not prepared to demonstrate a flexible and co-operative attitude there, what hope was there for admission or re-admission into other bodies? In 1988, at its Manila meetings, Taipei had broken the two-year boycott it began after the PRC was admitted, and its delegates had attended, even though they refused to wear the badges identifying them as humble 'Taipei, China'. So it was decided to go to Peking, and regulations restricting newspaper and television journalists and film-makers from going to the mainland were lifted, to enable coverage of the event.

What they saw was a piece of history. The ADB meetings coincided with what for a few short weeks looked like a victorious people power revolution in China's capital. Tian An Men Square at its heart was the scene of massive anti-government demonstrations, which the government seemed powerless to stop. The Taipei delegation was there for the second wave of protests, after the April marches prompted by the death of Hu Yaobang. Now it was the 70th anniversary of the May 4th Movement that provoked a resurgence. Many of the reporters who had accompanied the ADB delegation stayed on for the third wave, which accompanied Mikhail Gorbachev's historic visit for the first Sino-Soviet summit meeting in three decades, on 15–18 May. Most then remained to see martial law imposed on 20 May, and the people of Peking twice turning back the army from the outskirts of the capital. By the early hours of 4 June, Tian An Men Square was still watched by numbers of Taiwanese reporters, who were able to describe in graphic terms to their readers the army's brutal entry into Peking, killing hundreds or perhaps thousands of unarmed civilians as it crushed what had been a fundamentally peaceful student-led protest movement.

TAIWAN AND THE PEKING MASSACRE

The genuine grief and anger felt in Taiwan at the Peking massacre soon translated in the KMT into something approaching smugness. 'We feel vindicated', government spokesman Shaw Yu-ming said in June. But apart from proving to the world that the communists were as barbarous as the KMT had always said they were, the massacre also presented something of a domestic propaganda bonus to the KMT. This seems paradoxical. The KMT, after all, was formally committed to reunification with China, and still treats as seditious calls for Taiwan to face reality, and declare itself for what it is, an independent country. The spectacle of bloodshed and reprisal on the streets of the communist capital might have been expected to add weight to the independence movement. But in fact, the KMT gained new evidence to support its most damning argument against formal independence – that the Chinese Communist Party has never abandoned the threat of military force to reunify Taiwan in certain circumstances, one of which is a unilateral declaration of independence by Taiwan. If the communists will use tanks against unarmed students in their own capital, then surely they might well carry out their threat to subdue the Taiwan independence movement by force. So the massacre in Peking seemed to help the KMT's 1989 election prospects in two ways – by making the DPP, which included a strong pro-independence faction, appear dangerous hotheads, and, more generally, by increasing tension and enhancing the attraction of a vote for the status quo and stability.

Meanwhile, the serious rifts within the DPP widened further. The pro-independence 'New Movement' suffered a debilitating blow from the savagery in Peking. Whereas its leaders used to argue that invasion from the mainland was a KMT-inspired propaganda ploy rather than a serious threat, now their policy was closer to one of desperation. 'New Movement' stalwart Ch'iou I-jen, who until the faction's defeat in the 1988 Congress was deputy Secretary General of the DPP, said in June that he did believe mainland intervention was quite possible. But, he claimed, the mainland's military resources were inadequate, in particular their naval capacity. He pointed to Britain in the Blitz as an example of how a united people can withstand foreign aggression. This policy hardly seemed to be a vote-winner. Yet in the 1989 election campaign in Taipei City itself, the most enthusiastic rallies were those of Yeh Ch'u-lan – 'Taiwan's Cory Aquino'. The widow of a pro-independence activist who had burned himself to death in April rather than be arrested on sedition charges, Yeh was one of the 32 'New Nation Alliance' pro-independence candidates. She too was prepared to stare mainland military might in the face. 'In no country in the world', she told me, 'has freedom been won without a struggle'.

The election results, where the DPP fared so well, were in large measure a protest vote, and cannot be taken as a major indicator of pro-independence sentiment. However, it did seem that while the Peking massacre may have deterred some voters from backing the DPP, it swayed just as many away from the KMT with its constitutional commitment to reunification.

The KMT meanwhile tried to identify itself with the student movement on the mainland. Taiwan officials even began talking up the number of Taiwan residents who had visited the mainland, rather than, as in the past, playing down the boom in travel. The reason for the new official approach in Taiwan to describing the level of contact with the mainland was that the KMT was anxious to portray China's student demonstrators as inspired by what President Lee Teng-hui called the 'Taiwan experience'.

During 1989, this had become the theory behind the new mainland policy. It in fact represented a third major stage in the development of Taiwan's attitude to China. It superseded both the dreams of military reunification under Chiang Kai-shek, and of peaceful reunification through staunch isolationism under Chiang Kai-shek's later years, and the first seven or eight years of his son's regime. Dropping even lip-service to the idea of military recovery of the mainland, Taiwan now intended to win the mainland for capitalism by being a 'showcase' for what an allegedly free market economy combined with political liberalisation can offer the Chinese people.

In April and May 1989, there was a great deal of attention paid in Taiwan to a 'new idea' floated by Foreign Minister Lien Chan, and, improbably, by then Prime Minister Yu Kuo-hwa about the future relationship with the mainland. This was summarised as 'one country – two governments', and envisaged long-term co-existence of the two governments. This was to be distinguished from China's 'one country – two systems' approach, which required Taiwan's recognition of Peking's ultimate sovereignty. The 'new idea' was greeted with a predictably scornful rebuff from the mainland, as 'aimed at nothing less than splitting China'. But with an apparently pragmatic line in control in Peking it did not seem inconceivable that in the fullness of time some basis for negotiation with the communists over Taiwan's future could be found.

By the early morning of 4 June 1989, it did again seem just that – inconceivable. Of all the hopes and dreams buried under the tanks of the Chinese army in Peking, that of imminent peaceful reunification with Taiwan was one that was at first easy to overlook. And, paradoxically, the repression of the student movement awakened a sense of ethnic and cultural identity with the mainland in Taiwan as it did in Hong Kong, even among the native Taiwanese population. One of the journalists who was among those on Tian An Men Square on the night of 3–4 June, the Taiwan-born Yang Du, told me that his first thought on seeing the troops open fire was 'Why do Chinese kill Chinese?' But, this typical emotional reaction aside, the KMT back-pedalled fast from its tentative moves towards compromise with Peking. Pointing out that their characterisation of the Peking regime had been right all along, they also stressed that the 'one country – two governments' proposal was only an idea, a trial balloon. The KMT resorted to the argument that the status quo was the only viable solution to the 'two Chinas' problem. Reunification remained its ultimate theoretical goal, but was now almost openly acknowledged as a politically expedient means of staving off disaster, rather than as a realistic policy option. As one KMT legislator put it in June, 'It is just a goal. It may take thirty years, fifty years, a hundred years – so what? One hundred years in history is very short. So that's just a goal, so what we should do is make Taiwan the hope of China, and make Taiwan a showcase to influence mainland China'.

Undermining the argument that the students were inspired by Taiwan, and represented China's best hope, was the fact that the KMT were in fact very slow to express enthusiasm for the student movement, until its bloody denouement. There were a few lack-lustre government-organised pro-democracy demonstrations, but a very hands-off attitude prevailed. After the event, the official explanation for this reticence was that loud protestations of Taiwan support would have got the students into trouble. But oppositionists, like the DPP's 'Rambo' Ju Gao-jeng, argued that the KMT was inhibited by its similarities with the Chinese communists. It, too, he argued, was vulnerable to attack on the grounds of corruption and of the undemocratic exercise of power by a group of old hardliners. The average age of the mainland Legislative Yuan delegates, he pointed out, was 83, and they regarded senior Chinese leaders like Deng Xiaoping and Yang Shangkun as in their prime.

All such reservations were thrown to the wind after the massacre, however. Taiwan joined vociferously in the international chorus of outrage. But even here, policy was somewhat inconsistent. Taiwan urged Western governments to impose economic sanctions in China. But for its own part, it stepped up contacts, and said there was no intention of either tightening up on indirect exports to the mainland, or of reimposing the ban on the importation of strategic raw materials. The apparent contradiction between the measures demanded of other countries and Taiwan's own policy was explained officially by the nature of Taiwan's economic links with the mainland. The sanctions demanded were to cover high-level technology transfers and military sales. Since most of Taiwan's trade was in light industrial products, it felt justified in carrying on, in the spirit of flaunting the Taiwan showcase, and so of fostering a democratic revolution on the mainland. At the end of June, the Taiwan Ministry of Economic Affairs did something to rectify any bad impression caused by the policy inconsistency by announcing the establishment of a 'task force' to control high-tech transfers out of Taiwan, and reiterating the ban on technology sharing agreements (indeed, strictly speaking, on *any* agreements) with mainland partners. In the immediate aftermath of the massacre, direct telex and telephone links with the mainland were opened for the first time, and Taiwan radio broadcasts to the mainland expanded, as part of the effort to defy the Peking government's propaganda re-writing of the Peking massacre. However, presumably because of mainland incompetence or interference, only a small proportion of the phone calls got through, out of a massive number reported by Taiwan's telecommunications bureau in the first two days after the opening of the lines (170 000 calls of which 12 000 were connected).

In the shock that followed the massacre, Taiwan's people did demonstrate in large numbers. Large quantities of both blood and money were donated, with no means of reaching their destination. More tangibly, the government offered scholarships to pro-democracy mainland students already out of China, not just to study in Taiwan, but to carry on their studies elsewhere if mainland funding dried up. Some, too, seemed likely to win Taiwan passports. Taiwan was also quick to deny one report that a fleeing pro-democracy activist had been turned back from the Taiwan-controlled island of Kinmen early in June. However, it did acknowledge that 118 mainlanders had been stopped in June from illegally trying to enter Taiwan, none of them students. Sympathy and money were in good supply. But opening Taiwan's crowded shores to a potential flood of those evading repression was not on the agenda.

From the far right in Taiwan there were some calls for a resuscitation of the old militaristic dreams of going to rescue those suffering communist tyranny; but they were few. The military were put on full alert immediately after the massacre, and the President spoke of the danger of mainland provocation. It was speculated that a nationalistic venture such as recovering Taiwan might be what Peking needed to unify its battered people. But in reality, the Taiwan military alert was probably more concerned with keeping illegal immigrants out than any real fear of mainland adventurism. Fears did rise, however, when, as Peking flailed around in the search for culprits to blame for the so-called 'counter-revolutionary rebellion', in late June it arrested 13 alleged 'Taiwan spies' for their role in the democracy movement. Then in July a Taiwan journalist was briefly detained by the Peking police for allegedly meeting and helping a fugitive student leader. And the official New China News Agency carried a detailed refutation of some Taiwan reporting of the army action in Peking. But, otherwise, Peking was at pains to reassure Taipei, as other capitals, that nothing had changed. On 27 June, Tang Shubei, deputy director of the Taiwan Affairs office of China's State Council reiterated Peking's commitment to peaceful reunification, and its support for the expansion of contacts between people on either side of the Taiwan Strait. However, Yan Mingfu, who in his capacity as the head of the Communist Party's United Front office had been in effect the senior mainland official with responsibility for Taiwan, declined in influence as an ally of the ousted Party leader Zhao Ziyang. Meanwhile, travel agents in Taiwan were bombarded with invitations for inspection visits to prove that mainland tourism was still feasible.

10   What Next? Scenarios for the Future

INTRODUCTION AND OUTLINE: THE OPTIONS FOR TAIWAN'S FUTURE

The Peking massacre highlighted Taiwan's dilemma. It is not 'part of China', any more than the United States is part of Britain. Like settler colonies anywhere, the logic of its situation suggests a need for, and right to, self-determination. While China is ruled by Chinese, however, it seems impossible that any government in Peking could yield that right. There is no reason to disbelieve the repeated protestations of successive leaders in China that they regard reunification as a sacred duty, and would contemplate force to accomplish that if peaceful means were thwarted. The most likely way in which peaceful reunification could be seen to have failed would be if Taiwan declared itself independent. Moreover, Taiwan is ruled by a government whose legitimacy is founded on its claim to rule all of China. It, too, has a vested interest in side-stepping the self-determination question. In fact, it has become clear that the Kuomintang's main interests lie not in its stated goal, of national reunification, but in preserving and strengthening the status quo as long as possible. But how long is that? The status quo is under threat from at least three sources: the effects of political liberalisation on Taiwan, which give the independence movement a freedom to proselytise which it has not enjoyed for 40 years; the volatility of the Chinese scene, where sudden and violent changes in direction are more than possible, they are almost inevitable; and finally from the Taiwan government's own efforts to steer the perilous course between international isolation and separate nationhood.

In crude terms, there are six ways in which Taiwan's future could develop over the next two decades:

(i)   The status quo.
(ii) Reunification on Peking's terms, peacefully under the 'one country – two systems' formula.

(iii) Reunification on Taiwan's terms, under the 'three principles of the people.'
(iv) Independence for Taiwan as a separate nation.
(v) Reunification accomplished by military means.
(vi) Peaceful reunification on a compromise formula, preserving Taiwan's de facto independence.

It is the author's perhaps over-optimistic assessment that it is the last of these possibilities which will materialise. But that relies on taking a view about developments on the mainland. Taiwan's future was decided in Amsterdam in the early seventeenth century, in Peking 50 years later, at Shimonoseki in 1895, in Cairo in 1943 and is likely to be settled again in a distant capital, probably Peking once more. And it is likely to be settled yet again before anyone gets around to asking the people of Taiwan what they think. To explain the reasons for arriving at this conclusion, it is necessary to examine each of the scenarios.

THE PRESERVATION OF THE STATUS QUO

On the face of it, there is no compelling reason why the status quo should not be sustainable. Taiwan is not Hong Kong or Macao, with some foreign power feeling a legal or moral obligation to divest itself of a colony. There is no 99-year lease setting a time limit on the present arrangement. The Chinese Civil War is over. It is kept alive by a few men in their eighties who fought it, and for whom it will not be properly completed until the 'Chiang Kai-shek fascist clique' or the 'communist bandits' are wiped out. It is a piece of historical baggage that a subsequent generation will be only too happy to leave in the left-luggage locker.

After all, both sides have much to gain from the present arrangements. If Peking means what it says about granting Taiwan true autonomy under the 'one country – two systems' formula, then why push it? It can gain the benefits of co-operation without the need to press Taiwan into some formal recognition of its sovereignty. And Taiwan has negotiated its 'opening to the mainland' relatively painlessly. It has proved possible to deal profitably with the bandits without either relinquishing the KMT's ideological claim to legitimacy, or fundamentally altering Taiwan's international status of de facto independence. In both Peking and Taipei, a younger generation of pragmatic technocrats are gradually taking over the reins of power. Unlike their elders, they will feel no especial compunction to complete the job of national reunification in their lifetimes. So why not put it off indefinitely?

There are three reasons why the status quo might not be indefinitely sustainable:

1 Political liberalisation in Taiwan

The opening up of Taiwan's political system into a structure more genuinely representative of the people of the island is an irreversible process. A well-educated, affluent, cosmopolitan population will not readily acquiesce to being deprived of the freedoms it has been newly granted, short of a state of real national emergency or warfare. In a few years, Taiwan will have a parliament dominated almost entirely by Taiwan-born legislators. This will have a direct impact with the relationship on the mainland in two ways:

(a) The breaking of a constitutional link with the mainland
The claim of the Legislature to represent all of China will inevitably be weaker once there are no sitting deputies purporting to represent mainland constituencies. The KMT is probably correct in thinking that this change in itself is not crucial. Already, in the 1980s the absenteeism and debility of the mainland delegates make them no more than symbolic relics of the 1946 Constitution. However, their fading from the scene will undermine the credibility of that Constitution itself. Already the 1946 Constitution looks a threadbare cloak for KMT legitimacy. It was drawn up by the government of, at the time, just one part of China, by officials working for a government which was already on the brink of a disastrous civil war, in which a prime cause of their defeat was the haemorrhaging of popular support. Only a tiny proportion voted in the only 'national elections' held under the Constitution in 1947 and 1948. The results and conduct of those elections are both subject to dispute. The Constitution of the People's Republic of China may have been imposed on China by an undemocratic system of government, but in the early

1950s, there can be little doubt that the Chinese Communist Party had some kind of popular mandate for its rule. The various Constitutions it has imposed on China since then have not been in themselves any more self-evidently illegitimate than the KMT's effort.

(b) The growth of the 'self-determination' movement
It has been pointed out that the origins of the Taiwan opposition are in Taiwanese nationalist resistance to rule by a mainlander élite. The basic premise of its bid to win electoral appeal is that there is a divide between Taiwanese and mainlander, and that the KMT, for all its 'Taiwanisation' of recent years, represents mainlander interests. Although the opposition may also attack the KMT on the basis of domestic policy – pollution, corruption, media restraints and so on – it is largely organised around the questions of international status. Even the more moderate DPP factions' insistence on the issues of international political reform are founded on a sense of the injustice of a political system which does not give Taiwan people the right to self-determination. As, one by one, the KMT whittles away the worst symbols of mainland domination – martial law, mainlander domination of parliament and the executive – the logic of the DPP's strategy will drive it ever closer to uniting on 'self-determination' or independence.

There is no reason to believe that in the foreseeable future, the DPP could achieve an electoral majority, or even that if a 'self-determining' referendum were held, that it would opt for a change in international status. The benefits of the status quo are self-evident, and the dangers of antagonising Peking have been amply demonstrated by the Peking massacre of June 1989. However, once the Legislative Yuan and National Assembly are peopled by DPP firebrands and KMT 'young Turks', constitutional change becomes a possibility, calls for independence will become more common, and Peking is likely to take fright.

2 Mainland volatility

The Peking government in the 1990s will be in the throes of a fraught political transition. The problems of how to hand over power from the 'Long March' generation to younger leaders show no sign of resolution. After the popular uprising in China of early 1989, the communist leadership had to resort to the crudest of methods to demonstrate its legitimacy – first by proving that it could order the army to shoot the civilian population, and then by building a personality cult around the 85-year-old Deng Xiaoping, and his third designated successor, Jiang Zemin. Any successor leadership will have an even more tenuous grip on the popular mandate. One way in which it will be compelled to prove its strength is by demonstrating that it will uphold China's perceived interests internationally. The most sensitive of all international issues would be any effort by Taiwan, or by the international community on Taiwan's behalf, to effect some change in its status. Its attitude to Taiwan will be characterised by a heightened jumpiness, not just at any threat to the status quo, but at any hint that the status quo was solidifying into a permanent arrangement. Assuming the Taiwan question is not resolved before then, this edginess will become even more marked after the Hong Kong and Macao reversions to Chinese rule in 1997. Either the former colonies will be reintegrated successfully, in which case the pressure will mount on Taiwan to follow the same route; or, more probably, there will be considerable turmoil, in which case the offer of a similar arrangement to Taiwan will be revealed as a bankrupt policy.

3 Taiwan's 'flexible' diplomacy

Like its political reforms, the KMT's foreign policy shifts of the late 1980s are also in all probability irreversible. The experience of US de-recognition was not as bad as feared at the time. Indeed, the Taiwan Relations Act managed to lay a foundation for a legal relationship between Taiwan and its closest ally, even at the time when the US, in the wake of the invasions of Cambodia by Vietnam, and Afghanistan by the Soviet Union, most needed to 'play the China card'. Nevertheless, the US establishment of relations with Peking did give definitive proof that the cascade of de-recognition in the 1970s following its exit from the United Nations was unstoppable. Taiwan was condemned to diplomatic isolation. For a while, it survived this. But as China's stature and influence in the world grew, it became ever riskier for Taiwan to stand aloof from international diplomacy, and to leave itself without a voice in international affairs. There really was no choice but to try to manoeuvre for as large a residual influence in bilateral relations and multilateral forums as possible. 'Flexible' diplomacy was not really a matter of choice.

It is, however, fraught with danger. What it aims at is as much of the influence and status of an independent nation as possible, without the name. Hence the possibility for antagonising and alarming Peking is large. In this regard, the most sensitive areas are relations with the US and Japan, both of whom China suspects of harbouring influential elements who would like to see an independent Taiwan, as a bulwark against communism, and an 'unsinkable aircraft carrier' in their view of Pacific security. If, following the Peking massacre, China goes into a shell of greater political and economic isolation, then the right-wing 'pro-Taiwan' lobbies in both the United States and Japan are likely to gain ground. Correspondingly, China's influence with Washington and Tokyo is likely to shrink. US–Soviet *rapprochement* by 1989 had already led Chinese and American leaders to protest, plausibly, that Sino-US relations were no longer a question of either side 'playing cards' with Moscow. But in addition, economic isolation would deepen the disillusionment already felt with the commercial opportunities afforded by China's open door.

REUNIFICATION ON CHINA'S TERMS: PEACEFULLY, UNDER 'ONE COUNTRY – TWO SYSTEMS' FORMULA

One or more of the factors above is likely by the end of the century to lead to a smashing of the status quo. But will it lead to Peking's stated wish, that Taiwan enter the People's Republic of China as a 'Special Administrative Region', and carry on as before, with its own economic system, its own network of quasi-diplomatic relations, and its own army? For this to be achieved peacefully, one of two conditions would have to be met: either the KMT would have to renounce the 1946 Constitution, and recognise Peking's 1982 Constitution as subsequently amended or rewritten; or the evolution of the democratic process in Taiwan would lead to the people of

Taiwan choosing to accept Peking's sovereignty. Neither of these eventualities is likely.

1 Why the KMT is unlikely to drop its claim to legitimacy

It has to be remembered that the KMT relies on the 1946 Constitution not just for its claim to legitimacy on the mainland, but on Taiwan as well. Indeed its claim to Taiwan is much weaker. The savagery and chaos with which the KMT descended on the former Japanese colony in the late 1940s were those of an invading army. It cannot formally drop its claim to the mainland without acknowledging that for four decades it ruled Taiwan by a fraud. The KMT is trapped by its own history. The echoes of the past still ring around the traffic-clogged, neon-lit streets of Taipei. There are the protests by the old veterans of the Nationalist Army, who were compensated for their efforts with land bonds, redeemable when the mainland was recovered. There are the tomes produced by the elderly gentlemen toiling in Taipei's oldest office building, the 'Planning Commission for the Recovery of the Mainland'. there are the muck-raking efforts of the opposition, trying to throw doubt on the conduct of the 1947 and 1948 elections. There are the elderly generals like the once 'young Marshal' Chang Hsueh-liang, who have spent years in prison or under house-arrest for having crossed Chiang Kai-shek.

Even when the Peking massacre provided the KMT with its biggest propaganda opportunity in decades, the official media could not resist gloating that this is what the mainland got in return for ousting 'the best government China ever had', a characterisation so wild as to undermine the KMT's very real achievements on Taiwan. Of course, this need for a sense of historical continuity will diminish as time goes by. The old soldiers and bureaucrats will die, the old guard with their sense of 'historic responsibility' for the mainland will, like General MacArthur, just fade away. Soon, it is probable that the KMT will be able to point to its willingness to give the populace a real electoral choice, and still win a comfortable majority in the legislature.

But in a way, that gives even less reason to drop its claim to legitimacy. The KMT would be secure in its popular mandate, even if that mandate was based on an agreed silent contract with the electorate: if you do not vote for independence, we will not pursue reunification. Unless Peking were to force the issue, the KMT would face no compelling need to contemplate negotiation with the communists. The Peking government's own vulnerability has been clearly demonstrated by its need to resort to the army to control the civilian population. Not only does this make promises of non-interference under a 'one country – two systems' arrangement appear hollow; it also adds yet another reason to sit it out and see what sort of government emerges after the 'Long Marchers' finally hang up their boots.

2 The popular attitude in Taiwan to reunification

Nobody is likely to ask the people of Taiwan what they think about reunification on China's terms. Elections give them a choice between the KMT's proposals and the DPP's demand for self-determination. In the 1980s, on average, more than 60 per cent have voted for the KMT, which is implicitly also a vote against the CCP's reunification formula. Indeed, there is no evidence of widespread sympathy for the 'one country – two systems' approach in any sector of the population of Taiwan. Four decades of KMT-inspired indoctrination through the educational system have instilled an antipathy to communism. Now that some three per cent of the population have visited the mainland of the late 1980s, that antipathy is stronger. Living standards on Taiwan are so much higher than on the mainland as almost not to bear comparison. And by the late 1980s, the loss of faith on the mainland in the Communist Party and its leaders has left an ideological void. Few even in China are prepared to argue that Taiwan is, even in a political sense, worse off than the mainland. There is thus unlikely to be any popular pressure on the KMT from its electorate to concede sovereignty to Peking.

REUNIFICATION ON THE KMT's TERMS: UNDER THE 'THREE PRINCIPLES OF THE PEOPLE' (OR 'ONE COUNTRY – TWO GOVERNMENTS'?)

As suggested earlier, the KMT's stated position has to be distinguished from its actual policy. Whereas it continues to profess commitment to 'reunification under the Three Principles of the People', its actual policy suggests a dedication to the perpetuation of the status quo. This very nearly became explicit in early 1989, with the floating of the 'trial balloon' of 'one country – two governments', and the brief flirtation with a 'dual recognition' solution in the cases of Grenada, Belize and Liberia. The KMT leadership was quick to disavow the policy as any more than one among a number of ideas under consideration. It ruffled feathers both within the KMT and in Peking, which was quick to dismiss the idea as 'splitist'. However, it does represent the logic of the KMT's position. Once reunification becomes a 'distant goal', then the key policy imperative is to secure Taiwan's future in the interim. The 'one country – two governments' suggestion seemed aimed in part at testing reaction in Peking, to see if Peking was prepared to nudge forward from 'one country – two systems' to recognising the existence of two separate but equal regimes, each of which would implicitly or explicitly recognise the other. For the KMT's approach to succeed, again one of two conditions would have to be met: the CCP would have to compromise, or a new government in mainland China would have to welcome the KMT back on some version of Sun Yat-sen's three principles.

1 Why the CCP cannot renounce its claim to sovereignty

The CCP has its ghosts too, and one that haunts relations with Taiwan is a 'problem left over from history' that the Long March generation in Chinese politics can be assumed to feel strongly about. It is the last battle in the civil war, and one they were only prevented from winning by the intervention of the US Seventh Fleet. This generation seems to show no particular sense of urgency to complete the task of national reunification in their lifetimes. Like the KMT, they seem ready to take the long view. Deng Xiaoping once went so far as to talk about how China might catch up with Taiwan economically some time in the next century, implying that in that sort of time-scale, reunification would become more palatable to people in Taiwan. That generation, anyway, is fading from the scene. In its place, younger Chinese leaders are not just free of the legacy of civil war hatred of the KMT; many are actually attracted by the economic successes of the nationalists on Taiwan. Its style of authoritarianism combined with rapid modernisation is an appealing model for reformists in China as they witness the political upheavals their own efforts at 'taking economic development as the key link' have encouraged.

That is not to say, however, that they can effect another dramatic shift in Taiwan policy, to match Ye Jianying's 1981 'Nine Principles'. From their point of view, that offer is generous in the extreme. To go further they would have to incorporate some concession of sovereignty to the KMT government. To do so would be very difficult without in some sense 'losing Taiwan', and to recall the words of the 1979 'Message to Compatriots on Taiwan', 'Who among the descendants of the Yellow Emperor wishes to go down in history as a traitor?'. At the time of the initiatives his government launched in the early 1980s, Deng Xiaoping probably enjoyed greater popularity among the general public, and prestige within the top organs of state, Party and army than any ruler since Mao in the early 1950s. It is unlikely that in the turbulent transition to a post-Deng leadership, anyone will enjoy a comparable strength. As argued in the section of this chapter on the 'status quo option', this weakness is likely to lead to more, not less, intransigence on the Taiwan question. The only major concession short of sovereignty that China could make is to promise never to reunify by force. But for China's leaders, that promise, coupled with its implication that the Taiwan independence movement could flourish unhindered, is always likely to be tantamount to ceding sovereignty.

2   Why the KMT will not be welcomed back

In 1989, as Chinese pro-democracy activists around the world went into exile, parallels were drawn with Sun Yat-sen's revolutionary movement of the 1890s and 1900s. Once again, the best and brightest of China's intellectuals and students were organising to overthrow a corrupt and spent regime. Against repression at home, the movement's leadership set up shop abroad, ready to return to the motherland when the dynasty crumbles under the weight of its economic incompetence and loss of popular support. The communists, too, seemed to have 'lost the mandate of heaven'.

The KMT, flaunting its 'showcase of prosperity and freedom', naturally sought to identify itself with this movement. However, pro-democracy activists were keen, at first, to distance themselves from Taipei's overtures. Partly this was so as not to hand the CCP an easy propaganda tool with which to besmirch their campaign as provoked and financed by reactionary overseas forces. Again, the KMT and CCP had a common interest, this time in trying to show the importance of Taiwan for the democracy movement. But the distance from the KMT was not just a tactical move. China's young, too, have been brought up in an education system where the unity of the Chinese nation is drummed into them. Like the May 4th Movement, the 1989 student movement was inspired by patriotism as much as democracy. The KMT's historical record on the mainland, and its inability to separate itself from the past, make support for the KMT 'unpatriotic'. The democracy movement will not overthrow the Communist Party and invite the KMT to come back.

In public, however, Taiwan government spokesmen, encouraged first by the demonstrations in China and then by the upheavals in Eastern Europe in late 1989, continued to foretell the imminent collapse of the Peking regime, and the reunification of China on democratic principles before the year 2000.

INDEPENDENCE FOR TAIWAN AS A SEPARATE NATION

The author feels there is a very strong moral and legal case for Taiwan independence. The fact that most of the population is of Chinese ethnic stock should not be confused with an historic claim to legitimacy. Australia, Canada and New Zealand all have strong British connections stretching back a number of centuries, but are independent nations. What is more, Taiwan has been, in effect, an independent nation ever since 1949, and has fared very well. However, for Taiwan to declare itself independent, again two conditions would have to be met: an act of self-determination would have to decide on unilateral independence; and some or all of the world's major powers would have to support it.

1 Does Taiwan want to be 'independent'?

An act of self-determination as such is improbable in Taiwan in the near future. However, as suggested, elections for the Legislature will become more and more clearly votes for or against the status quo, including KMT policy on reunification. The electorate will be asked to make a relatively sophisticated choice. One party will be saying we are independent and should say so. The other party will be saying we are not independent, but will be meaning that we are independent, but if we say so, the mainland might take our independence away. One reason for the creeping pace of democratisation under the KMT is just this, that to make such an assessment the independence issue needs to be filtered out of the undoubted residual anti-mainland animosity among the Taiwanese population. The Peking massacre was a great help to the KMT in this respect. Hence the only way in which a pro-independence vote might win a majority would be if Peking were to renounce the use of force, and that, of course, is precisely why the mainland cannot do that.

2 Would the US and Japan support an independent Taiwan?

The communists are quite right when they say that there are powerful forces at work in Washington and Tokyo who favour a 'two Chinas' solution. However, the only circumstances in which these forces might win the open support of their governments would be those in which the whole triangular relationship between Washington, Moscow and Peking broke down altogether. This is not inconceivable. Moscow and Washington might continue their progress to detente, disarmament and co-operation. US strategic thinking might no longer be postulated on a Soviet threat. Meanwhile, China, starting with the Peking massacre, might find itself again forced into violent suppression of its population. As the economy suffered from the loss of popular enthusiasm, the cut-off of high technology transfers and a slowdown in investment, retrenchment and austerity might squeeze China back into its shell, out of which it would brandish a hostile fist at the imperialists, reactionaries and revisionists who had forced it into this pass. International support for Taiwan's right to self-determination would swell, bolstered by the arguments of those who argue that US and Japanese recognition of Chinese sovereignty was almost explicitly conditional on a peaceful approach to reunification, and that could not be relied on. This in turn would encourage Taiwan independence activists at home, and their potential voters.

This scenario, however, is what people in Hong Kong call 'Armageddon'. Just as likely in the short to medium term is that the instruments of social control available to the Chinese Communist Party prove effective, that protest is stifled and that China is allowed once again back into the fold of nations with whom the world is keen to do business. In those circumstances, international backing for the Taiwan independence movement is unlikely to precede a strong growth of the movement at home. It would be chicken and egg.

THE MILITARY OPTION

The KMT has, for the foreseeable future, abandoned any hopes of recovering the mainland militarily. Hence, if there is to be a military confrontation across the two sides of the Taiwan Strait, its most likely starting point is mainland aggression. China, of course, has never renounced the use of force. It has given various different formulations of the circumstances in which it would feel obliged to resort to force. Collating them, one arrives at six types of chain of events. None is wholly out of the question in Taiwan in the next decade.

1 If Taiwan declares itself independent

As argued in the previous section, the author does not believe this is likely in the near future. However, it is quite possible that the clamour by pro-independence groups, defying the ever-more obsolescent law making pro-independence rhetoric seditious, might sufficiently alarm Peking to take some action.

2 If there is a serious civil disturbance on Taiwan (on some occasions this has been qualified by making it additionally conditional on foreign intervention following the unrest)

The Chinese fear here seems to be that if the KMT is faced with serious social unrest, either by pro-independence protestors, or perhaps, far-fetchedly, by pro-mainland groups, it might call on the US to come in to prop up its regime. This seems improbable, because the degree of street protest that has sprung up since the lifting of martial law has never reached the point where it might actually threaten the regime. If it did, it is unlikely that the KMT would invite in the US, or that the US would unilaterally intervene. It did not intervene on behalf of its old allies in Manila or Seoul in 1986 and 1987, except to encourage them to take the path of reform, and to whisk the Philippines' President Marcos away from the mob by helicopter. Similarly in Taiwan, it is hard to see the US protecting the KMT against the apparent wishes of its people unless it was faced with a domestic communist threat, which it will not be.

3 A military alliance between Taiwan and China's enemies

This is a relic from the 1960s, of looming Sino-Soviet war, and the Victor Louis trips to Taiwan. By the late 1980s, China's only real enemy was Vietnam. Taiwan will not make common cause with Hanoi. Indeed, Taipei has offered to co-operate militarily with Peking in their joint claim to sovereignty of the Spratly or Nansha islands in the South China Seas against the competing claim of Vietnam.

4 If Taiwan develops nuclear weaponry

Despite frequent denials, Taiwan is almost certainly engaged in nuclear weapons research, as testified by the nuclear scientist Chang Hsien-yi who defected from Taiwan to the US in early 1988. While clearly of concern to Peking, the evidence of some nuclear research is unlikely to prod China into military intervention in the near future. It was one of the conditions rarely spelled out by the late 1980s.

5 If any country adopts a 'two-China' policy to an extent unbearable to Peking and which threatens the stability of the Taiwan Strait or the security of the Chinese mainland

Originally, this was probably directed at the Taiwan Relations Act, and added teeth to China's threats that it would not tolerate continued unlimited sale of US weaponry to Taiwan. However, it would also justify intervention if international moves to alter Taiwan's status were afoot.

6 If peaceful reunification is frustrated

This catch-all provision does not define either how long peaceful means are to be tried before being abandoned, or what would constitute the signal of their failure. In practice, this therefore re-duplicates the previous five conditions.

Both China and Taiwan are highly armed. In the late 1980s, more than 30 per cent of the Taiwain government's budget went on defence. This was despite a cut-back in the number of members of the armed forces from 600 000 in the early 1950s, to 500 000 a decade later, to 400 000 by 1989. The expenditure has been lavished on the most modern equipment, and where its access had been curtailed under the second Shanghai Communiqué, Taiwan has managed to develop an indigenous capacity in many areas, with presumed US help. The Indigenous Defence Fighter, a jet-fighter whose prototype was unveiled in late 1988, was the cornerstone of this policy. Meanwhile, the mainland's armed forces have, under Deng Xiaoping, been cut from 4 to 3 million men. Its navy was only beginning to develop a true blue-water capacity in 1987–8, when it flexed its muscles in the Spratlys. At about the same time, eased COCOM rules for China began to cut the technological edge that Taiwan undoubtedly enjoyed over China's armed forces.

Nevertheless, Taiwan does still enjoy that edge, and it was more than just bravado when its armed forces Chief of Staff, General Hau Pei-ts'un, in May 1988 declared that Taiwan could withstand an attempted mainland invasion. Taiwan's smallness, he said, meant that China's numerical advantages could not be brought into play at one time, but would have to attack in waves, where Taiwan's superior airforce and fire-power would beat them back. Military analysts seem to believe that invasion by the mainland, after a lengthy period of attrition, would be successful. It is not, however, an attractive proposition. Nor can it be ruled that a military confrontation across the Taiwan Straits would escalate into a global conflict. As noted, the United States tends to regard the Shanghai Communiqués as conditional on a peaceful approach by Peking towards reunification. In December 1989, the United States provided military support to President Aquino of the Philippines when she faced a military coup. Congressman Steven Solarz, Chairman of the House of Representatives sub-committee on Asian and Pacific affairs was at the time in Taipei, as part of a congressional delegation observing the elections. He made an interesting point: that the lesson for Taiwan of what had happened in the Philippines was that in the event of a threat to its security, a government is more likely to be able to call on United States assistance if it is a popularly elected democracy. He did not speak for the administration, but his views were probably sound. What he did not spell out is the corollary: that in Taiwan's case, the progress to representative democracy, inevitably entailing a more active pro-independence lobby, in itself makes an eventual threat to Taiwan's security greater. In other words: the more democratic Taiwan becomes, the more likely it is to face a threat from the mainland, and the more likely the United States is to defend it. More probable than military action by Peking as a first step, should any of the six danger points be reached, would be a stepping up of diplomatic pressure, accompanied by attempted economic sanctions. In the same remarks, General Hau expressed confidence that a mainland naval blockade to enforce economic sanctions would provoke such an international outcry as to be counterproductive.

However, at present China has an unused battery of diplomatic pressures. It does not intervene in countries' dealings with Taiwan except when it feels these encroach on its sovereignty, by containing an element of official recognition. Before the military option was tried, political pressure on China's diplomatic partners would presumably be tried in an attempt to isolate Taiwan. While pursuing 'peaceful reunification', this is not in China's interests. But if Peking decides it has to play tough, it will presumably not be too concerned with how opinion abroad or in Taiwan regards the justice of its actions. For a while, even trading with Taiwan might become 'meddling in China's internal affairs'.

A COMPROMISE?

If I might summarise the argument so far, it is that both the KMT and the CCP have an interest in maintaining the status quo, but that is most probably impossible. None of the other options on offer, however, seem workable and hence there must be some sort of compromise. The KMT under Lee Teng-hui seems only superficially moving towards compromise, with its hints that it might accept the sovereignty of the CCP over the mainland. That is the opposite direction from the one in which the CCP wants the KMT to move. The appeals to the spirit of Sun Yat-sen and the United Front, the partial rehabilitation of Chiang Kai-shek, and the warnings about the growth of the independence movement are all aimed at reminding the KMT of the bond to which it is committed by its own charter, that of 'one China'.

A compromise would have to involve at least two elements: (1) China would have to renounce the use of force as a means to reunification. (2) Taiwan would have to commit itself in return towards working towards 'one China'. Both sides would argue that they have already done this. China is offering peaceful reunification if Taiwan accepts the 'one country – two systems' formula. The KMT has never deviated from its rhetoric of national unity. But in reality neither side is giving the other the reassurance it is seeking – in China's case that Taiwan will recognise the Peking government other than as simply the de facto ruler of the mainland, and in Taiwan's case that negotiation on 'one country – two systems' is more than a ploy to lure the KMT into writing itself out of history.

The key questions then are under what conditions would Peking recognise Taipei as some sort of equal partner, and under what conditions would Taipei believe it. Both rely on a fundamental change in attitudes in both capitals. The Kuomintang has changed its political system far more extensively than has the CCP. Yet strangely, the change in attitude is more likely to result from upheaval in Peking.

The communist government in China has revealed itself as inherently unstable. The tensions which led to the 1989 uprising are now built into the system. First, economic reform has created the conditions for a flowering of vague democratic yearnings. These yearnings are an inseparable part of the economic policies still being pursued by the CCP. But without some structural political reform, they have no institutional outlet, and pose a threat to the whole system. Ultimately, they will have either to be accommodated by significant reform, or repeatedly repressed until the regime crumbles under the weight of its own unpopularity. Second, the failure of ideology and institutionalisation revealed by the Peking massacre has also left a void in the mechanism for the political succession. There seems to be no obvious way the transition can be handled without more turmoil.

What will emerge from this turbulent upheaval in mainland politics is unforeseeable. But as Deng Xiaoping himself said of the 1989 massacre, 'Sooner or later this storm was bound to come'. He did not explain why it will not come again, or what will be left after the next storm has blown over, but it is at least conceivable that it will be a government with whom the Taipei authorities feel they can deal. That is clearly also the unstated hope in Taiwan. Some day, the pressures for reform in China may result in a Chinese government that Taipei feels it can if not trust, then at least deal with in an atmosphere free from fear. Whatever such a government looks like, however, it will not give either the KMT or the Taiwan independence movement what they want. Rather, it will lie somewhere on the uneasy continuum between the status quo and 'one country – two systems'. Perhaps, for example, some kind of Chinese 'Commonwealth', where China, like the British sovereign, is its 'head' but has no power over its members – Hong Kong, Macao, maybe even Taiwan. More likely, however, is a compromise giving Peking more substantive sovereignty. Such a compromise does not appeal to a sense of natural justice or democratic impulses. Once more, it would imply that the political future of Taiwan's people is decided by negotiation between rival alien élites, and would foreclose the possibility of Taiwan's self-determination yet again. But until such a compromise has been achieved, Taiwan will remain China's last frontier.

Notes and References

Front and Introduction

1. Hu Yaobang's interview with Selig Harrison, *Far Eastern Economic Review*, 26 July 1986.
2. Ma Ying-cheou's interview with the author, Taipei, June 1989.

1 Geography and Early History

On Taiwan's topography, see Anon. (1960) and Hseih (1964). On pre-history, see Chai (1967), Davidson (1988) and Goddard (1966).

Early contacts with the mainland
Davidson (1988), Goddard (1966) and Reischauer and Fairbank (1958).

Early foreign contacts
Davidson (1988), Goddard (1966), Hsu (1970) and Reischauer and Fairbank (1958).

Taiwan under the Dutch
Campbell (1903), Davidson (1988) and Goddard (1966).

The Koxinga interregnum
Croizier (1977), Hsu (1970) and Kessler (1976).

The 'Wild East'
Davidson (1988), Goddard (1966) and Gold (1986).

Taiwan joins international politics
Broomhall (1982), Davidson (1988), Hibbert (1970), Hsu (1970), Wang and Hao (1980) and Yen (1965).

Early modernisation
Goddard (1966), Gold (1986) and Kerr (1974).

The Japanese annexation
Davidson (1988), Hsu (1970), Jansen (1980), Kerr (1974), Li (1956), Reischauer and Fairbank (1958), Smith and Liu (1980) and Wang and Hao (1980).

Taiwan under the Japanese
Behr (1989), Davidson (1988), Gold (1986), Ho (1978), Kerr (1974) and Mendel (1970).

REFERENCES
1. The 'Dragon Myth' is cited in Davidson (1988).
2. Quoted in Campbell (1903).
3. Quoted in Hsu (1970).
4. Quoted in Gold (1986).
5. Quoted in Davidson (1988).
6. Fairbank (1972).

2 The Kuomintang

The Kuomintang in 1945
Belden (1973), Bianco (1971), China White Paper (1967), Harrison (1976), Kerr (1974), Loh (1965), Seagrave (1985) and Tuchman (1972).

Sun Yat-sen and the origins of the KMT
Bianco (1971), Chan (1976), Creel (1953), Fairbank (1987), Gold (1986), Harrison (1976), Hsu (1970), Isaacs (1951), Schiffrin (1968), Spence (1982) and Tan (1971).

The Kuomintang reorganises
Bianco (1971), Gasster (1980), Jacobs (1976), Landis (1976), Schiffrin (1968) and Seagrave (1985).

The Kuomintang in power
Belden (1949), Bianco (1971), Ch'en (1967), Harrison (1976), Isaacs (1951), Loh (1965), Schwartz (1958), Seagrave (1985) and Snow (1938).

The second united front
Belden (1949), Ch'en (1967), Fairbank (1987) and Harrison (1976).

REFERENCE
1. Trotsky and Stalin are quoted in Schwartz (1958).

3 Taiwan's Political Development 1945—86

The KMT takeover of Taiwan
Bate (1952), Goddard (1966), Gold (1986), Kerr (1966) and Riggs (1952).

Defeat on the mainland
Fairbank (1987), Gold (1986), Loh (1965), Harrison (1976) and Tuchman (1972).

The KMT cleans up its act
Clough (1978), Gold (1986), Long (1989), Ho (1978) and Riggs (1952).

Political development in the 1950s and 1960s
Clough (1978), Gold (1986) and Riggs (1952).

The birth of the opposition
Clough (1978), Gold (1986), Huang (1976), Kaplan (1981) and Peng (1972).

Chiang Kai-shek and the succession problem
Goddard (1966), Winkler (1983) and contemporary press.

REFERENCE
1. Quoted in full in Huang (1976).

4 Taiwan's Economic Development

This chapter relies heavily on the research done for the author's earlier book *Taiwan: Politics vs. Prosperity*, using official statistics.

5 Relations with China 1945—76

The lines are drawn
China White Paper (1967), China and US Far East Policy (n.d.), Clough (1978), Hsiao and Sullivan (1979), Hsieh (1985) and Whiting (1968).

Hostility in the 1950s
Ballantyne (1952), China and US Far East Policy (n.d.),
Clough (1978), Jacoby (1966), Lasater (1986), Lee (1983) and
Stolper (1986).

Stalemate in the 1960s and 1970s
China and US Far East Policy (n.d.), Clough (1978), Cohen
(1971), Lasater (1986), Myers (1978) and Stolper (1986).

REFERENCES
1. China and US Far East Policy (n.d.).
2. China White Paper (1967).
3. Mao Zedong (n.d.).
4. China and US Far East Policy (n.d.).
5. Snow (1938).

6 Taiwan's Foreign Relations

Taiwan and the United States
Ballantyne (1952), Barnett (1981), Bueler (1971), Chan
(1984), China White Paper (1967), Chiu (1973), Clough
(1978), Cohen (1976), Fairbank (1972), Stolper (1986) and
Sutter (1982).

Taiwan and the United Nations
Chan (1984), Chiu (1979) and Hsieh (1985).

Taiwan and Japan
Bellows (1977), Clough (1978), Huang (1976), Long (1989),
and Newby (1989).

Taiwan and the Soviet Bloc
Clough (1978), Chiang (1937), Hsieh (1985) and contemporary press reports.

Taiwan and the overseas Chinese
Chiang (1988) and press reports.

Taiwan's current foreign policy
This section is derived from a close reading of the Taiwan
government's many foreign policy statements, reproduced in

the local media, and from press reports of its foreign policy initiatives.

REFERENCES

1. China and US Far East Policy (n.d.).
2. China and US Far East Policy (n.d.).
3. Reprinted in full in Chan (1984).
4. Reprinted in full in Chan (1984).
5. Reprinted in full in Chan (1984).
6. *Far Eastern Economic Review*, 26 July 1986.
7. Hsieh (1985).

7 China Changes Tack: Peking's 1980s Taiwan Policy

China's new approach
Benewick and Wingrove (1988), Chan (1984), Chiang (1988), Deng (1987), Gittings (1989) and Krug (1989).

The Hong Kong example
Bonavia (1984), Cheng (1984) and press reports.

China's pragmatic foreign policy
Harding (1984), Yahuda (1983) and press reports.

REFERENCES

1. Reprinted in full in Chan (1984).
2. Reprinted in full in Chan (1984).
3. Deng (1987).
4. Chan (1984).
5. Chan (1984).
6. *Beijing Review*, 16 September 1983.
7. Deng (1987).
8. Deng (1987).
9. Published in the UK Government White Paper 'A Draft Agreement between the Government of the United Kingdom and Northern Ireland and the Government of the People's Republic of China on the Future of Hong Kong' on 26 September 1984.
10. *Far Eastern Economic Review*, 26 July 1986.

8 Political Reform in Taiwan 1986—89
9 Taiwan's Opening to Mainland China
10 What Next? Scenarios for the Future

The account of recent developments in Taiwan in these chapters derives from study of the local press, especially the English language *Free China Journal*, the Chinese language *China Daily News*, and the independent magazine *New Journalist*. The author has also had the benefit of extensive interviews in Taiwan with many in politics, business, the media and academic life in 1988 and 1989. The opinions expressed, especially the prognostications in Chapter 10, however, are of course the author's own responsibility.

Select Bibliography

Anon (1960) *Area Handbook for the Republic of China* (Taiwan: The American University).

Anon (1989) *Republic of China – A Reference Book* (Taipei: Hilit).

Ballantyne, J. W. (1952) *Formosa: A Problem for United States Foreign Policy* (Washington: Brookings Institution).

Barnett, A. Doak (1981) *The FX Decision: 'Another Crucial Moment' in US–China Taiwan Relations* (Washington: Brookings Institution).

Barnett. A. Doak (1982) *US Arms Sales: The China–Taiwan Tangle* (Washington: Brookings Institution).

Bastid-Bruguière, Marianne (1980) 'Currents of social change', in *Cambridge History of China*, Vol. II, *The Ch'ing* (Cambridge University Press).

Bate, H. Maclear (1952) *Report from Formosa* (New York: E. P. Dutton).

Behr, E. (1989) *Hirohito – Behind the Myth* (London: Hamish Hamilton).

Belden, J. (1949, reprinted 1973) *China Shakes the World* (London: Pelican).

Bellows, T. J. (1977) *Taiwan's Foreign Policy in the 1970s, a Case Study of Adaptation and Viability* (Baltimore: School of Law).

Benewick, R. and Wingrove, P. (eds) *Reforming the Revolution – China in Transition* (London: Macmillan).

Bianco, L. (1971) *Origins of the Chinese Revolution* (Oxford University Press).

Bonavia, D. (1984) *Hong Kong 1997* (Hong Kong: Columbus Books).

Bouscaren, A. T. (ed.) (1967) *The Case for Free China* (New York: Twin Circle).

Broomhall, A. J. (1982) *Hudson Taylor and China's Open Century* (London: Hodder & Stoughton).

Bueler, W. M. (1971) *U.S China Policy and the Problem of Taiwan* (Boulder, Colo.: Associated University Press).

Campbell, W. M. Rev. (1903) *Formosa Under the Dutch* (London: Kegan Paul).

Chai, C. K. (1967) *Taiwan Aborigines: A Genetic Study of Tribal Variations* (Cambridge, Mass.; Harvard University Press).

Chan, G. F. (1976) 'Sun Yat-sen and the origins of the Kuomintang Reorganisation', in F. G. Chan and T. Etzold (eds) *China in the 1920s* (New York: New Viewpoints).

Chan, G. F. (1984) *China's Reunification and the Taiwan Question* (Hong Kong: Asian Research Service).

Chang, Parris (1983) 'Taiwan in 1982: Diplomatic setback abroad, and demand for reform at home', *Asian Survey*, XXIII, January.

Ch'en, Jerome (1967) *Mao and the Chinese Revolution* (Oxford University Press).

Cheng, Joseph S. Y. (ed.) (1984) *Hong Kong in Search of a Future* (Oxford University Press).

Chiang, David Wen-Wei (1988) *China Under Deng Xiaoping* (London: Macmillan).

Chiang Kai-Shek, Generalissimo and Madame (1937) *China at the Crossroads* (London: Faber & Faber).

China White Paper (1967) (Washington, DC: State Department).

Chiu, Hungdah (ed.) (1973) *China and the Question of Taiwan: Documents and Analysis* (New York: Praeger).

Chiu, Hungdah (ed.) (1979) *China and the Taiwan Issue* (New York: Praeger).

Chu, Yungdeh Richard (1986) *China in Perspectives* (Hong Kong: Asian Research Service).

Clough, Ralph N. (1978) *Island China* (Cambridge, Mass.: Harvard University Press).

Cohen, J. A. et al. (1971) *Taiwan and American Policy: The Dilemma in U.S.–China Relations* (New York: Praeger).

Cohen, Myron L. (1976) *House United, House Divided: The Chinese Family in Taiwan* (New York: Columbia University Press).

Copper, J. F. (1982) 'Taiwan's legal status: A multi-level perspective', *Journal of North-East Asian Studies*, I, No. 4, December.

Creel, Herrlee G. (1953) *Chinese Thought from Confucius to Mao'* (University of Chicago Press).

Croizier, R. C. (1977) *Koxinga and Chinese Nationalism: History, Myth and the Hero* (Cambridge, Mass.: Harvard University Press).

Davidson, J. W. (1903, reprinted 1988) *The Island of Formosa, Past and Present* (Oxford University Press).

Deng Xiaoping (1982) *Selected Works* (Peking: Foreign Languages Press).

Deng Xiaoping (1987) *Fundamental Issues in Present-day China* (Peking: Foreign Languages Press).

Fairbank, J. K. (1972) *The United States and China* (Cambridge, Mass.: Harvard University Press).

Fairbank, J. K. (1987) *The Great Chinese Revolution* (London: Chatto & Windus).

Gasster, M. (1980) 'The republican revolutionary movement', in *Cambridge History of China*, Vol. II (*The Ch'ing*), op. cit.

Goddard, W. G. (1966) *Formosa: A Study in Chinese History* (London: Macmillan).

Gittings, J. (1989) *China Changes Face* (Oxford Universty Press).

Gold, T. B. (1986) *State and Society in the Taiwan Miracle* (New York: M. E. Sharpe).

Gordon, Leonard H. D. (ed.) (1970) *Taiwan: Studies in Chinese Local History* (New York: Columbia University Press).

Gregor, A. J., Chang, Maria H. and Zimmerman, Andrew B. (1981) *Ideology and Development: Sun Yat-sen and the Economic History of Taiwan* (Berkeley, California: Center for Chinese Studies).

Harding, H. (ed.) (1984) *China's Foreign Relations in the 1980s* (New Haven: Yale University Press).

Harrison, J. P. (1976) *The Long March to Power, A History of the CCP Chinese Communist Party, 1921–1972* (New York: Praeger).

Hibbert, C. (1970) *The Dragon Wakes* (London: Penguin).

Ho, Samuel P. S. (1978) *Economic Development of Taiwan, 1860–1970* (New Haven: Yale University Press).

Hsiao, Frank S. T. and Sullivan, L. R. (1979) 'The Chinese Communist Party and the status of Taiwan, 1928–1943, *Pacific Affairs*, LII, No. 3, Autumn.

Hsieh, Chiao-Chiao (1985) *Strategy for Survival: Foreign Policy and External Relations of the Republic of China on Taiwan, 1949–1979* (London: Sherwood Press).

Hsieh, Chiao-min (1964) *Taiwan – Ilha Formosa, A Geography in Perspective* (Washington, DC: Butterworths).

Hsu, Immanuel C. Y. (1980) 'Late Ch'ing foreign relations', in *Cambridge History of China*, Vol. II, *The Ch'ing*, op cit.

Hsu, Immanuel C. Y. (1970) *The Rise of Modern China* (Oxford University Press).

Huang, Mab (1976) *Intellectual Ferment for Political Reform in Taiwan* (Michigan: Papers in Chinese Studies).

Isaacs, H. R. (1951) *The Tragedy of the Chinese Revolution* (California: Stanford University Press).

Jacobs, D. (1976) 'Soviet Russia and Chinese Nationalism in the 1920s', in Chan and Etzold (eds) *China in the 1920s*, op. cit.

Jacoby, N. H. (1966) *U.S. Aid to Taiwan: A Study of Foreign Aid, Self-help and Development* (New York: Praeger).

Jansen, M. (1980) 'Japan and the Chinese Revolution of 1911', in *Cambridge History of China*, Vol. II, *The Ch'ing*, op. cit.

Kaplan, J. (1981) *The Court Martial of the Kaohsiung Defendants* (Berkeley, Calif.: Berkeley University Press).

Kerr, G. H. (1966) *Formosa Betrayed* (London: Eyre & Spottiswoode).

Kerr, G. H. (1974) *Formosa Licensed Revolution and the Home Rule Movement, 1895–1945* (Honolulu: University of Hawaii).

Kessler, Lawrence D. (1976) *K'ang-hsi and the Consolidation of Ch'ing Rule* (University of Chicago Press).

Krug, B., Long, S. and Segal, G. (1989) *China in Crisis* (London: Chatham House).

Kuo, Ping-chia (1963) *China New Age and Outlook* (Harmondsworth: Penguin).

Kuo, Shirley W. Y. and Fei, John C. H. (1978) *The Taiwan Success Story: Rapid Growth with Improved Distribution in the Republic of China, 1952–1979* (Boulder, Colo.: Westview).

Landis, R. B. (1976) 'Training and indoctrination at the Whampoa Academy', in Chan and Etzold (eds) *China in the 1920s* (New York: New Viewpoints).

Lasater, M. L. (1986) *The Taiwan Issue in Sino-American Strategic Relations* (Boulder, Colo.: Westview).

Lee Teng-hui (1971) *Intersectoral Capital Flows in the Economic Development of Taiwan, 1895–1960* (Ithaca, Cornell University Press).

Lee, Wan-lai (1983) *The Taiwan Strait Strategy* (Taipei, Imperial Book Co.).

Li, Chien-nung (1956) *The Political History of China* (California: Stanford University Press).

Li, Victor H. (ed.) (1980) *The Future of Taiwan: A Difference of Opinion* (White Plains, NY: M. E. Sharpe).

Loh, Pichon P. Y. (ed.) (1965) *The Kuomintang Debacle of 1949 – Conquest or Collapse?* (Boston: D. C. Heath).

Long, S. (1989) *Taiwan to 1993: Politics vs. Prosperity* (London: Economist Intelligence Unit).

Mancall, Mark (ed.) (1964) *Formosa Today* (New York: Praeger).

Mao Zedong (n.d.) *Selected Works* (Peking, Foreign Languages Press).

Mendel, D. (1970) *The Politics of Formosan Nationalism* (California: Berkeley University Press).

Moore, Barrington, Jnr. (1966) *Social Origins of Dictatorship and Democracy* (Harmondsworth: Penguin).

Myers, Ramon H. (ed.) (1978) *Two Chinese States: U.S. Foreign Policy and Interests* (Stanford: Hoover Institution Press).

Newby, Laura (1989) *Sino-Japanese Relations* (London: Chatham House).

Peng Min-min (1972) *A Taste of Freedom: Memoirs of a Formosan Independence Leader* (New York: Holt, Rinehart & Winston).

Planning Commission for Mainland Recovery (1989) *Shi Nian Lai Zhongguo Gaige (Ten Years of Chinese Communist Reform)* (Taipei).

Reischauer, E. O. and Fairbank, J. K. (1958) *East Asia: The Great Tradition* (Cambridge, Mass.: Harvard University Press).

Riggs, F. W. (1952) *Formosa Under Chinese Nationalist Rule* (New York: Macmillan).

Sanford, Dan C. (1981) *The Future Association of Taiwan with the People's Republic of China* (Berkeley, Calif.: Center for Chinese Studies).

Schiffrin, H. Z. (1968) *Sun Yat-sen and the Origins of the Chinese Revolution* (Berkeley, Calif.: Center for Chinese Studies).

Schwartz, B. (1958) *Chinese Communism and the Rise of Mao* (Cambridge, Mass.: Harvard University Press).

Schwartz, H. (1964) *Tsars, Mandarins and Commissars* (New York: Lippincott).

Seagrave, S. (1985) *The Soong Dynasty* (New York: Harper & Row).

Smith, R. and Liu, Kwang-ching (1980) 'The military challenge: The north-west and the coast', in *Cambridge History of China*, Vol. II, *The Ch'ing*, op. cit.

Snow, Edgar (1938) *Red Star over China* (London: Left Book Club).

Snow, Edgar (1972) *Journey to the Beginning* (New York: Vintage Books).

Spence, J. (1982) *The Gate of Heavenly Peace* (London: Faber & Faber).

Stolper, T. E. (1986) *China, Taiwan and the Off-shore Islands* (Boulder, Colo.: Westview).

Sutter, R. (1982) 'U.S. arms sales to Taiwan: Implications for American interests', in *Journal of North-East Asian Studies*, I, No. 3, September.

Tan, Chester C. (1971) *Chinese Political Thought in the Twentieth Century* (New York: Doubleday).

Tuchman, Barbara T. (1972) *Stilwell and the American Experience in China* (New York: Macmillan).

Wang, Erh-min and Hao, Yen-p'ing (1980) 'Changing Chinese views of Western relations, 1840–1895', in *Cambridge History of China*, Vol. II, *The Ch'ing*, op. cit.

Whiting, A. S. (1968) *China Crosses the Yalu* (California: Stanford University Press).

Winkler, Edwin A. (1983) 'After the Chiangs: The coming political succession on Taiwan', in Bush, R. C. (ed.) *China Briefing* (Boulder, Colo.: Westview).

Yahuda, M. (1983) *The End of Isolationism: Chinese Foreign Policy After Mao* (London: Macmillan).

Yen, Sophia Su-fei (1965) *Taiwan in China's Foreign Relations, 1836–1874* (Hamden, Conn.: Shoestring).

Zhao, John Quansheng (1983) 'An analysis of unification: The PRC perspective', in *Asian Survey*, XXIII, No. 10, October.

Index

KEELE
UNIVERSITY

The
Library